THE ACADEMIC DEANSHIP

Individual Careers and Institutional Roles

David F. Bright, Mary P. Richards

JOSSEY-BASS
A Wiley Company
San Francisco

Published by

JOSSEY-BASS
A Wiley Company
989 Market Street
San Francisco, CA 94103-1741

www.josseybass.com

Jossey-Bass books and products are available through most bookstores. To contact Jossey-Bass directly, call (888) 378-2537, fax to (800) 605-2665, or visit our website at www.josseybass.com.

Substantial discounts on bulk quantities of Jossey-Bass books are available to corporations, professional associations, and other organizations. For details and discount information, contact the special sales department at Jossey-Bass.

We at Jossey-Bass strive to use the most environmentally sensitive paper stocks available to us. Our publications are printed on acid-free recycled stock whenever possible, and our paper always meets or exceeds minimum GPO and EPA requirements.

Library of Congress Cataloging-in-Publication Data

Bright, David F.
  The academic deanship : individual careers and institutional roles
/ David F. Bright, Mary P. Richards.— 1st ed.
    p. cm.—(The Jossey-Bass higher and adult education
series)
Includes bibliographical references and index.
  ISBN 0-7879-5350-4 (alk. paper)
  1. Deans (Education)—United States.   2. Universities and
colleges—United States—Administration.   I. Richards, Mary P.
II. Title.   III. Series.
  LB2341 .B648 2001
    378.1'11—dc21   2001001347

FIRST EDITION
HB Printing   10 9 8 7 6 5 4 3 2 1

THE JOSSEY-BASS

HIGHER AND ADULT EDUCATION SERIES

CONTENTS

PREFACE

A generation ago, achieving the academic deanship often meant a perma-nent alteration of one's role in higher education, a long-term shift into ad-ministration. But during the past decade the rate of turnover for deans has accelerated dramatically, with the significant result that becoming a dean is no longer a permanent, perhaps culminating, career choice but rather a phase—albeit a very important one—in an academic career. Together with the ever-changing landscape of higher education and the increasing technical demands placed on deans, this means that anyone contemplating an academic deanship must weigh a greater variety of considerations than did colleagues in earlier times, and with fewer sources of advice. The nature of the job has changed, as has the range of likely options at the end of a deanship.

We decided to write this book based on our experiences as academic deans at a variety of institutions, our extended involvement in professional associa-tions of deans, and our reflections on those experiences after stepping back into active faculty roles in our respective colleges. It quickly became clear that there are few other works available now on the topic of deaning, and those either focus on very specific kinds of administrative work or are relatively out of date (for example, giving no consideration to such basic tools as e-mail, or advising deans to neglect their academic careers) or else provide capsule information rather than a perspective on the job as a whole.

This book aims to provide a more current picture of deaning while discussing both the challenges and the rewards of the job. We hope it will give an aspiring dean the basis for an informed assessment of the job as a career option, provide a newly appointed dean with practical advice on beginning the job, offer a thoughtful assessment of the deanship in its wider context, and prompt experienced deans to reflect on their evolving career intentions so that they have control over the timing and manner of their transition out of the dean's office.

In short, the book is aimed first and foremost at aspiring and sitting academic deans. We have not tried to encompass the specialized responsibilities of other decanal posts, such as dean of students or dean of admissions; these are really on another track of professional training and of advancement. The academic deanship, rooted in the progress of a faculty career, is our focus.

At the same time, however, we hope this work will be of interest, and of use, to many others both on and off campus. Many faculty who have little direct contact with the dean have correspondingly little idea of what the dean does. Administrators across campus do have dealings with the deans, but for the most part on a limited array of issues. It may be helpful to those other administrators to see more clearly how the world looks from the dean's office. The same may be said of individuals, from trustees to legislators, whose work touches the interests of the university or college but whose perspective is determined mainly by their dealings with the president's office. The view from inside the academic programs is different and frequently hard to grasp. And finally, for most people who do not have any regular dealings with a campus, "dean" is merely the answer to the stock crossword puzzle clue "campus bigwig." We hope that this account of the most enjoyable job in higher education can help to make the campus seem a bit less strange, at least in one sense of that term.

The ideas, experiences, and advice that form the substance of the book come from various sources. In addition to drawing on our own experience at six institutions, we have profited from countless seminars, workshops, and panel sessions offered by professional organizations for higher education, years of conversations and shared advice with our fellow deans across the country, and reading in the literature about deaning and higher education issues. The result is not a work that lays out research in the usual sense of the term. Rather, the heart of the book is the experience of hundreds of deans with whom we have had the privilege of working over the past fifteen years. It is constructed from interaction in the community of deans.

We begin (Chapter One) by evoking ways to think about the institutional role of the dean, including its intriguing contradictions, and then (Chapter Two) focus on qualities of mind and temperament, experiences as a faculty member and skills and duties required, that should influence any decision about whether to aim for a deanship. Assuming this assessment lends encouragement, we look at what is involved in the process of candidacy (Chapter Three). In particular, how is pursuing a deanship different from being a candidate for a faculty position?

The next part of the book takes up the role of the dean as chief administrator of the college, with emphasis on questions that may arise for a new dean. Chapter Four treats the transition to the dean's role, in particular the tasks to undertake in the first six months and how to evaluate progress at the end of that period. Then we look more closely at the administrative fabric of the college—the dean's staff, faculty governance, and faculty unions (Chapter Five), and the critical role of department chairs in the life of the college, including selection, evaluation, and support of chairs (Chapter Six). Here, as throughout the book, we illustrate the topics with real situations reported by deans—with details changed as discretion required—and consider alternative approaches to common problems.

Chapters Seven through Twelve address the variety of challenges that every dean faces, beginning with planning (Chapter Seven). We point to alternative models for planning, the steps in a typical process, and potential pitfalls for deans. Chapter Eight discusses the basics of budgeting and allocating resources from personnel to operating funds, technological support, physical facilities, and external grants and contracts. Then Chapter Nine takes up the dean's crucial role in faculty matters, including recruiting, mentoring, evaluating—especially for tenure and promotion—and rewarding, as well as encouraging excellence in teaching and research, building a culture of good academic citizenship, and assisting faculty members toward retirement. The academic programs themselves are the focus of Chapter Ten, together with the dean's role in ensuring their quality and viability.

Students are no less important to a campus than faculty. What is the dean's role in recruiting students and ensuring they have access to the best possible programs? What is the role in handling allegations of sexual harassment procedures, promoting effective faculty advising, and recognizing student accomplishments (Chapter Eleven)?

The most delicate part of the dean's job, and the one for which faculty life may give the least preparation, is in the legal realm. Chapter Twelve outlines some of the legal issues that most concern deans, gives specific advice about sexual harassment involving colleagues, and discusses the special challenges that may face female and minority deans.

Chapters Thirteen through Fifteen look outside the confines of the college, beginning with relationships elsewhere on campus. Chapter Thirteen discusses how to establish a good working relationship with the provost, with an eye to open communication, emergencies, planning, and performance review. The other crucial on-campus working relationship is with one's fellow deans and directors, who form a natural cohort for everything from program development to professional growth; this is the topic of Chapter Fourteen. And then we move on to the wider vista of alumni, parents, the media, and the community at large. The dean is constantly developing and maintaining relationships with each of these groups, from staying in touch with alumni to placating distressed parents and conveying information to the media about both emergencies and happy events. Not the least of the dean's challenges is seeking financial support from prospective donors, an art in itself. Chapter Fifteen offers some specific suggestions for working in all these situations.

At the end (Chapter Sixteen), we return to the idea that being a dean is only a part of a full career. The dean needs to bear this in mind while in office, especially by maintaining an active academic identity—which is a constant theme among both sitting and former deans—and by looking beyond current activities to the next career step, whether that is more administration or a return to full-time teaching and scholarship. One of the trickiest aspects of being a dean is deciding when it is time to make a move and then choosing the next step; moving hastily or rashly can be damaging, but far worse is lingering in office until the college community echoes the Bard: "Nothing in his deanship became him like the leaving of it!"

Above all, we hope that we have conveyed the adventure, the exhilaration, and the continual learning that come from being a dean. This is indeed one of the most satisfying roles on campus, especially when conjoined with the satisfaction of a faculty career, not interrupted but enriched by new perspectives!

January 2001   DAVID F. BRIGHT
                                                      MARY P. RICHARDS

ACKNOWLEDGMENTS

Many friends and colleagues have contributed their ideas and experiences to this book.

Sarah R. Blanshei, Jennie Skerl, and David R. Hiley were particularly valuable sources of information and help on a host of matters.

We are also eager to acknowledge the many contributions of Dale Abadie, Susan Anker, Nora K. Bell, David F. Brakke, D. Heyward Brock, Bonnie Buzza, June Cason, Roger Cason, Susan Coultrap-McQuin, Donald Cress, Peter W. Dowell, Holly Downing, Richard Edwards, Leila Fawaz, P. Geoffrey Feiss, John Flocken, James Frey, H. Frey, David C. Glenn-Lewin, Irwin L. Goldstein, Stanton W. Green, Sharon Hahs, Paul Hain, Wayne Hall, Mary Healey, Gordon Hedahl, Richard J. Hopkins, Irwin T. Hyatt, Jr., Elise Jorgens, Joel Kassiola, Gary W. Krahenbuhl, Rosemary Magee, James McMillan, Charles R. Middleton, Barbara Montgomery, James Muyskens, Ernest J. Peck, Peggy Pittas, John W. Prados, Michael Renner, Steven M. Richardson, Beate A. Schiwek, Barbara A. Shailor, Holly M. Smith, Praria Stavis-Hicks, David Stocum, Dale J. Trela, Alvin O. Turner, and Harriet Wall.

And we are very grateful to Gale Erlandson both for her initial interest in the project and for the clarity of her advice at every stage of its progress.

Any collaborative project presents special challenges: coordinating activities at a distance, adjudicating among options, and achieving consistency as well as clarity. Nobody deserves more thanks than Jason B. Jones, whose remarkable skills—both linguistic and technological—were a constant boon in helping us say what we actually wanted to say.

THE AUTHORS

David F. Bright is professor of classics and comparative literature at Emory University. He earned his B.A. degree from the University of Manitoba (1962) and A.M (1963) and Ph.D. (1967) from the University of Cincinnati, all in classics. He taught at Williams College (1967 to 1970) and the University of Illinois at Urbana-Champaign (1970 to 1989). At Illinois, Bright twice served as chair of classics and was director of the program in comparative literature, as well as acting director of the School of Humanities and acting dean of the College of Liberal Arts and Sciences. In 1989 he moved to the Iowa State University of Science and Technology, where he was dean of the College of Liberal Arts and Sciences (1989 to 1991). In 1991 Emory University appointed him vice president of arts and sciences and dean of Emory College, a post he held for six years. From 1996 to 1997, he was president-elect of the Council of Colleges of Arts and Sciences. Bright has also held offices in several scholarly associations. He is currently chair of classics at Emory.

Bright's academic honors include fellowships from the Woodrow Wilson Foundation and the American Council of Learned Societies, and membership in the Society of Fellows of the American Academy in Rome. He has written four books and two dozen chapters and papers on classical and medieval literature, from Homer to the Renaissance, and has also given numerous presentations and seminars on higher education.

Mary P. Richards is professor of English at the University of Delaware. She earned her B.A. degree (1966) in English at Southern Methodist University and both her M.A. (1967) and Ph.D. (1971) in English from the University of Wisconsin. Richards began her academic career at the University of Tennessee-Knoxville in 1971. During her seventeen-year tenure at that institution, she was promoted to associate professor and then professor of English and served in a number of administrative positions from the departmental through the system level, most extensively as associate dean of the graduate school and associate dean of liberal arts. From 1988 to 1991 Richards was dean of liberal arts at Auburn University in Alabama. In 1991 she joined the University of Delaware as dean of arts and science, a position she held until 1997. From 1995 to 1996 she served as president of the Council of Colleges of Arts and Sciences.

A specialist in Old English language and literature, Richards is the author of two books and numerous articles in that field and in higher education administration. Her honors include a Woodrow Wilson Fellowship and a Huntington Library Fellowship. From 1988 to 1991 Richards served as executive director of the International Society of Anglo-Saxonists. She is currently on the editorial board of *The Department Chair* newsletter.

PART ONE

BECOMING A DEAN

CHAPTER ONE

THE MAP AND THE CROSSWORD

Ways to Think about Being a Dean

"I have to see the dean!"

This sentence is uttered every day on every campus. Sometimes it is even true. More often, the correct statement would be "I want to see the dean" or even "I want to say something to the dean" (although I may not want the dean to say anything in reply). The dean constantly risks being idealized as the ultimate authority or sentimentalized as the source of all wisdom both academic and practical; that selfsame dean will also be glibly denounced as the cause of any distress and the source of all bad decisions.

Moreover, "I have to see the dean!" is voiced in a wonderful variety of inflections and emotions: from the elated faculty member bringing news of well-earned recognition, to the unbridled rage of another faculty member who feels slighted by a meager salary increase or a denied promotion; from the despairing student who has flunked out, to the bullying parent who cannot believe the college was so stupid as to deny admission to the smartest kid in town; from the nervous sophomore reporter for the campus paper who wants to interview the dean in hopes of a scandal or a scoop, to the state senator who just got wind of a course that sounds like a waste of taxpayers' dollars—the week before the appropriations bill is to come up—and the athletic association adviser who hopes to find some way to work out the starting center's inexplicable failing grade in calculus, and so on.

As this catalogue suggests, deans occupy an especially visible place in the academic world. Despite this perhaps unwonted prominence, however, deaning can bring much enjoyment, a widening of personal and professional horizons, and a whole new perspective on the workings of the academic world. Many say without hesitation that being dean is the most interesting and satisfying job they have had. They are called upon to be pseudoparents (and not just to students), colleagues, midlevel executives, intellectual leaders, strategic planners, politicians, counselors, and conflict resolution managers. And virtually all of it is on-the-job training.

Our purpose in this book is to reflect on the place of the dean in the academic cosmos and on the place of deaning in an academic career. What do deans do, and why should anyone consider doing it? What are the qualities of mind and temperament, of experience and outlook, that make deaning a plausible step in a career? More important, what constellation of abilities and ambitions, what achievements and closure, will make it enjoyable?

Two images capture the essence of a dean's job, one for the way the world fits together as seen from the dean's desk and the other for the kinds of activities that are conducted from behind that desk. The first is the map, and the second is the crossword puzzle.

The Map

Maps are so useful, so filled with information—and often so artfully rendered— that we may treat them with more deference than they deserve. In planning a trip we find destinations and routes by consulting the map, and on the road we rely on it where accuracy of information is critically important. We consult the atlas to learn or verify a single fact or to understand complex ideas and events, such as a war on the other side of the globe. Above all, we take for granted that the information a map provides is true, even or especially if it is a depiction of something that we would never be able to verify for ourselves.

In short, maps are usually viewed as factual accounts of some area or some topic. Although there is no reason to begin by assuming that what a map shows is inaccurate, there is equally no reason to think that it tells the whole story. All maps are artifacts of someone's priorities; the cartographer must select the area depicted, the features shown in that area, and the relative emphasis placed on types of information (natural features, highways, political boundaries, cities of varying size), and then lay them out and draw attention to specific details for particular purposes. This makes neither the cartographer devious nor the map unreliable. It places the responsibility on the user to pick a map with relevant information and a suitable format.

Similarly, prudent deans are in constant need of reliable maps while exploring, traversing, developing, mining, or trying to transform the face of the college. They must consult all available maps before setting out on any of these activities and refer to the best sources of information for refining their position along the way. Where is the highway clear for speedy progress, and where is it washed out by the ravages of fiscal rescission or political storms? Where lurk dragons and trolls? What areas offer the best prospect for growing new crops and sustaining the enterprise? Where can resources for building new communities be found, and are these resources lying ready to hand? Are they already in use but subject to reassignment? Or must they be excavated at much toil and risk? The dean will want to gather information from all possible sources in order to build a detailed mental map of the college, but as with all maps, the information must be recognized as privileging certain themes or parties—in short, as partial in both senses.

But even as deans are travelers relying on maps prepared by others, they also change the terrain not only of the college itself but also of the adjoining territories with which the college has relationships on the rest of the campus and in the wider community. That is, deans must not only read and use maps but be makers of new maps. This requires three qualities: a keen eye for understanding the current lay of the land; the ability to see what previous cartographers have not seen, or at least not seen fit to record; and the steadiness of purpose to sell that new mental map to the college and the campus. The successful dean will not merely have programs and take action but will transform the landscape in the minds of its inhabitants—faculty, staff, and students. No dean can draw a new map in disregard of current facts or the advice of the longtime population of the region, but eventually the map will show new places of settlement and growth, new routes linking parts hitherto unconnected, newly discovered resources and features. Some will always have been there but gone unnoticed, others will be freshly created. Creating such a pathbreaking map is the hardest single project of any deanship—except for persuading others to start using it.

The Crossword Puzzle

This image developed out of the personal enjoyment one of us takes as a crossword puzzle enthusiast. For the enthusiast, scarcely a day goes by without at least one puzzle to amuse and frustrate. Moreover, something in that daily mental challenge corresponds to the way deans spend their days at work, and like the crosswords in *The New York Times* the challenges grow steadily more challenging throughout the week. In fact, the correspondence may be greater even than the normal mystery-solving impulse of the academic (the favorite amusement of the scholar is the murder mystery, which permits harmless personal fantasies along with the pleasure of outwitting the author). But what makes crosswords so apt a metaphor for deaning? Several things do.

The most obvious feature of a crossword is its framework. Solving a puzzle requires working within constraints that are not of one's own design, and no solution, however ingenious, can run beyond the puzzle's border. A pity that one of the most highly prized skills in the academy is thinking outside the box! We are always thinking of inventive answers, and even inventive questions; the dean may hear a dozen stimulating ideas a week and wish to act on some or most of them. The constraints within which we work, whether fiscal, political, organizational, or intellectual, are not less real for being irksome, and they have the beneficial effect of keeping us focused on the problem (or the opportunity) as it is, not as we would like it to be.

Furthermore, even in the overall frame of the puzzle, the way is studded with limits and impediments; answers can be of only a prescribed size and run in a prescribed direction. If we consider an unworked crossword simply as a visual object, we are confronted with a positive and a negative image playing against each other. At first glance, we see the blocks more than the spaces; indeed, the design of the blocks can have an aesthetic appeal arising from its symmetry and its contrasts, rather like a quilt pattern waiting to be worked. It simultaneously tempts the puzzle solver with opportunity and limitation.

Like an Escher design, the puzzle contains two contrary patterns; seen one way, it is an invitation to participate in completing the pattern by supplying answers to the clues provided. As we fill in the spaces, our perception of the pattern shifts from a picture of lack and openness to one of resource and plenitude. As puzzle solver, we become one of the architects, or rather the authors, of the resulting work. From another perspective, we also experience the blocks themselves, the limitations on our inventiveness, as positive components of design, not merely as curtailments on the free rein of our answers. The ground of the puzzle is a fact in its own right, a reality to be not merely accepted but appreciated, lived in, and worked with. In just such a way, the grounding pattern of a college as the new dean encounters it will have a strong effect on his or her attitude toward possibilities, priorities, and relations with those who make up the local reality (or the details of the map, to revert to our previous image).

Although the job of a dean brings puzzle after puzzle, each must be solved by starting from the realities, the traditions, and the logical prospects of the college. A dean is never (well, hardly ever) given a blank slate to fill in at will—and any dean should be very concerned about a college with so little sense of its own identity or resources that it presents neither pattern nor limit to the imagination and ambitions of the dean.

A crossword does not proceed on the basis of fully formed questions but with clues, teasing and enigmatic hints. The good news for the puzzler—better than the usual situation of a dean—is that these clues, properly interpreted, always yield the correct answer. The puzzle is not intrinsically unworkable nor is any clue a false datum. However, clues are frequently both obscure and misleading, built on bad puns or tricky definitions. These may not require any more specialized knowledge than would a straightforward clue, but they do call for a keen sense of the humorous possibilities in a statement and for flexibility to follow a sudden change in the subject one thought was under discussion.

It is equally true that an academic administrator, in working through the issues of the college and dealing with the wider campus context, is more often confronted by clues than by direct information or even clearly formulated questions. This situation is the result of two influences. First, the academy, for all its structural conservatism, is committed to the discovery and dissemination of new knowledge. It lives on a routine of discovering answers that are immediately treated as the next generation of questions. Thus the subject matter under consideration is constantly shifting before one's gaze, and the academic community's view of any given question shifts at the same rate. We may feel fortunate even to get clues that lead us toward a definable result.

The second reason is closely akin to the first: our work as academics is a kind of semantic and logical game, and this inevitably carries over into the way we talk. Academics take a frequently maddening pleasure in ambiguity, wit, and other forms of verbal play. As a result, discussions of new ideas, suggestions—and even strongly stated requests—sometimes seem more like a trail of bread crumbs than a well-formed loaf of bread to chew on!

Because the crossword is intended for a wide audience, its subject matter is correspondingly sweeping. The puzzle solver needs a broad range of general knowledge to make much headway or to derive much satisfaction, but because many topics reappear from puzzle to puzzle, we acquire a storehouse of facts and words that may never cross our path otherwise (who ever uses "anoa" outside the world of puzzles?) but are a part of our working vocabulary in this setting.

In the American style of crossword, all answers are fully interlocking. This means that every entry not only must be correct but also will contribute to constructing—or distorting—the answers to several other intersecting questions. Every dean knows the painful applicability of this comparison. Most frequent are the allocation choices: Should the expansion line go to Spanish or mathematics?

Should the precious open office be kept for faculty use, assigned to TAs in English to tutor hundreds of undergraduates in their discussion sections, or converted into a computer lab where graduate students in history, political science, and sociology can do their research?

In each case, progress for one unit may mean stasis, or even retrenchment, for the others, but such a shift of resources may allow judicious adjustments to the size or focus of a unit that has grown beyond its sustainable dimensions, and that is progress too. In fact, the decision may well have a greater impact on the unit that does *not* get resources than on the unit that does.

More appealing is the challenge of advancing more than one ambition with the same decision—supplying letters for words in both directions, as it were. Faculty appointments that link a stronger department with a less mature one can give both of them a new capacity and a shared sense of engagement in new activities; support for academic programs that cross disciplinary boundaries, physical facilities that benefit several units, and scholarship funds that help both underrepresented student groups and undersubscribed programs are other good illustrations of the process.

And finally, whatever success or failure with the current puzzle, tomorrow morning will bring a whole new puzzle, with its own design, constraints, clues, and answers. Experience steadily builds both a knowledge base and adeptness at interpreting the clues. Just as the Sunday puzzle has a hidden theme or gimmick, so there are unspoken themes, nuances, and familiar topics on the job.

Still, there is at least one crucial difference between the crossword puzzle and the dean's job: the puzzle comes preconstructed. Each clue can have only one answer, and that answer is known—to the puzzle maker, but not to you—before you ever consider the first clue. It is a very good thing that deaning departs from puzzle solving in this respect. Instead of hoping to catch up with a predetermined course of action, deans have the freedom to devise solutions as numerous and as creative as the constraints of resources, institutional policy, and political reality will permit, and choose among them. In this way, they get to be puzzle maker as well as solver!

Deaning as Part of an Ongoing Academic Career

A glance around the room at a gathering of deans, or any extended conversation in such a group, will suggest that deans fall into three broad groups, reflecting the needs of their particular college, their motivation and attitude upon entering the job, and their career plans as the job progresses.

The Faculty Citizen-Dean

A very traditional view of the deanship, now mostly seen in smaller liberal arts colleges, is that it should be a short-term engagement, not intended to last more than four years. Most faculty who become deans in this context would not think of moving to another institution simply to be a dean; it is a role that a senior faculty member takes on at home, an act of *noblesse oblige*.

In this model, the dean is on loan from his or her department, a role akin to that of an ambassador to a small and placid island republic. Everyone understands from the beginning that the ambassador will go back to the department and resume the full-time life of teaching and scholarship that made him or her an appropriate choice to become dean in the first place. Such a dean is almost invariably a well-respected scholar and a model academic citizen. The record may include service as chair of a major department or leadership in faculty self-governance, but the appointment as dean is not primarily in recognition of administrative adeptness. Instead, it is a simple statement of confidence in a senior colleague who understands the place and its people, and can be relied on to do The Right Thing.

This is the quintessential faculty member-dean. During this time away from normal faculty service, the incumbent tries not to weaken any significant tie to the academic world to which he or she is accustomed but rather to carry the experience and habits of a skilled academic, undiluted, into a new role, and work from the same premises, priorities, and (as far as possible) procedures as before.

The Corporate Dean

This approach is (very loosely) based on notions of corporate management that have swept through academic administration at an accelerating pace in the past two decades. Faculty usually would not endorse, much less adopt, the corporate management mentality for the academy; indeed, the two worlds seem starkly antithetical to most faculty.

The impetus for a corporate approach comes rather from the senior leaders of campus administration who are keenly aware of the need for competent, prudent administrators to lead the component parts of the enterprise. As presidents have been cast more often in the role of corporate executives (reflecting the personal habits and preferences of the trustees, transmogrified by the aspirations and anxieties of the university), so the view of the academy as a business first and an intellectual beehive second has become normative for virtually all research universities and for most others as well.

This style of managing the academy entails a different view of how the institution is structured, of the roles that various groups should play, and of the basis on which decisions are made. A faculty member who becomes a dean in this setting is more likely—eventually if not at the outset—to see academic issues as defined by resources and policies, leading to solutions and actions that are cast in quantitative terms, rather than starting from the familiar faculty perspective of programs, colleagues, external stimuli, and local ambitions, and casting outcomes in terms of values.

This is not to suggest that one approach is inherently better than the other; however, they will look very different and have different value to the two populations with which the dean must deal: the faculty and the campus administration. Of course, where resources are scarce and ideas plentiful—that is, in nearly every college—careful stewardship and planning are essential, and all deans will be conscious of fiscal constraints and tantalizing opportunities. The difference will be one of emphasis, presentation, and justification.

Of more personal significance, this style of deaning will put the college and its operations in a new light; indeed, serving as a dean in a "corporate" setting is likely to create a permanent change in one's view of the university as an institution and even of one's priorities for an academic career. Returning to a full-time role as scholar-teacher may bring a strong sense of relief or a lingering sense of regret, but the view of the campus will never be the same.

The Accidental Tourist-Dean

This is the most common model. Faculty who have had extensive and at least sporadically satisfying experience with departmental administration or faculty governance see deanship as a logical next step. They realize that the role of dean is not a simple extension of the normal faculty routine but rather one that builds on the administrative world glimpsed from the department chair's desk. Accordingly, the new dean expects a new distribution of time and effort (little or no regular teaching, for example) but may expect no big surprises in the administrative content of the job. Usually, the new accidental tourist-dean plunges into the world of administration with little or no systematic preparation and swiftly discovers how high the stack of obligations really is, how unforgiving the calendar, and how varied the range of activities.

The nearly inevitable result is a dramatic attenuation of the activities at the core of the faculty member's life—teaching, ongoing research, regular involvement in disciplinary organizations and meetings, supervision of graduate students. There is no conscious intent to make a break with one's familiar life as a faculty member, but there is also no definite timetable or resolve to return to the status quo ante. The unwary dean may quickly wonder whether there has been a ghastly mistake. It is extremely important to come to grips with the realities of the transition and become comfortable with the nature of the new job.

The central feature of each of these models is the degree to which one sees deaning both as an academic role and as something different from a slightly recast faculty role. Different institutions will have expectations that will determine to a great extent what kind of dean will succeed, or even get appointed. Anyone hoping to become a dean needs to be conscious of these expectations, deliberate in accepting the model, and comfortable in what it will require. If a corporate dean ends up at an institution that wants a faculty member who will keep up a fair amount of teaching, vigorous research, and strong ties to the disciplinary department, that dean is likely to have a short and frustrating career as a dean. A scholar who cannot tolerate a reduction in research time yet is called on to spend 40 percent of the week in external development efforts will leave the deanship on a sour note, with a damaging hole in the part of his or her career that matters most.

But if there is a good fit between what an institution wants in its dean and the individual's own long-term values for a career in the academy—not just for the next few years or for the past few—then deaning can be the most interesting job on campus. The following chapters will explore facets of that job, from the decision to try for a deanship through the decision to leave it behind for better—or, at least, other—pursuits.

Suggestions for Further Reading

Axtell, James. *The Pleasures of Academe.* Lincoln: University of Nebraska Press, 1998.

Hines, Samuel M., Jr. "What to Read." In George Allan (ed.), *Resource Handbook for Academic Deans* (pp. 36–40).Washington, D.C.: American Conference of Academic Deans, 1999.

Kolodny, Annette. *Failing the Future: A Dean Looks at Higher Education in the Twenty-First Century.* Durham, N.C.: Duke University Press, 1998.

Rosovsky, Henry. *The University: An Owner's Manual.* New York: Norton, 1990.

Tucker, Allan, and Robert Bryan. *The Academic Dean: Dove, Dragon, and Diplomat* (2nd ed.). Phoenix: American Council on Education/Oryx Press, 1999.

CHAPTER TWO

WHAT IT TAKES TO BE A DEAN

A s even the most cursory survey of deans will show, there is no best or clearest route to a deanship. Many kinds of positions provide useful experience, but much also depends on the traditions of one's academic discipline and
the kind of college seeking a dean. A college of arts and sciences may prize
range and diversity—the ability to understand and work with faculty over
the vast span of the traditional disciplines—as greatly as it values administrative experience or depth of scholarly record. A college of engineering will
normally require a record of research funded by a range of external sources,
including industrial and federal grants, which are the lifeblood of any such college. By contrast, colleges of fine arts are frequently led not by creative artists
but by administrators from arts-related backgrounds who are able to persuade
creative people to work together. A dean of business will often combine experience from the business world with academic credentials in order to have
credibility with constituencies inside and outside the institution. Small colleges
often will look for deans who, as students or faculty members, have experienced
a similar type of institution and are prepared for their specific challenges. Thus
everything in this chapter must be set in the context of field, college, and institutional type.

Relevant Credentials and Experience

As when traveling to a new country, one needs the proper credentials to gain admission, but here these consist as much of experience as of documents. The process thus begins with a critical but appreciative scan of one's overall record, always bearing in mind that preparation for a deanship can come from a wide range of activities both inside and outside the academy. No part of the record should be disregarded until it has been measured against the expectations of this new line of work.

Chair

It is a common article of faith (especially among department chairs) that service as a chair is the most direct route to a deanship, and in fact, assuming that the chair is more than a figurehead or a rotating obligation, this position does offer the opportunity to gain valuable experience in a number of key areas, such as budget, personnel, and planning. Working closely with one's peers on common issues, learning how to say no, and perhaps even having to fire colleagues, offers preparation for many aspects of deaning, including some of the less pleasant. The chair must negotiate with students, faculty, and staff every bit as much as a dean does and must be prepared to defend decisions to those above and below in the chain of command.

Moreover, today's department chairs are involved more than ever in fundraising and grant-seeking, not just for their own projects but for the department itself. They learn how to handle effectively and efficiently the relentless demands on time and energy that all academic leadership positions impose. Perhaps most important, many of the competencies necessary for a deanship can only be gained through holding a line position where one is directly accountable for the success of the unit. Small wonder, then, that experience as chair discourages as many people as it encourages to become deans.

Given these facts, a chair has a distinct vantage point for viewing the deanship. The chair reports to the dean, and over time sees how the dean performs every function, from conducting meetings to allocating resources, participating in the numbing round of ceremonial tasks, and—more rewarding if also delicate—listening to concerns. In this observation, there is as much to learn from negative as from positive examples. Department chairs know how it feels to receive the dean's requests and decisions, and their own responses as chairs can instruct their behavior in the other role. Unworkable deadlines that make the blood pressure rise, for example, will make a chair vow never to act this way as dean; it is an idle vow because the academy marches on impossible deadlines, but it illustrates how only a chair can know the frustration stemming from an unreasonable dean's regime. Still, for better or for worse, observing the dean from the privileged position of chair and analyzing strengths and weaknesses of style can be an invaluable way both to understand the dean's role and to decide whether to pursue it.

Staff Positions

If the department chair is seen as the most probable point of access to a dean's office, the opposite view is commonly held for academic staff positions: they are dead ends in campus administration and aspiring deans should not trap themselves in this area. In truth, although any position can be a dead end in the right hands, there is no reason to see staff roles as inherently barren. An academic staff position such as assistant or associate dean in a college, or perhaps in the central administration, in the provost's office or graduate school, provides a broader view of the college's place in the campus and the overall workings of the institution than does the chair's closer but narrower perspective in the college.

One disadvantage is that staff positions often entail relatively few line responsibilities and thus, in that sense at least, they provide less direct preparation for accountable leadership. Nevertheless, assistant and associate deans see the dean's office from within, and they take on shared responsibility for its operation. They learn its dynamics, the efficiencies and drawbacks of its structure, and the interplay among priorities and personnel in a complex administrative office (see Chapter Five on the organization and management of the college office). This can be a valuable opportunity to consider what works and what does not, to gain insights that can permit more rapid and accurate appraisal of the situation elsewhere as a new dean.

The "A-dean" (as assistant and associate deans sometimes style themselves) performs a number of decanal responsibilities, both those that are permanently delegated and those that require standing in for the dean. From this flexible role, it is easier to know whether a deanship would be enjoyable or merely tolerable (a simple test is to contemplate representing the college at official functions such as commencement or student awards ceremonies, or providing gracious and appropriate remarks on nearly any topic with little or no advance notice).

Furthermore, as part of the academic staff, A-deans participate in the planning and assessment so vital to the health of the college, and some are involved with personnel issues, including the inner sanctum of academic judgment, promotion, and tenure. Others have a voice in budgeting and have separate accounts to manage. Academic staff are brought in to witness discussions, such as investigations into sexual harassment, where a third party is needed. Thus, taking a college staff position can be a good way to get a complete sense of the dean's job and its relationship to the institutional structure.

The larger hierarchy on campus is naturally found in the central administration, and that setting can also afford vital experience to the aspiring dean. Working in the campus administration offers a perspective on the entire enterprise: how the various colleges are structured, how they relate to each other and the institution, and where their strengths and weaknesses lie. All of this information is of crucial importance to a dean, who must relate the college's needs to the full institutional enterprise, especially the academic areas. Anyone who holds a post in the campus administrative structure and then decides to change institutions has an advantage in sizing up positions elsewhere and can shorten the learning curve in the new situation. For those aiming at a deanship in a doctoral research university, experience in graduate school administration is especially helpful because it requires hard thinking about issues of research quality, evaluation by the stern jury of national reviews, and the necessity to work at the forefront of knowledge. Because the office of the dean of graduate studies or vice chancellor for research opens a window onto the role of research in every part of the campus, staff positions in this part of the central administration often serve as training ground for aspiring administrators. Taking advantage of this expectation can lead to participation in institutional planning, budget building, and resource decisions.

Another benefit of working centrally is the chance to build relationships with the institutional leadership and learn from expert practitioners of the administrative art; when one is seeking advice about the most reliable instructional technology or the fairest and least incendiary procedure by which to distribute named professorships, these colleagues are ideal mentors. They are also informed, and usually sympathetic, sources for career planning. And not least, when the time comes to interview for a deanship at another institution, encounters with the campus leadership there will lead more readily to a comfortable and productive interaction if the candidate is accustomed to dealing with those at the top.

One final benefit of a staff position, often unappreciated by those who have not had the opportunity, is simply the hands-on experience of researching and writing reports, letters, proposals, position papers, speeches, and related documents. As it happens, many in the professorial ranks have little notion of the challenge that comes with writing the varieties and volume of expository prose required of a dean's office, nor do they know where to obtain the information needed for administrative reports and proposals. This kind of work, therefore, yields further competency for a deanship by inculcating and refining both the content and processes of academic administration.

All these advantages notwithstanding, an aspiring dean should not remain, even inadvertently, in a staff position for more than a few years. A lengthy sojourn in a staff role is often read as a sign of career complacency or limited capacity for leadership and can actually detract from an otherwise convincing candidacy.

Faculty Governance and Committees

Many faculty view committee work and participation in faculty governance with disdain. Committee assignments may befall those who are not there to refuse them, and campus governance sometimes seems to attract those without enough projects to do. Hardly the stuff of which deans are made! Yet, ironically, that service, if conscientiously performed and focused on pursuits beneficial to the department or college, can be both a useful credential and a training ground for such a move.

For example, serving in the faculty senate, participating in union activities, and working in other governance structures on campus provide critical knowledge of how the institution works from the faculty perspective. The dean who understands and respects the role of faculty governance in higher education will be able to involve faculty in the essential business of planning and achieving goals for the college. Valuable lessons in working with difficult colleagues and gauging faculty opinion come through such service, not to mention a greater understanding of the esoteric world of athletics on campus. These activities on one's record show an ability to work productively with faculty colleagues in areas of dispute, an essential skill in any form of deaning. Moreover, because such work is putatively voluntary, it shows an interest in the health of the institution and a willingness to invest time and energy to improve it.

No less beneficial is the effect of encountering the astonishing variety of faculty perspectives on one's institution: the further afield one goes on campus the more remarkable the anthropological encounters. There is no substitute for a classicist's exposure to the academic worldview of a mechanical engineer or agronomist (and vice versa!) while grappling with a tough case on the campus promotion and tenure committee, or hearing the vice president for business explain to a faculty committee why the university's budgeting process allows construction of new buildings but not recruitment of faculty to work in them. Such exposure is part of the education of a dean and cannot all occur after one is sitting in the dean's chair.

Even within the world of the college, work on curriculum, promotion, and tenure, program review, and faculty searches are especially useful assignments, impelling a broader and more balanced view of a college that most faculty members know mainly from the perspective of a single department. It is no remarkable discovery, for example, that building, maintaining, and reforming the curricula of individual departments in the college, and of individual colleges vis-à-vis the campus, is a profoundly interdependent activity—the burden of a new mathematics prerequisite for engineering majors will fall mainly on the arts and sciences college, and the recasting of the psychology major will have ripple effects throughout the institution. But faculty who have worked only on presenting their own discipline to students and defending it from the depredations of external forces will bring a fatal parochialism to the dean's desk.

Yet another avenue to this broader comparative and analytical view is service on an institutional program review committee for another discipline. However the assessment process is structured on any given campus, there are opportunities for learning about the various disciplines in depth and to consider ways to evaluate mission, goals, quality, and institutional contributions of academic units. For example, despite the great differences in method and subject between the sciences and the humanities, an English department can gain much from learning how a superior chemistry program maintains its excellence and adds value to the institution through its research funds, cooperative projects with industry, and support for other science-related disciplines on campus.

All these activities lead to greater awareness of how less familiar parts of the enterprise work. In the college itself, for a faculty member who is pondering a move into administration, the best opportunity for scouting the terrain is to serve on a dean search committee. This assignment not only provides a clear and detailed view of institutional expectations but also gives a ringside seat to watch the recruitment process and see the best candidates perform. As the next chapter will discuss, being a candidate for dean is a rather different activity from being a candidate for a faculty position, and there is no better test of one's own interest than serving on a search committee.

Committee service can also include more painful activities, such as grievance panels or judicial boards for such issues as sexual harassment or dereliction of duty. The unhappy wisdom gained through this kind of responsibility can spare the dean, as the responsible officer for adjudicating the follies and worse to which a very few faculty succumb, from being caught unawares by fatal naiveté.

Other Experience

Participation in faculty development workshops may likewise enhance readiness and credentials. Many institutions offer these at little or no cost to faculty members. Topics range from teaching techniques, computing skills, general education, and leadership skills to the future of higher education. Even though workshops are no substitute for hands-on experience, there is considerable value in simply being familiar with some of the burning issues facing higher education. In some fields such as engineering, nursing, and business, professional accrediting organizations offer insights into the latest issues and prospects. Preparing materials for accreditation reviews on one's own campus and serving on visiting teams elsewhere are two excellent means for keeping up with the field. The ability to analyze, compare, and evaluate programs in their institutional settings cannot be overestimated. Quite apart from learning more about the institution, team members gain important experience in analyzing programs by meeting with campus leaders, reading self-studies with a critical eye, and asking the hard questions about assessment procedures or the imbalance of women in leadership positions, for example.

Finally, professional experience outside the academy itself is important for some disciplines such as nursing, education, and social work, but less important for others. One can often gain credibility in one's own area by working in the field, but at the dean's level the nature of the responsibility held is more important than the simple fact of having worked in a professional area. Supervising employees, managing a large budget, or leading teams of coworkers will clearly build skills relevant to a deanship, whereas simply practicing as an accountant or a chemical engineer outside the walls of the academy offers little that is of distinctive merit for the decanal candidate.

Necessary Skills and Expected Duties

Whatever one's background, the surest measure of preparation is to place all these possibilities in the light of the necessary skills and expected duties of a dean. In the last analysis nobody (not even a search committee!) can know better than you whether deaning is a sound decision for you, although it also makes sense to consult trusted colleagues, plus a spouse or partner, for an informed, if not necessarily detached, opinion. Equally important, this kind of honest self-scrutiny is vital once in the job. Skills and interests will evolve, as will the responsibilities of the role, and careful, periodic reflection on the match between one's own predilections and the requirements of the position one holds can preserve one's sanity and one's post!

Leadership

The biggest day-to-day challenge for most deans is keeping the big picture in mind while attending to the details that keep the college functioning efficiently. Ronald Heifetz has called such leadership, which is at the center of 99 percent of discussions among deans, "active and reflective. One has to alternate between participating and observing" (1994, p. 252). He compares leaders to star athletes who are able to observe and influence the patterns of the game while still playing skillfully. So also a dean as a player-coach must take sufficient time-outs for analysis and reflection even while doing the job, either to gain perspective for the next steps or to make a strategic adjustment in the midst of a play. Thus even when confronted with unexpected budget cuts (a midyear rescission, for example) the dean must be able to reposition key resources in order to continue addressing the college's priorities.

A good dean is an optimist who focuses on the college's strengths even while addressing its weaknesses. That positive outlook will become the perspective of the faculty, staff, and students, or at least those who will make the greatest difference. To tip the balance of outlook, the wise dean will remember to recognize publicly the accomplishments of faculty and staff, and to sustain a sense of momentum especially when times are hard. As Heifetz observes, this positive approach "provides the ongoing capacity to generate new possibilities" (1994, p. 275). Indeed, setbacks can be the most energizing source of fresh initiatives. Imagine an initiative to reconstruct the economics department where the search for a new chair to lead the effort has failed amid rising gloom and apprehension from both supporters and critics of the plan. Rather than insisting on the plan and turning to a reliable but unexciting internal candidate, the dean decides to recast the description of objectives and devises new strategies to find the right person (including in all probability new inducements to attract an even stronger candidate for an even harder task).

Advocacy

The dean is equal parts deviser and advocate of leadership. Above all, to be an effective advocate for the college, the dean must believe in its work, know where it is going, be able to speak to its strengths, and most importantly, be able to persuade skeptics and opponents that it is an enterprise worth the investment of time, energy, and resources.

Few deans have faced this challenge with greater zeal than deans of the colleges formerly known as home economics. In the early 1970s, attempts to professionalize fields such as textile studies or domestic sociology that had long lived in the shadowy edges of colleges of agriculture were greeted by skepticism, along with calls for colleges of home economics to justify their existence. The response has been a proliferation of creative nomenclature (for example, home ecology, or human resources and family sciences), and the champions of change have been the deans. They knew they had to overcome prejudice as they tried to recruit male students and demonstrate that their curricula are both relevant and substantial in today's world. Many of these colleges offer important science in their nutrition courses and research, for example, but rather than buck the reputation of the mainstream curricula and research in agriculture, they have put out their message by touting the kinds of careers their graduates enter, offering tours of teaching and research laboratories, and showing the practical relevance of the various fields of study, such as the development of more durable textiles.

To perform this kind of advocacy, a dean must obviously have—or develop— a college infrastructure that can sustain claims about its promise, but further must personally take the time to master the details of the college's strengths and identify the resources needed to move ahead. Effective advocacy cannot rest on enthusiasm or optimism alone, and will be fruitless without the faculty and their work, for they are the only convincing evidence for the quality of the college. If the dean does not know the college in intimate detail and with ready illustrations but instead falls back on generalities or fudges answers to specific questions, the case is dead on arrival. Conversely, a clear purpose, an arsenal of detail at hand (but not mercilessly inflicted), and a passionate advocacy for the cause can move mountains. The final link in this chain is the articulation of the college's place and ambitions in the larger picture of the institution.

Planning

Obviously the dean's advocacy will be tightly tied to leadership in developing a vision, plan, and goals for the college. We will return to this crucial topic later (see Chapter Seven), but should include a word here on planning as a central activity expected of every dean. The hallmark of any individual dean is his or her vision for the college and plan for realizing that vision. A consultant can be very helpful in the process, eliciting ideas, identifying steps, and building a timetable, but the dean bears ultimate responsibility for both the process and the final document. Moreover, planning, like advocacy for the plan, is an ongoing process that includes monitoring and updating on a regular schedule and commissioning subsidiary plans as necessary. The college budget is an annual expression of this subsidiary planning process; each year the dean ensures that it reflects the priorities of the college plan and drives progress toward the achievement of those priorities.

Assessment

The dean must be fully acquainted with the institutional, state-mandated, and regional accreditation reviews that will affect the college and be prepared to make them work to the college's benefit. External evaluations can easily be seen as hostile and uninformed by the units under review, so only the dean's dogged engagement will ensure that they are taken seriously and that recommendations and other findings will have a response.

Just as departments and individual faculty may feel that evaluation is an overworked tool, so deans often believe that their colleges are overreviewed, particularly at state-supported institutions with aggressive higher education commissions. But it is also true that many institutions lack any useful system of formal review and evaluation. In those cases, the dean needs to develop processes for assessing the quality of departments, programs, chairs, faculty members, students, and staff. These processes should involve external advice, as a matter of both practicality and credibility. National assessment workshops and conferences are a very useful source of advice on evaluation in the college.

Personnel

A vital ongoing form of assessment is personnel review. Faculty are notoriously sensitive to the annual review of their performance and it is a matter of universal belief that administrators face less severe, even less interested or less honest performance reviews than faculty. Thus the dean sets the example for personnel evaluation in the college, and however the institution constructs administrator reviews the dean must be fair, exacting, and open in evaluating staff members, department chairs, and others who report to the office. Woe to the dean who conveys the impression (still less can it ever be true) that the dean's staff is immune to the standards of accountability used for other personnel in the college! By example and training, the dean ensures that department chairs and other supervisors are versed in procedures for evaluation and staff development.

The dean's worst nightmare is a personnel crisis (especially a termination) in which the record does not indicate that problems were identified and brought to the attention of the employee or faculty member. Some supervisors find it hard to believe that they are doing a disservice when they give a positive evaluation to "encourage" a person whose performance is substandard. The dénouement of that play is always bloody and hard to watch.

When it comes to personnel, the dean's responsibilities also include structuring the college office, appointing department chairs, approving new or replacement positions, interviewing candidates, and participating in the promotion and tenure process. Although each of these important functions will be addressed in more detail later (see Chapters Six and Nine), an aspiring dean needs to weigh the prospect of settling personnel issues for all parts of the college. This is not a simple matter of obeying the institution's rules for position approval, searching, and hiring. The dean must provide leadership in both allocation of precious resources and quality control in the recruitment process.

Budget Management

The topic of money is never far from a dean's mind, starting with the simple fact of responsibility for a budget that may run well over a hundred million dollars per year. Although all but the smallest of colleges have a budget officer, the final responsibility for maintaining a balanced and rational budget resides with the dean. This fact is dramatically underscored each year when the dean presents the college's formal budget request to the central administration. Here is an opportunity for a compelling but restrained presentation of the facts, and a reminder and update of the college's vision. It is also a powerful temptation for rhetoric and histrionics, which are to be avoided at all costs for the simple reason that the most compelling budget presentations can still find the least hospitable reception because all colleges are in competition for finite resources (see more on this in Chapter Eight).

Outreach

Whether in a public or private institution, every college is increasingly dependent on the generosity of others. The dean plays an important role in determining what those linkages will be and then establishing, cultivating, and finally, concluding them. These arrangements will be part of the college plan and will serve a variety of goals.

Fundraising in particular is claiming an expanding part of deans' time, especially at private institutions. Professional development staff will play crucial roles in shaping plans, identifying prospects, and devising strategies, but it is the dean who must first determine the purposes for which funds are needed and establish priorities. Furthermore, the dean's role includes endless receptions and special events, private lunches and public appearances to underscore what is needed and to acknowledge what is given. It is a blend of planning, cheerleading, team managing, and overeating (see more on development in Chapter Fifteen).

But friends are as important as funds. Partnerships with industry can facilitate the exchange of researchers and opportunities for student internships and practica. The pharmaceutical industry is a natural ally, for example, for a program in molecular biology. Public service partnerships can lend needed expertise to state and local government while bringing real-life problems into the classroom for study. Programs that bring the expertise of faculty members to the community in clinics, reading groups, lecture series, and commemorative events likewise build important alliances with individuals and groups outside the campus. Some deans appoint a staff member to coordinate and develop outreach efforts, but once again the dean's responsibility is to lead, to plan, to communicate, and to evaluate.

Time Management

In view of this lengthy but by no means exhaustive catalogue of the skills and duties that a college deanship entails, it can be no surprise that time management is a significant issue in the dean's life. In fact, the only resource in shorter supply than money—even in badly underfunded colleges—is the dean's time. Everyone wants the dean's ear (if not head), but the dean cannot be available to everyone who arrives at the door.

A discreet and diplomatic assistant, operating under clear guidelines, should control the calendar and telephone. According to the dean's preferences, certain times will be blocked out for quiet work or handling emergencies, the latter tending to subsume the former. Specified types of inquiries go to the dean's staff or other appropriate personnel on campus. Regular meetings and other obligations are entered on the calendar. From there, the dean needs to set priorities. Appointments with supporters of the college, consultations with students, talks at departmental faculty meetings, discussions with department chairs—what is most important to the job at the moment? The dean does not want a reputation for being inaccessible or so hurried during meetings that the essential work does not get done. However, the dean needs to set limits on "face time" to avoid becoming a sounding board for everyone with an agenda. And realistically, the dean will develop a list of people who are not to receive appointments under any circumstances.

One dean established her relationship with the college early in her term by announcing that during two ninety-minute periods each week her door was open to anyone—faculty, staff, or student—who wanted to talk with her on any topic. No appointments, no boundaries on subject. If nobody was waiting outside, her time was yours until someone else came; if someone was waiting, you had at least ten minutes and then had to yield to the next person. This simple and ingenious policy allowed her to meet a large number of people quickly, hear about issues while they were still fresh, and convey the unmistakable message that she was genuinely interested in all issues and all people of the college.

Smart deans are assiduous about meeting deadlines. Therefore, at times they clear the calendar in order to complete a project and do it well. Their assistants maintain "tickler files" as reminders of forthcoming obligations and set up the necessary meetings to get the work done. Life is not always predictable, however, and some deans maintain the pretense of a regular existence but then bump scheduled items from their calendars when something more urgent or interesting comes up. This practice reveals a leader who is caught off guard or spooked by the unexpected. In practical terms, less exciting work goes neglected, and people who have been bumped several times will get the message not to return. If that really is the intended message, then there are more polite and less damaging ways to send it without gaining a reputation for capriciousness, bad manners, and weak communication skills.

Communication

Skillful communication is the most important single weapon in the dean's arsenal. Fortunately, all teachers are familiar with the need for clear communication and many are superb at it—articulate, comfortable, and well-informed without being pedantic. The natural teacher has famously been characterized as good at understanding those who are not very good at explaining, and explaining to those who are not very good at understanding. There could be no better description of what is needed in administration. Unfortunately, administrators have (and sometimes deserve) a reputation as murky or devious. Whether the problem arises from poor writing or speaking skills, unfamiliarity with the issues, defensiveness about an unwelcome message, or indifference to the audience, the dean will appear to be hiding something or prevaricating, and the reaction will be hostile.

But accuracy, clarity, focus, consistency, and a dose of wit will serve any situation and show that the dean puts thought and care into dealing with all groups. Written materials such as reports, formal presentations, or letters should create no problem because they call for a polished, formal style that will assure care with both detail and form. Speaking creates more problems owing to the variety of audiences a dean faces. Because deans have so many speaking obligations, there is a strong temptation to keep a storehouse of remarks and deliver them off the cuff. After all, it seems easy enough for a practiced teacher to talk ad lib on any topic and at any length. This leads some to make inadequate preparations for specific occasions, giving an impression of indifference or ineffectiveness. Brief greetings to an alumni luncheon may be every bit as important as remarks at the faculty meeting; it is important not to shortchange or overdo either.

Ironically, given the cynical popular view that administrators do nothing but talk, the reverse is closer to the truth. Deans become immersed in issues that fall to their lot and may forget they need to keep others involved or at least informed. Those others may not understand the issue or may view it quite differently. Often this is a fault of time management: the dean is pressed for time and focuses on solving the problem or producing results rather than engaging all parties. In short, a dean may be tempted to skimp on communication in the heat of a project and create unnecessary difficulties. Far better to find some way—perhaps by consciously taking stock at the end of each day—to avoid this trap and use communication as a potent ally.

How Do I Match Up?

If the preceding pages offer a fair sketch of what is needed in a dean, the question for anyone contemplating a deanship now becomes: How does my own dossier compare? Here are two points to consider in this regard:

How Strong Are My Faculty Credentials?

Aspiring deans should take a hard look at their faculty credentials. Simply put, most faculty expect their deans to have convincing dossiers as faculty members because the dean is the embodiment of the faculty in dealing with the university leadership. A weak record as a faculty member makes an unconvincing basis for leading the college, especially for such responsibilities as presiding over judgment of the academic achievements of its faculty. It is an issue of the dean's credibility as the college's leader and stature as its representative. Furthermore, the dean should have earned the rank of full professor by exactly the same standards as the best faculty in the college. For good reasons, faculty respect academic achievement above all else, and a candidate for dean who has a deficient academic record is an implicit affront to the standards of the faculty he or she aspires to lead.

To every statement there is an exception. In colleges of arts and sciences and most others, there is no substitute for extensive accomplishment as a faculty member—in scholarship, teaching, and academic service—in the kind of arena where the deanship is set. But colleges of business, for example, sometimes recruit a dean with substantial corporate experience and valuable connections that match the emphases of their programs. Law and engineering schools likewise sometimes take particular records of external experience as suitable replacements for a full faculty cursus. But no dean can step into a role of academic leadership without being able to address issues of teaching, scholarship, and service and to understand the challenges that faculty members face in these areas.

Have I Enough Relevant Experience?

Most who consider deaning have had experiences such as executive officers or faculty leaders or significant academic staff officers. But how much is enough? Even the most candid and stern self-critic may not be able to answer that question with confidence because the answer entails assessing what has been done and how well. Trusted colleagues, including one's own dean, can be invaluable if they will be candid. But beyond that, there are questions that only the individual can answer about self-confidence, aptness, and motivation. The self-assessment process is important because dean candidates are invariably quizzed about their readiness for the job in every sense of the term (and unfortunately the questioning is sometimes especially sharp if the candidate is female or a member of a minority group). Knowing one's strengths and deficiencies and being able to discuss both of them frankly is a great asset.

If there are substantial gaps in preparation, such as experience in budget matters, but none weighty enough to crush ambition, there may be ways to remedy them in a reasonable amount of time without forcing neglect of current responsibilities, such as an internship with the current dean or a national workshop that offers training for future administrators. Examples of these include the American Council on Education's internships, which run for a full academic year, and summer programs such as those sponsored by Harvard University and Bryn Mawr College. These latter programs normally require the endorsement of the president, whose reaction to the request will offer another built-in reading of one's aspirations.

Do I Want a Deanship?

In the end, the hardest question is that which stood at the head of this chapter but can only be asked at the end of this discovery process: Knowing what is needed and what I have to offer (and assuming that the two are compatible), do I want to make the trip? Following are some cautionary notes, not intended to discourage but to lend perspective to the impact this job will have on one's personal life.

Will I Enjoy Working on Behalf of Others?

Most faculty derive satisfaction from pursuing their own intellectual agenda and achieving their own devising. In that sense, even though we all work for the institution and more narrowly for the college in which we are faculty, we actually work for ourselves. A dean, in contrast, works for others and must take satisfaction from their accomplishments. That is to say, the dean must be able to feel rewarded by the successes of those who have received the college's assistance, whether from funding, staffing, or other resources—or perhaps simply by the smooth administration of the college that allowed the faculty to concentrate on their work.

Can I Live with the Impact on My Teaching and Scholarly Career?

Working for the college rather than for oneself can require a new way of thinking for those who have been long-term faculty members. Even deans who remain active in research will do so at a reduced pace, and inevitably will reflect, "I could have finished that book, or won that prize, or obtained that grant if I had had the time to work on my own project." If that realization will be a cause of ongoing distress, deaning is not a wise choice. Likewise when it comes to contact with students. At larger institutions, the dean's interaction with students is less than a faculty member's except for problem resolution and ceremonial occasions. Meanwhile, deans at small colleges may continue direct student contact, but not through the preferred medium of the classroom. Most deans do some teaching each year, but the crowded administrative calendar, combined with unpredictable intrusions, limits both the kind of course and its scheduling. Teaching after 10 A.M. can be especially problematic as the diurnal crises and preset meetings build up. Even if these activities do not actually conflict with class time, the distraction can diminish one's effectiveness as a teacher. Introductory courses, where students need consistency and nurturing, can be problematic for dean and students. Similarly, a dean who cannot give graduate students the sustained attention they need in their work should step back from that responsibility rather than jeopardize the students' progress.

Surprisingly, it may be easier for a dean to continue a minimally satisfying level of scholarly activity than to teach. A laboratory team can function without constant close supervision; one can hook up with collaborators who can fill in as need be. For research or creative work that is portable, there can be some work time on trips, out of reach of the usual distractions. But deadlines for completing manuscripts or other projects can be harder for deans to meet because they have less control over their time than faculty members. Thus deans must be careful about accepting commitments, because a reputation for being slow or unreliable will mean fewer invitations to work on projects. Finally, the scope of scholarly work and expertise will inevitably narrow: while deans strive to stay in the forefront of their defined research area, they cannot keep up with the whole field the way they did as faculty members. Those considering pursuing a deanship therefore must also consider how they will manage those components of their career that they want to maintain.

What Will Be the Impact on My Personal Life?

With meetings before and after the business day, evening events such as lectures or performances, semiofficial social occasions, athletic events, and weekend recruiting activities for prospective students, the deanship can easily dominate all waking hours, at least for the incautious or compulsive. Attendance at some activities is optional or can be delegated to an associate, but the presence of the dean is often requested even if it is not required. At certain times of the year, especially the six weeks preceding graduation, deans seem to eat nothing but chicken for days at a stretch and may wonder whether to leave the name tag on to be recognized at home.

There is also the impact on spouses or partners. Unless they love attending these kinds of functions, it helps to offer them a choice if their participation is not essential. Spouses or partners would normally be expected to attend cocktails and dinner for the trustees at the president's home, but not a staff awards dinner. The dean must do some entertaining, though not necessarily at home. The hardest part is having so much of the calendar dictated by external forces and therefore having limited choices regarding personal, family, and social life outside the institution. The dean who plans to remain sane will set priorities for time away from the deanship and accept the intrusion that the job brings to the rest.

Am I Ready for Constant Scrutiny?

We laugh at the absurdities that appear in the tabloids and wonder how anyone could take such reports seriously, or why anyone would care, but an allegedly gentler version of the rumor industry operates on campus. The dean's behavior, appearance, and formal and casual remarks in public and private settings are the topic of reports both true and invented. To be sure, comment and judgment are to be expected when the dean is on the job and representing the college, but colleagues will scrutinize everything—a slight change in appearance after a poor night's sleep will bring inquiries about one's health. Private comments to individuals—requests for assistance or confidences to help them understand a problematic situation—circulate and transmogrify like a secret whispered around a dinner table. Individuals of both sexes will try to determine whether the dean favors male or female colleagues in the strong belief that neutrality is impossible. Some will go so far as to grill the dean's spouse or partner for confidential information. Inevitably, false impressions will circulate. In most cases, they are prompted by idle curiosity rather than malice, and a dean can learn to screen the absurd and idle from the intentional and cruel, but an occasional stone will still strike the glass house.

Can I Accept a New Relationship with Colleagues?

The dean is thrust into a new place in the world of the college, and this can strain or even distort individual relationships. Many colleagues, of course, accept the shift, often with mordant witticisms about selling out or fading out, whereas others assume that the individual has not merely taken a new position but become a different person. One faculty member who accepted a year's assignment as acting dean of his college had been collaborating on a book with a colleague, and they ate lunch together every week to discuss the project. When the temporary administrative stint was announced, the colleague said, "I will see you in a year." The almost-dean assured her that he would have time to continue the project, but she said, "That is not the point. I do not eat with Them, and you have become a Them. Call me next year." She stuck to her aversion to administrators but cheerfully resumed lunch and project the next summer when his administrative contagion had passed.

It is very difficult to "be yourself" and be dean. Suddenly people want to socialize with "The Dean" and dimly imagine that, once away from the office and with drinks in hand, they will glean crucial details about the person and his or her decisions. Others view any occasion as a chance to bend the dean's ear on pet peeves or personal ambitions. Frustrating though it can be, one needs to maintain a kind of distance from others because, in their minds at least, they are no longer equals. This can be especially difficult with long-standing colleagues and may best be handled by addressing the subject directly with them. In particular, it is awkward and problematic to have close personal relationships with people you must evaluate. However clear the distinction between personal identity and professional performance may be in the dean's mind, it will not matter when the time comes to deny a promotion. To help avoid this problem, some deans choose friends outside the institution; others focus on their families. To maintain friendships with colleagues, however, it is important to set limits and be careful about observing them.

Am I Ready to Change Locations?

For many reasons it makes sense to embark on a deanship at a new institution. Deans appointed internally tend to carry a certain amount of baggage from the past, including perceived biases and ready-made enemies. There can also be a perception that the dean was anointed rather than chosen honestly from a search, even if that search included external candidates. Conversely, changing institutions means encountering a new system and all its people. This will lengthen the learning curve and perhaps diminish what can be achieved in the first weeks or months. That may feel like a disadvantage to both the dean and the college, or it may seem like a breath of fresh air to both parties.

In order to find a good match of talents and interests, the aspiring dean must be open to a range of possibilities, in geography as well as institutional type. Families, especially spouses or partners with careers of their own, must be full partners in the decision to relocate and that concurrence must come before there is an offer on the table. In one particularly frustrating sequence of events, a very large college ran a lengthy and exhausting search for a dean, and the provost called the winning candidate to make an offer. The candidate accepted at once over the phone, and the considerate but incautious provost immediately called the other finalists to tell them that the search had been concluded. An hour later the successful candidate called back; his wife simply could not bring herself to leave their current location and with much regret he withdrew from consideration. The moral: even having discussed a prospective move in advance, one should never accept a position without conferring about the specific offer with family and others who will be directly affected by the change.

Because faculty members in many fields have enjoyed considerably less mobility over the past three decades than previously was the case, many aspiring deans will have worked at only one institution. The exhilarating prospect of a new role and the alarming thought of leaving the town and the campus where perhaps two decades have been spent (which is about the average single-campus career of those who finally uproot only for a change to administration) can be wrenching. Selling and buying a home, finding new physicians, and reestablishing life in a new community take time and energy. The change is usually invigorating rather than depressing, but not if the upheaval catches the family by surprise.

Can I Handle the Stresses of the Deanship?

Some amount of stress is simply built into being a dean. Hundreds, perhaps thousands, of faculty, students, and staff depend on the dean's leadership for the college to thrive. Because very few situations are unambiguous, a dean may be tempted to revisit or even brood over decisions long after the issue has been handled. There are times when only the inside of your automobile should be privy to your real thoughts and what you would do if you had the power. And no amount of prudent preparation can help a person to foresee all the effects that an action will have. Omniscience is not a part of the dean's skill kit, even if others expect it!

As with all middle managers, the stress comes from both directions. A change in campus leadership could easily mean the end of a dean's tenure in office. The same result can come of arguing against plans that the dean believes to be misguided or even wrong, but failing to defend the college's best interests will lose the confidence of the faculty. All is made harder if attended by misleading statements that cannot be publicly corrected. The dean must plunge ahead with plans and decisions and rise above the swirl of problems. Success in such conditions will be all the more gratifying.

Am I Ready for a New Social Life?

Most academics can gear casual socializing to personal preferences and time available for relaxation. Such a social calendar is feeble preparation for the rigors of a dean's life, as already suggested. At an institution that emphasizes athletics, the football or basketball season may be the focus of constant activity, both for cultivation of supporters and recruitment of students. At smaller colleges, deans are expected to attend alumni functions and report on academic developments. Mingling with trustees, donors, government officials, and community leaders at a variety of events introduces a level of formality far from the casual mores (in dress as well as habits) of faculty life. For those who like more formal occasions, hobnobbing, and meeting new people, this part of the dean's job will be especially enjoyable.

Am I Interested in Community Service?

Deans regularly receive invitations to serve on boards of community organizations. For the dean newly arrived in a community, this is a good way to meet community leaders and become a committed citizen. Such organizations often want to hear the perspective of higher education, and a dean in turn may be able to identify links that offer opportunities on both sides. Some institutions, especially private ones, expect deans to maintain a high level of visibility in the community. Thus a dean whose college includes fine arts may look for service with local arts groups. In any case, the dean needs to find an extra store of time and energy for community activities—it will certainly help the college and may prove very enjoyable.

This litany of qualifications, considerations, and self-scrutiny puts into context the question of whether to pursue deaning. Is it a journey for which I am suited, one I can endure and enjoy? What must I carry in my bags? We have said nothing yet about the journey itself. That is the theme of the next chapter: picking a destination and testing the waters.

Suggestions for Further Reading

Austin, Michael J., Frederick L. Ahearn, and Richard A. English (eds.). *The Professional School Dean: Meeting the Leadership Challenges.* New Directions for Higher Education, no. 98. San Francisco: Jossey-Bass, 1997.

Birnbaum, Robert. *How Academic Leadership Works*. San Francisco: Jossey-Bass, 1992.

Bowen, William G., and Harold T. Shapiro (eds.). *Universities and Their Leadership*. Princeton, N.J.: Princeton University Press, 1998.

Eble, Kenneth E. *The Art of Administration*. San Francisco: Jossey-Bass, 1978.

Heifetz, Ronald A. *Leadership Without Easy Answers*. Cambridge, Mass.: Harvard University Press, 1994.

Keller, George. *Academic Strategy: The Management Revolution in Higher Education*. Baltimore: Johns Hopkins University Press, 1983.

Kolodny, Annette. *Failing the Future: A Dean Looks at Higher Education in the Twenty-First Century*. Durham, N.C.: Duke University Press, 1998.

Tucker, Allan, and Robert Bryan. *The Academic Dean: Dove, Dragon, and Diplomat* (2nd ed.). Phoenix: American Council on Education/Oryx Press, 1999.

CHAPTER THREE

FINDING THE RIGHT POSITION

$\mathbf{F}$inding the right deanship requires many of the same attributes as being a dean: tolerance for confusion, comfort in dealing with strangers on one's turf, ready imagination, careful preparation, and limitless energy.

Dean of What?

Now the scrutiny of personal credentials gives way to an examination of opportunities. First perhaps the question is more structural than critical: Dean of what kind of thing? There is great variety in the way institutions distribute the parts of their academic enterprise, especially the arts and sciences: professional schools are far more constrained by national accreditation standards, but even there one finds surprises. In many schools, for instance, economics is in the business school rather than the arts and sciences; some have educational studies in the arts and sciences college, and many others include the fine and performing arts. At a few places, physics is in the engineering school; in the University of Illinois at Urbana-Champaign, chemical engineering is in liberal arts and sciences with the rest of the chemical sciences rather than in the college of engineering. (In fact, one dean of engineering there was in chemical engineering, and therefore held his disciplinary appointment outside the college he headed!) A campus with both health sciences and arts and sciences will probably have cross-appointments between the basic science departments in the medical school and such departments as biochemistry, molecular science, or psychology in the arts and sciences college. This arrangement likewise broadens the scope of responsibility for the arts and sciences dean, and can have an impact as well on the mission and operations of the medical school departments.

Thus one cannot assume that the dean at another institution would have the same range of disciplines as on one's current campus. Taking a deanship may involve shifting into a different sort of college, or one that includes a different constellation of disciplines. Large universities such as the public members of the Big Ten often break up the arts and sciences into two or more pieces, most often separating the physical, mathematical, and life sciences from the humanities and social sciences. Some go further and have a separate school or college for each of the three traditional divisions (humanities, social sciences, natural and mathematical sciences); Ohio State's massive Columbus campus has five separate fiefdoms that collectively handle the arts and sciences. A college of liberal arts may encompass the arts and sciences or a subset thereof.

The range and variety of smaller colleges and universities is also considerable. Some have maintained a predominantly liberal arts focus, whereas others have added professional curricula such as business or engineering, so that a prospective dean could well have to learn widely disparate fields. Also, at smaller institutions the dean of students may report to the dean of the college, and in effect, the latter serves as the institution's chief academic officer. Sectarian institutions may have ecclesiastical representatives in the administrative structure with whom the dean will relate. Thus it pays to examine the descriptions carefully as a prelude to applying for a deanship.

The next question becomes: What breadth or configuration of college will be appropriate or satisfying or feasible? This will depend on many personal factors, starting obviously with the candidate's own academic field, but including such matters as feeling prepared to take on responsibility for unfamiliar fields (not all deans are comfortable providing leadership in disciplines that are not normally in their colleges—studio and performing arts, physical education, educational studies, military science, speech pathology, and so on).

The size and type of institution should normally correspond to the kind of campus where the candidate has worked. Large or small, public or private, research or teaching-intensive, religious or secular, the list of features that will matter to both candidate and committee is long and fraught with significance. The public-private divide seems to be somewhat more important in the minds of private institutions, but both sides are cautious about a dean who may not understand the differences between the two traditions in culture and procedure (especially budgetary methods). Small liberal arts colleges are wary of candidates who have had no comparable institutional experience and might make grandiose assumptions about resources, staffing, faculty size, or other crucial matters; conversely, colleges in large public universities are equally concerned lest the scale of operations and scope of responsibilities might be too big a leap for someone who has worked only at small, private colleges.

Some institutions have a defining mission or characteristic. For example, a historically black college or university, a single-sex college, or one with a religious affiliation seeks candidates who can connect well to their particular environment. Moreover, geography may play a role for both search committees and candidates. In the southeastern United States, previous experience at a southern institution is especially valued at all but the most cosmopolitan places. On the other hand, the candidate may have regional, sectarian, or other preferences or even conditions, and should factor those in before pursuing a position, however appealing it may seem. The frustration on both sides will be all the more acute if these issues only come up during the endgame. By the same token, it is important for candidates to keep as wide a perspective as possible because dean searches are very competitive. If an aspirant has strongly held personal limitations at the outset, including geography, institutional type, size and quality, and other factors, the perfect job will never come up while an excellent opportunity may slip away unappreciated.

What Is Available?

Personal preferences in any case must take a backseat to the realities of the positions that are actually open. The chief resource for this question is the weekly listing in the *Chronicle of Higher Education,* although *Change* magazine (from the American Association for Higher Education) and other more specialized outlets can be helpful as well. Here we should notice an important difference between recruitment of dean and faculty searches: the great majority of faculty searches begin in the fall. The process moves to the rhythm of the school year and annual disciplinary conventions, especially the many in the humanities and social sciences that fall between Christmas and New Year's. Because most faculty leave regular positions over the summer and new faculty start regular appointments in the fall, this single hunting season works well. This is not so in administrative searches.

Although announcements for administrative positions appear year-round, two "seasons" bring especially large rosters of opportunity. The first, not surprisingly, is in the fall, from early September to late October when institutions that are managing an expected, orderly turnover form search committees and advertise their positions. Traffic remains brisk until the end of the fall semester, but then after a lull in announcements it picks up again in late February. Why? Because many of the openings announced in the fall, not only for deans but also for provosts, vice chancellors, and other senior officers, have now been filled, many of them by sitting deans. This creates a second wave of openings, and if a college knows soon enough that its dean is leaving, there may be an opportunity to run a search that will attract candidates already on the market and receptive to appointment for the fall.

A sample weekly "Bulletin Board" in the *Chronicle* during the high season announces a few dozen deanships covering all sorts of colleges and schools. The notices may give a more vivid sense of the institution than of the dean's position itself. Again, this is different from most faculty notices that concentrate on the desired field of study and may convey only slight information about the department. A deanship is often described less by desired qualifications and more as a reflection of the broader institutional self-image and intentions. Thus the ad may say surprisingly little about the college beyond its scope and size (number of departments, faculty, students) and the qualities needed in the successful candidate, which tend to be described in nearly identical terms from one place to the next. It will tell more about the overall nature of the institution, including distinctive features of its mission or prospects, and the most alluring features of the city, town, or region. There is usually no indication of salary range other than some terms such as "competitive" or "commensurate with experience," which can leave a faculty member unsure about what financial implications this career move might have.

In several ways, then, position notices give the impression that an institution is recruiting a member of the overall administrative structure rather than an individually distinctive leader for a specific part of the institution. That would be a false impression, but a university cares far more that the dean of a college will fit into the campus administrative team than large departments usually do when recruiting one more faculty member. In the end, however, any competent search will look for the person who can bring distinctive gifts to a difficult role.

Often the topics not mentioned will be of real importance to the outsider: Is there a history of acrimony or of cooperation among the departments of the college? Is the trend in resources downward or upward? Is this a unionized campus on which the dean, as an administrator, is not offered tenure? Is the campus about to launch a capital campaign that could mark a turning point in the fortunes of the college? Although all these matters will, or at least can, come up during an interview, any one of them may determine whether a potential candidate wants to enter the race. At least two sources may help to supply the information: colleagues at the institution itself, who will usually be candid, if not always sanguine, about their own college, and the dean of one's own college, who may know the situation at the other campus well, and even more important, be able to translate the administrative complexities there into more familiar terms. Even a bit of inside perspective will be very helpful in deciding whether to apply, and how to cast, the application.

Application and Nomination

Many universities and colleges engage executive search firms such as Korn/Ferry, Heidrick & Struggles, or A. T. Kearney to manage searches for deans and other senior officers, and the position notice will direct inquiries to an associate or partner of the firm. So-called headhunters may have an excellent understanding of the academic scene, because many senior partners have previously served as provosts and presidents and will maintain an extensive roster of potential candidates. Their role is first to help the institution decide and articulate what it is looking for and what the position has to offer (not in terms of resources but as a professional opportunity). They then shape the process, from placing announcements in the *Chronicle* and elsewhere to scheduling and orchestrating the interviews both off campus and finally on campus.

But their most important role is to find and screen potential candidates. Search firms have a remarkable network of contacts across the country and a detailed familiarity with institutions of all kinds. As a result, they maintain a roster of people both incumbent and aspiring and can bring dossiers forward for consideration for appropriate jobs in appropriate places. Because many searches take place each year, the search firms are always looking for additional prospects in order to provide the best possible pool for consideration by their clients. It is important to remember that the consultants are working for the institution that engaged them, not for the position-seekers, but they are remarkably generous and helpful in dealing with candidates. The interaction of search firm and prospective candidate thus can be a productive symbiosis, yielding information to the firm and invitations to candidacy for the individual.

The process of considering a move is always a discreet matter. By working through the network of the search firms, one can avoid the roiling waters of rumor resulting from inquiries to colleagues elsewhere, and perhaps avoid causing one's own dean needless alarm (or optimism). In addition to providing accurate, tactful, and dispassionate information about a position, the search firm consultant can offer an objective assessment of an individual's overall prospects and credentials. This can encourage appropriate searches and help avoid hopeless causes or jobs that would turn out to be unappealing once the situation was better known.

This personal screening process is important because, as already noted, despite the range of opportunities available dean searches are highly competitive. Whatever preferences an aspirant may have about type or location of institution, or type of deanship, it is as unwise to narrow the search prematurely as to pursue professional unicorns—unattainable or mythical posts perfectly suited to one's peculiar talents. Furthermore, many institutions with prestige and the necessary resources prefer to recruit sitting deans and avoid gambling on promise without experience. And many sitting deans are more than willing to advance to a better decanal post before or instead of a provostship.

Finally, a willingness to be a candidate for more than one position at a time will allow comparison among various places and their ways of operating, which in turn will yield a sharper picture of one's own competitiveness—as well as further experience in the demanding world of administrative interviews.

Résumés and References

Dean searches may differ from faculty experience in two other significant respects: résumés and references. It may seem axiomatic that a candidate needs to paint the best possible portrait of his or her professional credentials and experience in a clear, strong curriculum vitae, accompanied by a list of references. But a typical faculty curriculum vitae presents achievements and projects as seen by a faculty member, cataloguing the activities of a teacher-scholar-academic citizen to be read by other faculty. It emphasizes scholarly papers read and published, courses taught, dissertations directed, and so forth. All these accomplishments are vital parts of the candidate's case for selection as a dean, but other dimensions of the record may play a decisive role for the committee as it chooses among candidates who are equally strong in academic terms.

The dean's résumé should not be shy or dismissive about administrative effort but rather lay it out in more detail: the number of personnel supervised in the lab group, the size of the budget of the institute, information on leading external review teams. Faculty are likely to understate participation in campus-level task forces as being less important to their academic record. For an administrative position, that difference is if anything tilted in the other direction. The question is not simply whether the candidate is a strong faculty member or a widely respected scholar, important as those are. The question is whether the candidate has the skills and perspective to bridge the world of the faculty with the world of administration.

All résumés tell a story, by both what they include and how they state it. The résumé is the candidate's advocate during the first stages of the search and screening process, especially if the process is in the hands of an experienced search firm consultant. Like a diplomatic intermediary, the résumé should introduce its subject sympathetically but without fanfare, exaggeration, or undue length. It should also speak the language of the land to which it travels; that is to say, it must move administrative experience close to the beginning of the record and highlight it with brief descriptions of the responsibilities in each position, with special emphasis on the most recent accomplishments. International experience and community service, if significant, can enhance the story.

Likewise, references function a bit differently in administrative searches. In a faculty search, the candidate will probably have a set list of about five referees (until they weary of the role) because the nature of the position and the kind of reference needed will be more or less the same from one faculty position to the next. But dean positions vary so greatly that it is wise to have a larger spectrum of potential referees—as many as ten in all—who can speak in varying combinations depending on the nature of the deanship. For example, a computer scientist might be a candidate for dean of engineering, arts and sciences, or applied sciences, and therefore need to tailor the list of references accordingly. The references should include at least one woman who can address the candidate's record on such issues as affirmative action, and also people who have worked with or for the candidate as well as his or her own supervisors.

In contrast, it is unwise to supply a long list of referees to any search committee. Not all are needed, and not all will be well-suited. Even worse, a committee that has asked for a specific number of names may simply approach the first three on the list, whether or not they are the most appropriate references for the position. A compromise approach is to provide a longer list of up to eight names, with a brief notation by each entry indicating the connection (former provost, head of department, current dean, research collaborator, head of foundation). There is nothing to be gained by coyly hinting that references will be provided only if and when the committee smiles on the application. Whatever names the candidate chooses should be sent forthwith to avoid the impression of archness or inability to follow instructions.

Furthermore, search firms and committees conduct much of the preliminary screening through phone calls to references rather than by letter. This allows the consultant or committee member to gain a more vivid picture of the candidate and concentrate on issues at the institution in question. Referees thus need to be well informed on topics that might never come up in a faculty recruitment. At a minimum, they will need a copy of the résumé as it has been recast for this new line of candidacy. They will also appreciate being kept abreast of impending calls or requests for letters.

A third difference in administrative searches is that they involve nomination by others at least as much as direct application by candidates. In the last analysis, it will probably not matter much whether a candidate emerged from a third-party suggestion or by self-nomination; the dossiers, references, and interviews will make or break any case. Nevertheless, search consultants rely heavily on suggestions from persons they have dealt with before, whose judgment they have tested and can trust. Nomination by a known source can make a difference in catching the attention of the consultant early in the process. Similarly, nomination to a campus search committee by a well-respected faculty member at that campus can yield early interest among committee members. But there is finally no substitute for the quality of one's credentials and references.

Letter

Together with résumé and references, the third leg of the tripod is the candidate's letter, whether as direct application or in response to an invitation from the consultant or the committee. The differences in approach from a typical faculty search that we noted earlier come into play here as well. Where a faculty candidate might stress his or her distinctiveness of field or novelty of research agenda, the decanal aspirant must convert those qualities into a good fit with the larger situation of the college and the institution, elucidating the strengths of the academic record in a single discipline as a basis for providing academic leadership across the entire college and showing how experience as an academic citizen at the current campus has readied the candidate for the challenges of the position under review. Generalities and self-congratulation are fatal. The candidate is uniquely positioned to point out specific experiences or interests that match what the hiring college has asked for, and the candidacy letter is the critical moment to make that linkage for the committee. In particular, if the candidate has any existing ties to the hiring institution—research colleagues there, past involvement in institutes, colleagues at one's own campus recruited from that place, guest lectures or visiting appointments—now is the time to bring these facts to the forefront.

Many committees invite candidates to provide a statement of philosophy, either as a part of the letter or separately. This is a very difficult assignment, if only because of its vagueness, but once composed this statement can be revised for a host of settings and purposes. It provides an opportunity to reflect on (but not dwell on) current issues in higher education and a dean's options in addressing them. This is not the time for simple autobiographical memoirs, nor for abstractions or generalizations, but rather a crucial opportunity to describe one's approach to administration, including the issues of greatest importance to the candidate and the intellectual and organizational tools that could be brought to bear on them in this specific context. It is the best chance to catch the search committee members' attention with a thoughtful, creative account of their own world.

Interviews

All faculty are familiar with the rituals of interviewing, having been on both sides of the conference table all their careers. Once again, a dean search will differ significantly.

Committee

The committee deputized to hire a dean is notably different from that seeking faculty. First is the composition of the search committee. Instead of a panel of disciplinary colleagues, perhaps including a graduate student, a dean search committee will normally include a dozen or more faculty from across the college, an undergraduate and a graduate student, a representative of the staff, and perhaps even an alumnus and a trustee. In some places a dean from another college on campus may be involved. The roster of members is always provided in advance, and the prudent candidate will garner from the Web or from colleagues a fuller picture of the group. Often the membership of a search committee will reflect current issues in the college, whether that is the desire to enhance interdisciplinary programs, a need to increase external funding, or the aspiration to incorporate a new department.

The practical effect of this heterogeneity, and the second difference from a faculty search, is that unless one of the faculty members of the committee happens to be in the same field, there may be nobody who understands the candidate's academic work. Because research is the one topic about which all faculty feel confident in talking with strangers, especially on a job interview, this can produce a powerful sense of isolation. There are always opportunities in the course of the interview to speak of one's academic work, and any sensible screening committee will want to hear the candidates describe their work to nonspecialists—explaining complicated matters to uninformed strangers is one of a dean's most frequent tasks—but the purpose of the interview with the committee lies elsewhere, and the candidate must beware the temptation to hijack the conversation.

Furthermore, a faculty search committee is selecting a new colleague to do what the members themselves do, but the dean search committee includes perhaps fifteen people from as many different units, charged with selecting someone for a role that none of them performs. In that sense, people on both sides of the table lack a comprehensive view of the dean's job (or if the candidate is a sitting dean, the advantage may lie with him or her).

Third, because faculty search committees are all in the same field as the candidates and thus the experts in assessing credentials and aptness, and because the appointment will normally be in the same department as the committee, the choice virtually rests with the faculty themselves, subject of course to the dean's approval of the procedures and the interviews with the finalists. In the case of a dean, however, the primary appointment is as an administrator and the selection will rest with the provost or chief academic officer. Thus the committee is frequently asked to provide an unranked final list of recommendations rather than pick a winner. In short, they are a screening and advisory committee rather than a true search committee.

Off-Campus

Most search committees conduct their interviews in two stages. In the first phase, they meet with as many as sixteen persons who seem promising on the basis of their dossiers, letters, and references. This first round of the tournament may take place by videoconference, or by telephone conference call, but most frequently at a site away from campus. The easiest and most common venue is an airport where candidates can arrive and leave conveniently—and discreetly. Committees use this round not only to see their top priorities but also to gamble on one or two unusual prospects. More importantly, many candidates wish to keep their participation in the search confidential unless and until something comes of it. Off-campus interviews serve everyone's interests.

Airport interviews allot about two hours to each candidate, a brief time for a large committee to meet and assess sixteen strangers and keep them all separate in their minds. For the candidate, the interview is like sudden-death overtime with no regular game beforehand: one cannot really win, but one can lose at any moment, for unlikely reasons.

One such cause is ill-aimed or ill-timed wit. Here is a case in point. One dean recalled an interview for which he had prepared meticulously. He noticed that because of serious financial concerns a few years earlier, mentioned in the provost's report, a well-regarded unit of the college had almost been shut down. The crisis passed, and as it happened, the head of that unit was on the search committee. The candidate, wishing to show his detailed knowledge, commented in passing that the unit had "passed through the valley of the shadow of debt." One member of the committee thought he said "death" and was alarmed, the representative of the unit was offended that his past problems were being thrown up at him, and the candidate was out of the running because of a bon mot.

Preliminary interviews tend to be tightly scripted, for both economy of time and consistency, with questions assigned to individual members but leaping from topic to topic—capital campaigns, curriculum reform, start-up costs in surface chemistry, views of student grievance procedures, and so on. Fortune favors the mentally nimble candidate who can be informative but concise, conveying a sense of individuality without rampant eccentricity. There is no substitute for a careful reading of the bulky envelope of materials that the college provides, even though it is hard to guess what questions will emerge from so disparate a collection of data and self-promotion.

A conference call presents the special challenges that committee and candidate cannot see one another and must depend on choice of words without body language or eye contact. This leaves the candidate with more responsibility for initiative but less control over the conversation in the matters of interpreting topics, developing illustrations, or qualifying what has been said.

On-Campus

Out of the preliminary interviews will emerge the four to six finalists invited to campus for the full treatment, running two days or even longer. Here we may note a fourth feature of the decanal marathon that strikes a novice candidate: the range, variety, and public visibility of activities in the interview process. In states with sunshine laws, most or all meetings are public, and if there is any suspicion that the candidate might be interesting, the press may even show up for comments (this is far more common in searches for provosts but not unknown in dean searches as well). The candidate is whisked from the committee to the college staff consortium, the dean's staff, student government officers, diversity advocates, alumni, a general faculty assembly, and private interviews with the provost, senior staff members, perhaps the president, and almost any of those on campus with a nameplate on their door and a title.

In most cases, candidates are asked to make a presentation to either a faculty meeting or a general assembly open to staff, students, and all who care to attend. Topic and performance seem almost equally important. Everyone realizes that the inner workings of the campus will still be a mystery to the parade of visitors, so the talk takes on more the air of the compulsory round in an ice-skating competition than the polished individual pyrotechnics of a seminar. The candidate is expected to be relaxed but ready for the most unexpected questions, even those testing patience and tact as well as knowledge; informed about some local issues without being pedantic; able to introduce new wisdom from elsewhere without distorting the issue or scorning the local culture; seriously interested in joining the new setting but never seeming to disparage current affiliations. Many deans recall this element of the interview process as the most enjoyable—and the most challenging.

A typical itinerary for a campus interview, as suggested earlier, includes meetings with representatives of all parts of the campus with whom the dean interacts, but especially the faculty and the provost. In the past decade, colleges have placed much greater emphasis on student concerns, and the student members of the search committees are frequently among the most perceptive and trenchant interviewers.

The process is intended to test the candidate's versatility, adeptness at learning nuances, ability to interact with a wide array of personalities (all deans suspect that the committee planted the most notorious curmudgeons in the college in various meetings to watch for signs of weakness), public poise, and stamina. From an early breakfast session to an evening of "relaxing" conversation, the pace of each fifteen-hour day is deliberately taxing, not least because each of the many audiences wants a candidate with high energy and personal engagement. The slightest sign of weariness is seen in the most unfavorable way; a moment of mental drift signals lack of interest in the job. Many deans recall exit interviews at which they were apparently the only ones fully awake. Again, this is not a sign of boredom but rather proof that everyone works very hard in these; the candidate is just not allowed the luxury of showing it.

The most difficult part is casting the same issues or information in an endless variety of ways for very different audiences who have different stakes in the matter, all the while assimilating reactions and refining one's take on the whole situation. Amid the continual temptations to change an answer in order to placate or impress a difficult audience, Mark Twain's admonition is useful: when in doubt tell the truth (as is another dictum: "I was gratified to be able to answer promptly, and I did. I said I did not know."). By the end of the visit, the adept candidate will have pulled together key concerns, formulated a very provisional account of priorities and strategies, and spotted the key figures who can help or hinder such plans.

Last but far from least, the candidate is also being considered for a senior, presumably tenured faculty appointment. Some unionized campuses do not offer tenure to persons recruited for administration, and any candidate who is leaving tenure for this new dispensation must weigh the decision with care. The campus visit provides the appropriate department a chance to meet, scrutinize, and interview its prospective new colleague. At many places this includes a request to give a seminar. Whether or not the dean normally teaches in his or her home department while serving as dean, membership in the department is a permanent fact, and may be more than titular when the dean leaves office. No department should view this process lightly, and no decanal candidate should gloss over the importance of the faculty appointment that is the long-term basis for affiliation with the college.

Offer

Interviews do not always go well. One side or the other may conclude, even while the candidate is on campus, that there has been a mistake. In such a situation, a swift, graceful severing of the line is far preferable to groping diplomacy. In any case, both committee and candidate want to move quickly once the last visitor has boarded the plane, but whereas in a faculty search this may require only one department meeting, the members of the dean search committee need to gather impressions from a wide population as well as discuss their own thoughts. Knowing whether a candidate remains interested or has been disenchanted is a most helpful piece of information. The enthusiastic candidate can follow up an interview with brief notes to the chair of the search committee and provost expressing continued interest, and conversely, one who decides not to pursue a position should send a letter of withdrawal. Here, in contrast, there is no compelling need to dwell on the truth—a visceral antipathy for the provost, for example, or a conviction that Houdini alone could escape the budgetary snares in which the college is trapped.

Still, for those who are interested, a waiting game is inevitable. Scheduling interviews with so large a cast of characters may mean spreading them over several weeks. The collection of responses and shaping of recommendations to the provost will add another week. And then the process shifts to the provost, who usually makes additional phone calls, confers with the president, and consults the candidate's academic department before approaching the candidate of first choice. Many a candidate is startled to hear from the provost long after concluding that the prize had gone elsewhere. Even then the news may be that although the college has identified a different lead candidate the process is not settled. Enough candidacies founder on the rocks of negotiation (or ego) that it is worth staying in the hunt despite any bruises to one's pride.

A word about ethics. Even as candidates are expected to be forthright and honorable in all searches, the campus committee, provost, and other responsible parties must treat candidates fairly or expect undesirable consequences. In one spectacular breach of that principle, a chief officer's executive aid who was managing the search process for the campus contacted the lead candidate and said, "You are our first choice, but we are required by state law to bring at least two candidates back for second interviews. Can you come next week?" When the candidate explained that previous commitments prevented a return visit for two weeks, the campus functionary said, "The other candidate can come this weekend. While you are our top candidate, if you do not come for two weeks you may step off the plane to learn that the job is filled. On the other hand, if you can come before this weekend, you can steal a march on the other guy and leave *him* standing at the airport." Not surprisingly, the "top" candidate withdrew and shook the dust of that place from his feet, grateful to have learned its moral code before accepting a job!

Even if the approach is in good faith, however, important challenges remain. When someone is invited to take up a first deanship, everyone concerned is keenly aware that this is a major career change and may be accompanied by cold feet, rash acceptances, and other ailments. The successful candidate and spouse or partner are normally invited to visit the campus again to talk further with key administrators (including any who may have been unavailable during the first visit), gain detailed information on benefits, examine lab space or other facilities, and scout out housing and schools.

Because many aspiring deans have hitherto experienced little if any mobility in their careers, the steps preliminary to the decision should be taken with special care so as not to learn later that there were vital questions they should have asked before changing institutions. This can easily happen in the matter of benefits, in which there are startling variations often involving real but unadvertised disadvantages to newcomers to the system.

There are two aspects to the negotiation process, for the college and for the candidate's own situation. The dean's new colleagues will watch eagerly to see how skillful a hunter their new leader is and judge the success of the search by the new resources that come to the college, a factor that first-time deans can underestimate. They will signal both the dean's skills as a negotiator and his or her grasp of local realities. There will probably be no more favorable moment for presenting pressing needs such as new faculty positions, renovation, or construction of facilities essential to teaching and research, and increases in equipment funds or technological support. No dean would expect to get all of these, but it is a moment for making progress—in the resources of the college and the support of the faculty. As long as the requests have a strong rationale, the newcomer should be able to gain some resources for the college. If the provost or president is reluctant to make any commitments, dean and college alike are justified in reading this response as an omen.

Negotiating for oneself is always a delicate matter, and guidelines are slippery at best, but it would be a rare (and disconcerting) offer that did not include relocation expenses. Because the administrative position is year-round it should naturally represent a substantial advance from a nine-month faculty base, and in most cases will translate into real progress even when compared on equivalent bases (the prevailing impression is that a 20 percent increase in the base is a modest achievement, but we lack data to test that claim). Such factors as comparative cost of living, comparable positions at the institution, or a statewide salary scale will help clarify the value of the offer.

Finally, because deans now rarely remain in office until retirement, it is imperative to have clear agreement on the conditions under which the dean will take up full-time faculty status if that step occurs. It is not churlish to ask for clarity in these matters: this is the dean's prenuptial agreement, and it is no time to be squeamish about discussing delicate matters. Many incipient deans fail to get these issues stipulated in writing, and perhaps we should attribute that to misplaced modesty rather than naiveté. Perhaps not.

The last piece of business is announcing the appointment. Selecting a new dean is a matter of high significance to a college, and reporting a successful recruitment usually involves the press as well as on-campus organs. The hiring institution must have control over the timing of the announcement. Naturally, the new dean can declare the news at home simultaneously, but should not jump the gun even out of understandable zeal or a desire to share good news with colleagues. The final days on the old campus are a good preparation for the ceremonial side of a dean's life, marked as they are by numerous farewell events and fond words from long-term colleagues. Or, if they are not, it will be confirmation of an unexpected sort that the decision to leave was a good one!

Suggestions for Further Reading

Nelson, Cary, and Stephen Watt. *Academic Keywords: A Devil's Dictionary for Higher Education.* New York: Routledge, 1999.

Readings, Bill. *The University in Ruins.* Cambridge, Mass.: Harvard University Press, 1996.

PART TWO

ADMINISTERING
THE COLLEGE

CHAPTER FOUR

THE SHIFT TO THE DEAN'S OFFICE

The process of negotiating for a dean's position has now been completed, and the position accepted. Now, two fresh questions come up: What have I done? And what do I do now? The answer to the first is relatively simple: I have embarked on one of the most exciting professional adventures of my life. The answer to the second question is the subject of this chapter.

Setting Up and Settling In

Preparation for this role shift and candidacy will have made it clear that a dean inevitably faces real changes in responsibilities, point of view, and professional life in general. Accepting that need to change can be a very difficult mental shift. Best to face the fact well informed: it will help to sit down and actually list the areas in which change looms, and then to note the kinds of actions that these changes require.

Calendar

For example, having another person control one's calendar may feel intrusive as well as confining after the flexibility of faculty life, but it is no longer possible to come and go freely or impulsively. A dean is unlikely to have the freedom to operate without the constant engagement of an administrative assistant or secretary to schedule appointments and meetings. That staff person needs to know the dean's schedule and have reliable contact information in case of changes, emergencies, or calls from a superior that need to be returned at once. Given the wide freedom of movement and personal scheduling that academics enjoy, many a dean instinctively resists surrendering the workings of life—or at least of the business day—to another's management, but it is far better to consider how to manage that necessity than to fight it. Even as simple a step as not scheduling appointments before 9 A.M. in order to allow for phone calls and e-mail will make life easier and restore some sense of shaping one's time.

Delegating

A related but larger issue is assessing the workload in the office and then preparing to deal with it. Even experience as an associate dean still will leave room for significant adjustment, given the demands of the dean's role and especially the dean's final accountability for the college. Fewer tasks will seem routine or casual, and taken together they can seem overwhelming. One way to begin is by reviewing the yearly calendar of set meetings and deadlines for the institution and for the college; this will provide a map of the year (it is important to make a full twelve-month scan, preferably from the start of fall term through the following summer). Because many deanships begin July 1, this step is particularly important for the novice. Although the change of pace in the summer is not nearly as pronounced as for faculty, the summer workload still bears little resemblance to that of the academic year. Fall sends a tidal wave of activity through the office, and it will be too late then to take precautions against drowning in the paperwork, correspondence (computers have done little to reduce the deforestation), appointments, and crises. When a new dean sees gridlock on the calendar, stacks of phone messages, e-mails numbering in the hundreds, and mountains of written requests and memos, there is a strong temptation to reduce access just to get through the day. Far better to plan ahead about people, problems, and opportunities that must have priority on the dean's own calendar and delegate other matters to the decanal staff.

Delegating, however, can also be a challenge. Most positions prior to a deanship, including departmental leadership, do not sufficiently prepare a novice to sort out delegated responsibilities for a staff the size of a large college office. It would be rash to offer hard-and-fast rules for this, because it is an evolving process of relationships as much as of work assignment. A good grasp of the job and sense of the people available, their competencies, and changing priorities for the office will continue to affect the picture, but how to get started? What style of delegation will work best with a new dean's personality and still-tentative grasp of the job? Some prefer to assign to associates large but clearly defined areas of responsibility, such as grant proposals or the curriculum, and ask them to report regularly on their activities; some feel reassured by getting copies of most communications the office sends out; others are glad to be spared that deluge if confident that any concern or problem will be flagged and discussed. Still others delegate by function—correspondence, troubleshooting, budget proposals—with less regular reporting.

In contrast, department chair experience is directly related to the situations of deans in small colleges. These, especially the independent ones, tend to have relatively few staff positions, especially at the assistant-associate dean level. This means that fewer large responsibilities can be delegated, and the staff will have to be assigned as many routine ones as possible to free the dean for budget oversight, planning, and so forth. Fortunately, many such colleges have a strong tradition of faculty governance to help with such matters as faculty development, but deans still need to look carefully at the issue of delegation to see what is feasible to get the job done.

It remains true that a major pitfall for new deans is a tendency to micromanage. Despite good intentions, and even with implicit confidence in the staff, a daunting sense of accountability can make a dean reluctant to assign big tasks to others without compulsively looking in to make sure all is well and offering advice (quite possibly less expert than what the associate already has). The predictable result is exhaustion and even worse, gridlock, which is not likely to make a positive impression on new colleagues. The antidote is to begin with the realization that a dean *must* delegate, and decide how to accomplish that most comfortably. More suggestions will appear in the course of this chapter.

Office Environment

The physical environment of the dean's office needs careful attention, both because so much time is spent there and because the office speaks for the position. Furnishings and arrangements that are comfortable and even reflect the occupant's personality can genuinely contribute to what gets done in that office. Some institutions provide decorating funds to new administrators, although in most cases the college will end up covering the costs of any changes. But renovations are easier to arrange and to complete at the outset; later on they will surely strike someone as unnecessary extravagance. If funds are not forthcoming at the outset, the dean should not expect them once other claims intervene. For some deans—business, engineering, and the health sciences lead the way—the office is expected to reflect a certain opulence; for others, this would be anathema. More important is the physical setting in which to conduct business. The formality of a conference table, the more relaxed atmosphere of a sofa and chairs, the symbolism of working across a desk—all of these will help to say who the dean is and what happens in the office. The most important point is to choose furnishings that reflect preferred working styles.

Is the computer equipment sufficient to handle the online resources for the office along with any special needs the dean may have? This must include a personal printer for confidential materials. Some deans extol the virtues of handheld dictating machines. Although it may take a little practice to become proficient with them, they can save time when answering correspondence, writing reports, and noting down reminders to the staff while they are fresh in mind. And a dictating machine that can be accessed remotely offsets some of the disadvantages of traveling without a laptop and thus without e-mail access.

Availability

A prominent claim on the new dean's time will be meeting people across the campus. Those whom he or she does not visit will come calling, especially people with grievances, real or imagined, from the previous regime. A workable policy on availability is imperative, to preserve both time and sanity. In the case of faculty whose sole purpose is to lament the past and dread the future, the dean's assistant will screen requests for appointments to be sure the matter has gone through the normal chain of command before coming to the college office. Often, a concern can be redirected to an assistant or associate dean, providing of course that appropriate assistance is available through that route. (The dean who simply fobs off troublesome visitors onto an associate will soon run out of associates!) Most deans do not make their direct phone extension public knowledge, which allows the assistant to screen or even handle calls in advance.

E-mail is another matter. It is so pervasive, so swift, and so necessary to the conduct of daily business that it would be a hindrance to limit access through that path. In any case, e-mail anonymity is almost impossible, because all addresses are presumably listed in the online campus directory—and in most cases follow a simple pattern (jones@campus.edu)—and one iota of ingenuity will enable anyone to contact the dean. But e-mail is not risk-free. Messages sent to one person can be forwarded to the immediate universe, including the most inappropriate sharing of information; all correspondence, even casual and ill-considered outbursts, are stored on the server and are retrievable, admissible files in the case of formal complaints or litigation. Moreover, the risk of accidentally misdirecting an e-mail and sending an embarrassing or damaging message should at least make a dean cautious before committing discreet material to e-mail. Some deans are loath to do business by e-mail for fear that it will lead to all kinds of problems from individuals who do not work through channels. That is true, but shrinking from e-mail for fear of mishap is a crippling mistake considering the necessity and convenience of direct access with the rest of the academic and business world. Although overly hasty or ill-considered e-mail can be damaging, even a carefully crafted noncommittal response to messages is better than none at all. The very cautious could route all e-mail through an assistant for screening if this is a problem, but one dean set up such a screening process and then consistently failed to benefit from it by picking up the phone whenever he got riled up!

Personal Adjustment

Last, but still important, the new dean needs time for personal settling in at home—grappling with the myriad details related to moving. Every dean can recall the struggle to keep up the energy level on the job while cleaning and organizing at home each night. Add to this finding a dentist, physician, reliable mechanic, and so forth to preserve both vigor and mental health! Fortunately, experienced locals will have suggestions on each item. If the routine tasks of life, now suddenly difficult and unfamiliar, stack up, this new adventure can begin to feel like a mistake for trivial reasons. A half-day set aside each week for a couple of months to make the ordinary again seem familiar will be time well spent.

Needing Immediate Attention

Experienced deans are full of stories about what they encountered when they first arrived on the job. Although any thoughtful executive would like time to learn the new situation and evaluate the current personnel, policies, and organization before taking any action, some issues cannot wait. The following is a sampler of the kinds of challenges that may face the dean immediately and require quick action.

Office Personnel

Not infrequently, the dean's assistant or secretary—the one person who knows all the procedures, the annual calendar of deadlines, the idiosyncrasies of chairs and other administrators, in short, the one indispensable person—leaves when the new dean arrives. This is probably not a personal comment on the newcomer, but no matter the reason, it can be unsettling to arrive only to discover that the office mainstay is gone. With little but a job description, the newcomer has to make an appointment that could be critical to the success of his or her regime. What to do? First and obviously, whichever office staff member is best able to manage complex matters with little guidance should be asked to fill in temporarily. Second, it should be clear to all, including the temporary appointee, that a search for a permanent replacement will follow as quickly as possible but not before a thoughtful revision of the job description so that it meets the new dean's office needs.

Someone new to the college, or even to the dean's office, may wish to look first at internal candidates (not merely from the dean's office but from the institution) who bring a good working knowledge to the position. Still, relying too much on local advice in making the selection can easily result in rewarding a well-liked but unsuitable employee backed by friends who cannot step back and see the need for fresh approaches. So much depends on chemistry and compatible working styles that the dean must make all the important decisions in filling this critical position. The quicker the search, the better; the new team can develop office structures and routines together, and speed will avoid fostering the impression that the temporary has a lock on the job (or if that person is indeed the right choice, all the more reason to move swiftly in making it official). In any case, unsuccessful candidates from inside the office may start looking to leave, and the office may face an extensive turnover in staff within the first six months. The dean can try to avert unwelcome departures by speaking with staff members individually and encouraging them to stay; this may help to retain valuable employees, but there may well be some losses.

Past the confines of the college office, the new dean may also find one or more department chair searches that have foundered. These issues should have emerged in the advanced negotiations and not come as a surprise, but the details often remain murky and the whole case may have been inadequately explained. Given the importance of department chairs to the health of the college, these searches can be emergencies. After a briefing by the search committee chair and possibly the full committee, the search may prove to be still viable and can move ahead. If candidates have already been to campus for interviews, for example, and one or more has been judged strong, the dean should speak with the finalists both to reassure them about the transition in college leadership and to make his or her own assessment. Unless there are strong countervailing reasons such as a stringent lack of funds, the dean should meet them personally before making an offer. However, the cause of the problem could be disagreements within the department over the candidates, and the only sensible course is a new search.

No matter who the new dean is, there will be disgruntled candidates for the position on-site. This can be a very difficult personnel problem. Often, there is a long-time associate dean who believes that he or she has earned the deanship and is angered at not being chosen by the search committee or chief academic officer.

Again, local loyalty can produce resentment: department chairs may have supported this person for the job as a known quantity, someone to whom they felt allegiance. Because of lengthy service in the dean's office, the associate dean may not have stayed current in scholarship or even teaching, thus becoming an inadvisable choice for the position. Does the dean try to work out a cordial détente or look to replace the associate dean? There are pitfalls either way. A disgruntled senior staff member in the office can be very destructive to both routine and morale, but there may not be a good alternative role for the person, even back in the department, and a bad situation will not be improved by placing a well-informed and ill-humored exile into a vital department. The chief academic officer can play a crucial role by resolving such an internal problem in advance. Not all CAOs are interested in reaching into the affairs of the college in this way, but if the pretext for inaction is respect for the autonomy of the college it is a foolish specimen of that notion.

Despite Machiavelli's advice to hang your most dangerous enemies on the public square early in your regime, the dean may try a softer approach—offer the incumbent a six-month trial period on both sides to see if a satisfactory partnership can be developed. That way the newcomer cannot be accused of treating a longtime staffer cruelly without a hearing, or conversely, allowing an incompetent person to stay because that was the expedient thing to do.

Campus Leadership

Turnover above the dean may seem even more ominous. The same spring recruitment season that sets deans to migrating also affects provosts and presidents. If there has been a search for a president or chief academic officer concurrent with the decanal recruitment, candidates for both posts will be aware of the situation, but incumbents in those senior roles may be selected for glory elsewhere only after the deanship has been filled. Either case is awkward and potentially problematic, because the dean ends up working for someone who had little if any role in the hiring process. In general, if an institution is searching simultaneously for a chief academic officer and one or more deans, the relationship between CAO and dean—in terms of both chemistry and authority—can be weakened or at least take longer to become firm. Candidates for both positions ought to be concerned about this situation. In a small institution, concurrent searches for president and dean can be equally problematic.

Practicality is superior to lamentation. If the new dean arrives to find a turnover in the senior administration, he or she might ask how to be helpful to the search process, although if there are several colleges on campus such an offer will strike others as brash. The chair of the search committee may be glad to have fresh advice (this is far from a sure bet, however); in a search for CAO one could also check in with the president. Participating in the search will help to create a necessary relationship with the campus administration in general and the new CAO in particular. In any case, even if the search proceeds with exactly the same cast as before—which is not unlikely—all sitting deans will be in the same position vis-à-vis the new leader, and that can lead to stronger ties among the deans themselves.

Sizing Up the Crowd

First impressions are lasting and honeymoons are short-lived. The first weeks on the job will hinge on intangibles as well as actions; everything from casual words to choice of drink will contribute to an image that may prove hard to live up to—or overcome. In general, everyone will expect to see tireless energy and steady, confident enjoyment. This is the time to build trusting relationships with higher administrators, fellow deans, and department chairs; doing so is best achieved through individual visits preceded by a request for briefing materials. In many ways these early encounters with new colleagues are an extension of the interview process. Time consuming as such meetings have to be, they provide both personal contact and vital knowledge of other parts of the enterprise. New colleagues are eager to tell more about their province than was feasible in a quick meeting with a candidate, including fuller perceptions of the college. Even if those perceptions are wrong, they can alert the dean to unsuspected issues.

Among all these meetings, none has a greater impact on daily life than time spent with the members of the dean's staff, learning about their responsibilities and accomplishments and finding out what must be kept and enhanced, what altered or halted. The simplest approach is to ask what all of them like most and least about their current jobs. The answers will provide clues for revising job descriptions or even reorganizing the office. Perhaps the dean's assistant never felt comfortable with budgetary tasks that the last dean had assigned, or an associate dean who was handed the college plan may not know how to begin but is too game to complain. Some assistant deans have said that they are regarded as clerical help with fancy titles.

As suggested earlier, staff members are likely to have specific ideas about improvements they would make in their jobs. Given the opportunity, an associate dean might offer to oversee the development of interdisciplinary programs. An assistant dean might want to coordinate outreach programs and enhance her potential for fundraising and alumni relations. In short, asking staffers to reimagine their roles can generate many creative responses.

Any reconsideration of individual positions must obviously fit with a rethinking of the entire office, in image as well as in reality. Much as when the eyes adjust to a change in lighting, it may take a while to see how the staff looks to others. Are they knowledgeable, optimistic about the college and the institution, responsive to queries, careful about deadlines, supportive of college goals? All of this requires a balance among assistant or associate deans and secretarial or clerical positions. A top-heavy staff is unhealthy and could need quick adjustment; so too with personnel who are clearly not doing their jobs, such as the office manager who does little but preside, to the great resentment of the secretaries. Department chairs are a good source of information about the effectiveness of the dean's office, and some will be eager to share their knowledge. Looking in another direction, the CAO's office, where deadlines are set and important reports are submitted, will know of any problems in dealing with the college office. In these ways, a new incumbent can move quickly to communicate expectations to the office, size up its effectiveness as a unit, and make necessary changes for smooth functioning.

Budget Surprises

Unless the college and the campus are in fiscal straits, a new dean is likely to have additional resources to distribute on arrival. These may be a one-time bonanza to address specific existing problems or to give the dean a chance to make an early mark on the face of the college. They may result from canny negotiations, or include funds that the CAO recognized as necessary but kept in reserve until a permanent leader was named. In the former case, the dean will already know where to put the resources; in the latter, however, the dean should be ready to make a relatively quick decision on allocation that is convincing to the CAO and to the college. There is obviously room for consultation with college staff and key faculty leaders, and the supplemental funds can be segregated from the normal review and the normal flow of the budget, but in some sense this windfall is a test of the dean's ability to move expeditiously in assessing the whole college situation, formulating plans, and deploying resources. Assuming he or she made careful notes during the recruitment process, urgent priorities and looming opportunities will have shown themselves. Ironically, although the CAO expects to hear the dean's plans in some detail after due consideration, this found money constitutes an invitation—even at some level a challenge—to the dean to show initiative and creativity. Conversely, the CAO, if consulted too tentatively, may feel invited, or challenged, to urge particular uses. It is always better to know where the money *should* go before being informed where it *will* go! A final warning about nonrecurring funds in the hands of the new dean: the recipients will regard them as permanent, recurring, and inalienable rights. This gift horse will not only be looked in the mouth—it may be kicked in the teeth.

The alternative and less welcome scenario is a budget reduction that hits while the dean is en route or newly arrived. This may reflect unexpected developments—a legislative session that turned nasty in the late stages, for example—or may simply be a monument to human nature—an institution that is striving to recruit the most effective new leadership may not wish to spell out the worst side of its situation as part of the courting process, and not all candidates will become more enthusiastic about a position by learning that their first task will be to savage the budget. Even if a candidate inquires about potential budgetary problems, the answer may merely suggest difficulties rather than detail them.

If budget cuts are indeed a hard fact awaiting the dean, the first thing to do (after swallowing hard) is to understand the parameters of the reduction—not just the amount but the principles behind the cut, such as the need to reduce personnel costs. Other deans may be a good source of advice at this point because they are probably undergoing the same process but do not have a vested interest in decisions outside their own college. In fact, a new dean without prior entanglements may be able to devise a dispassionate approach to reductions that would be more difficult later. The areas of flexibility, and hence potential reduction, in most college budgets are mostly confined to operating and equipment funds, personnel dollars generated by vacant positions and fringe benefits, and the number of positions for support staff. Because across-the-board cuts send a message that the dean avoids hard decisions, the best option may be to absorb any vacant positions and scout for programs whose budgetary support outweigh their contribution to the mission of the college. A sharp and dispassionate eye—and a good budget officer—are indispensable.

Student tuition is the largest single component of income in a college, whether assigned directly to the college or used as the basis for allocations by the state or the campus. Accordingly, the budget issue is closely linked to enrollment. Many a dean is recruited with a mandate to rescue declining student numbers. Enrollments are not secret, and the topic will not be a surprise, but the dean will still need some ideas for action. These may include negotiating added scholarship funds to attract more strong students with financial need or asking regional employers to put up scholarships or internships. The alumni office will be glad to identify graduates who can help by spreading the word and even assist with recruitment, and despite traditional qualms in graduate programs about admitting students who did their undergraduate work in the same department, it may prove beneficial at least for a limited period. Moreover, the local papers are often interested in doing features about the new dean, and thus about the college's programs, career prospects for its graduates, and so forth.

Finally under this heading, an incoming dean can actually leverage the fact of his or her newness as a way to deal with certain crises. If, for example, a program has recently lost its accreditation or certification, the dean may be able to negotiate an extension to allow time to address the situation. Likewise, the dean may defer imminent deadlines for nonemergency issues. This tactic should be used sparingly, not only because the patience of the campus not will be unlimited but also because deferral merely increases the pile of short-term obligations in the near future.

The First Full Round

Calibrating the College to New Leadership

As we all know, change is threatening. For some who work closely with the dean—members of the college staff, department chairs, and directors—the arrival of a new dean may be little short of traumatic. Chairs in disciplines far removed from that of the dean will suspect that their fate is in the hands of someone who does not understand or sympathize with them. Staff may fear that their valuable contributions to the college will go unappreciated.

Every dean, experienced or not, should be sensitive to the level of anxiety produced by change and confront it directly. First, it helps to be forthright about one's management style and values from the beginning. But second, this must not come across as cocksure confidence that the dean knows how to do it all. A "listening tour" of both the college office and the chairs can yield ideas and gratitude. "Here is the way I have preferred to handle issues of this type; how does that look in this setting?" will show an approach born of experience but leave room for advice from colleagues who are more familiar with the immediate context. The challenge is to have actions follow words. Many deans report having declared a philosophy about, say, avoiding micromanagement and then being unable to follow through. Making strong initial claims that fall away in the face of local realities only highlights the problem and raises questions about credibility.

Second, the new dean should make the prospect of change an explicit topic of discussion by laying out a provisional plan for the first year, then eliciting and listening carefully to discussion. But change should never be trumpeted as a rescue operation after an inept predecessor (even though some deans are explicitly told that is the role they need to play, and virtually all deans feel that way sometimes). Far wiser and better is to show respect for the work of a predecessor and for long-standing traditions and move cautiously, only exorcising after recognizing the true demons. Obviously, this does not lessen the need to address concerns as they arise.

Third, no matter how extensive the disarray of the college, any newcomer and especially one selected from outside must choose carefully among the big problems to tackle first. No sense of urgency should spur the dean to act in advance of understanding the problem or before touching the necessary political bases, and nothing short of general calamity should prompt action on numerous problems at once. A few necessary and visible accomplishments early on will set the dean and the college on the right course for continued reform and achievement.

Widening the Circle of Acquaintances

Another large demand on time comes from the social realm. At the outset the new dean should accept as many invitations as possible, with the goal of meeting people and learning the landscape. Again, caution is necessary because some invitations will be from people with an agenda. One new dean accepted a dinner invitation from a department chair only to discover that the whole evening had been planned to give a second department chair the chance to plead for an endangered program. It is also wise to accept a generous variety of speaking invitations so as to introduce oneself to the institution and the community at large. No matter what the circumstances, however, the dean must be mindful that first appearances are lasting. Events of all sorts will call for appropriate remarks and good-humored but noncommittal responses to entreaties.

Still another set of meetings on campus will pay rich dividends: sessions with the faculty of every department and reporting unit to hear their aspirations and concerns and let them meet the dean on their own turf. This is the best chance to enlist the support of the faculty, provided it is not a mere courtesy call. Faculty will not take kindly to platitudes or evasive answers. They will want to be satisfied in their own minds that the college has a dean ready to lead and able to understand them. The former may come from what the dean says, the latter only from how well he or she listens. However distressing the college's problems, they will not improve by being blamed on the previous incumbent. Suffice it to say that new leadership requires a fresh look at the challenges of the college, and that in turn may bring new approaches. The worst mistake for a former chair, now a new dean, is to dwell on that previous experience as the source of all his or her ideas. Every chair in the college can claim the same credential and will feel very skeptical about seeing a used chair instead of encouraged by meeting a new dean.

Visibility in the community is especially challenging but can be very rewarding. The new dean may need advice from colleagues about the major players to meet but should begin the process as quickly as possible. It helps to identify one person who can help with introductions. A senior officer in institutional advancement will probably offer to arrange some key introductions. A department chair or distinguished faculty member in the college can help as well. More generally, a new dean should be eager to speak at Rotary Club and similar organizations as a good way to meet a cross section of local professionals. During this initial period of becoming known, the dean will receive invitations to join such organizations and perhaps even to sit on nonprofit boards.

These community contacts are inevitably linked to development, especially when the college development officer provides the initial introductions. The interest will run both ways, as community figures take the measure of the dean, looking for ideas that may spark their imagination. If the dean can be specific about strengths in the college and ask for advice on challenges to be addressed, significant community figures can contribute to the learning process, and eventually in more tangible ways (see more on this topic in Chapter Fifteen).

The trustees will want to meet the new dean, but the amount of interaction will depend on institutional tradition. In general deans do not communicate directly with trustees except at the request of the president. It is necessary to establish a cordial relationship with them, but contacts generally are filtered through the president or CAO.

Finally, most deans have at least one external advisory group of alumni, corporate, community, or educational leaders. A fuller discussion of these groups will come later (see Chapter Fifteen), but for the moment the crucial point is that any advisory council is the product of growing relationships with individuals who want to work with the dean who invited them. That relationship does not necessarily or readily transfer to the next dean. To maintain continuity with a busy group of volunteers, the dean should open the conversation with the leader of the council without delay but be genuinely open to a variety of possibilities: wholehearted support, wariness, or at worst a need to reshape the group entirely. But such decisions can come later. The immediate task is to keep the communications open with an important body of supporters.

More closely focused on the dean's profession proper are myriad state and national deans' organizations, higher education groups, and disciplinary organizations (see Chapter Fourteen). A new dean ought to sample the appropriate deans' groups as soon as possible to enter a network of helpful colleagues from around the country. In addition to college-specific groups such as the Council of Colleges of Arts and Sciences (CCAS) and the Council of Graduate Schools, deans at land-grant institutions can benefit greatly from the National Association of State Universities and Land Grant Colleges (NASULGC).

Developing an Agenda

Though it may hardly seem possible amid the welter of introductory meetings, new faces, and environments, a routine will be emerging and the important topics that form the fabric of the job will be taking shape. Most of these activities will be the subject of individual chapters in this volume: budget, curriculum, student affairs, faculty development, strategic planning, and so forth, and need not detain us now. But taken together, they are the task at hand from month to month and year to year. In the very process of courting exhaustion in pursuit of reliable intelligence, the hard work of preparing the college for planning has begun. The more modest, first stage of that planning is the establishment of an agenda for the first year. Even if the college already has a plan in the files—or in the works—it will require a fresh assessment. As the dean accumulates knowledge and forms opinions, he or she will recognize some priority issues in the state of the college, its role in the institution and its external relations. From those observations will arise a *few* key issues to tackle during the first year. The list must touch on problems that are substantial but can be addressed in a relatively short time—not more than the first year in office. They should be relatively uncontroversial but substantive. They may range from promoting international study in a variety of ways to addressing a nagging problem of leaky roofs, improving undergraduate or graduate advising, or enhancing the service role of the college while increasing opportunities for internship and practicum experiences. And the projects must have visibility. Ideally, they will affect positively a number of faculty members and students and solve problems that have prompted complaints, and they will make a measurable difference in the college's commitment to high standards in all its activities.

The sooner a new dean can begin to show results and deliver on initial commitments, the better. If unexpected difficulties come up in accomplishing something important, it is far better to be forthright about the problem and break the goal into smaller, manageable steps. Stonewalling and making excuses are not acceptable substitutes for momentum in the first year!

In the end, however, no achievement ranks beside an increase in the quality of the college: everyone from parents to president will share in this conviction. Because excellence is the one essential requirement for any priority, the dean's agenda should include a meaningful assessment of the college's strengths and weaknesses during the first year. If a vigorous system of program evaluation is not built into the institutional agenda, the dean should immediately begin planning one. Whatever the fiscal state or prospects, a college can design a system that sharpens resource decisions and clarifies college planning.

One of the biggest tasks for the dean in the first year is to think through development goals and shape them into a plan that matches the internal plan for the college as an academic entity. The enthusiasm and generosity of donors are precious assets, but they must never steer the college in directions that do not coincide with its agreed purposes. The formulation of a college agenda and the shaping of a development plan cannot blur each other or both efforts will be the poorer for it. Above all, benefactors are most gratified by the opportunity to support well thought-out ambitions.

How Am I Doing?

The last and most difficult chore of the first year is to evaluate how well the first year has gone. A rule of thumb is that very early on, the dean will hear mostly good things from those who want to be encouraging (adverse comments will be heard elsewhere but not reported directly). By the end of the first year there will be a mix of grumbles and cheers, and thereafter the floor is open for comment. Thus if colleagues come forward with specific positive comments, they are probably true but partial. If seldom is heard an encouraging word, the dean may have cause for concern. But assessment is not purely a matter of public reaction. A checklist of intentions set against a factual record of things done will provide an objective, if not very textured, picture of the year's work. The courageous (or rash) dean can circulate questionnaires to be completed anonymously by department chairs, assistant and associate deans, and others who report. One can only and earnestly hope that the CAO will offer an honest assessment along with pointers for the future. Deans, like the rest of humanity, cannot satisfy everyone, especially in one year. The critical question is whether the initial approach is working. Finding the answer requires asking questions of people who will speak truth to power, and it requires a dean who will respect and act on what they say.

Suggestions for Further Reading

Eble, Kenneth E. *The Art of Administration*. San Francisco: Jossey-Bass, 1978.

Plante, Patricia, and Robert L. Caret. *Myths and Realities of Academic Administration*. New York: ACE/Macmillan, 1990.

Steeples, Douglas. "So Now You Are a Dean: The First 100 Days." In George Allan (ed.), *Resource Handbook for Academic Deans* (pp. 89–91). Washington, D.C.: American Conference of Academic Deans, 1999.

CHAPTER FIVE

BALANCES OF POWER

Although maps, trips, and crosswords are useful metaphors for the conceptual understanding of deaning, in practical terms the best image may still be the badly overworked one of the team, with its connotations of painful training, coordination, strategies, huddles, cuts, competitiveness, and in the end, wins and losses. The image also sets up the most difficult conundrum that a college administrator faces: if there are several teams, they are presumably competing against one another. Every dean has had the conviction that the other deans are opposing coaches in the campus league, but what happens when the other team is inside the college? In nearly every college about which we have information, faculty and administration see themselves as adversaries at least part of the time and in bad cases deeply, almost inherently. The first time a dean of a major midwestern university addressed his faculty and spoke of common goals, a career curmudgeon rose and said, "Do you not realize that you are the enemy? Do you not know that the campus administration is the Evil Empire?" (This was in the 1980s.)

The dean's staff is the central grouping of administrative personnel, but there are in fact three layers of participants in the management of the college: the college administration, the department chairs, and faculty governance. It is very much in the dean's interest—and the college's—to prevent these from becoming competing teams. Time spent on one team is useful experience for signing up with another, but in this league the key to success is reducing the sense of competition or mutually exclusive victory.

One aspect of the cooperation vital to a successful administration is obviously communication, but not merely in order to know what is happening in other parts of the office. Although everyone in the office—the dean, any assistant or associate deans, and the office staff—must have clearly delineated areas of responsibility and be expert in performing their assigned duties, the most challenging but beneficial effect is the ability to substitute in emergencies for one another despite the range and complexity of individual portfolios. We all have dealt with (but if we are lucky, not worked in!) offices where no one can help in the absence of a given individual, or where the staff seem not to communicate and give conflicting answers to the same question. The college administration cannot afford to function like that; the credibility of the enterprise depends on regular, sound communication and the cooperation that follows it.

Similarly, college committees must have a clear mission and well-defined goals, along with an understanding of the way their work affects the operation of the college. This chapter will focus on the development and performance of the college office team—the decanal staff and major nonacademic staff members—and on the governance structures in the college as a whole, and include a note on faculty unions. Departmental leadership and function follow in the next chapter.

The Office Staff

The office staff, structure, and methods of working are critical to a dean's success.

Structure

In all but very small colleges there are three levels of college office personnel, including the dean at the top. The second level is made up of associate and assistant deans, assistants to the dean (if any), and sometimes directors of such specific aspects as the budget. Nomenclature varies enormously, and there is no standard or normal pattern. The assistant to the dean, for example, might be the budget officer, a development officer, or the executive assistant to the dean. Either of the first two might equally be designated a director, as is also the person in charge of admissions and advising in some colleges. Normally, titles other than associate or assistant dean indicate that the staff member does not have an academic appointment but is a professional administrator.

At the third level are administrative assistants, secretaries, clerical staff, and in some colleges, professional academic advisers (although these also may have the title of assistant dean depending on their credentials and whether they hold any academic title and do any teaching).

The dean of a small independent college might read the previous paragraph with amusement or envy—or relief. Many colleges have just a dean and an administrative assistant, plus a small number of clerical workers. Many do not have a separate budget officer or any full-time academic advisers. All the management functions that are not under the business office of the campus fall on the dean's shoulders, and all academic functions reside with the faculty. In such settings, the highest virtues are versatility and low blood pressure. The advantage of so intimate an administrative structure is that the person in charge is aware of all the issues that need attending, and communication with the staff is constant, detailed, and unavoidable. The disadvantage, needless to say, is the pressure on the dean to maintain all aspects of the college's mission without enough time for the reflection or experimentation that can make the role so rewarding. But the dean of a very small college will know the students far better than his or her counterpart on a large campus, and the satisfaction of knowing all members of the community for which one is responsible is no small blessing.

Responsibilities

We begin with the middling assumption that the dean is neither utterly alone nor overstaffed. How to deploy personnel over functions? Whatever the size of the decanal staff, responsibilities can be distributed in several ways. The three most frequent are by academic area, by administrative function, and by constituency. None is ideal, but all can work. The first model imagines the college as a collection of academic associations even as the campus is a collection of schools and colleges. The second and third models imagine the college as an administrative entity emulating the central administration of the campus, presiding over facilities, business office, and so on. The problem is that the campus has separate staff and resources for both kinds of management, but the college does not. How to play two games with one deck?

Large colleges of arts and sciences often have a triad of associate deans who handle the three major academic divisions—humanities and arts, social and behavioral sciences, natural and mathematical sciences (some large and comprehensive colleges, such as Kansas, have two associate deans just for the humanities). Often business schools will distribute undergraduate and graduate programs to associate deans. If (as is usual) the associate deans are already experienced members of the college faculty, the advantage of this arrangement is that they will know the departments and programs in their division well and will probably have worked already with the departmental executive officers; they have a natural interest in the welfare of the division. The learning curve for procedures, personnel, and issues will be less steep.

The concomitant disadvantages of divisional subdeans are not trivial. First, such a structure conceives of the whole college administration in academic subject terms, which is clearly not appropriate. The administration of the college is precisely the point at which issues must be approached and handled across the boundaries of academic field or fiefdom, but everyone—faculty, students, and staff—may read such an administrative structure as downplaying the unifying purpose of the college's central operations. Second, and potentially more serious, departments and faculty will normally deal with the associate dean for their division except in problematic situations, and this can isolate the dean from the departmental executive officers and other key decision makers of the college for normal operations, making her or him seem remote and uninterested in the activities of individual departments. Naturally, the dean wants to stay in productive contact with the chairs and directors and will surely take the time to do so. In that case, the arrangement does not reduce the number of people reporting to the dean, even though it creates a sense of distance between the two levels of administration. And third, the associate deans' portfolios will still need to include the administrative functions (for example, curriculum). There is a real risk that the college will either tax its decanals to the limit or appoint more associate and assistant deans to handle this more complex administrative structure.

Nevertheless, we should emphasize that the divisional arrangement works very well in many large colleges. Everything depends on the administrative acuity of the dean in retaining good communications with the departments and selecting associate and assistant deans who understand the demands and the limits of their positions.

A second model proceeds from function: associate deans for research administration, budget planning, advising, and so forth. This approach has the advantage that faculty who become associate deans work on issues that affect the entire college, and thus no member of the decanal team can keep (or develop) a parochial outlook that may hinder the effectiveness of the entire administration. Many faculty are committed to the welfare of the whole academic enterprise and find this wider perspective comfortable and even familiar, but others—though solid citizens and brilliant scholars—retain powerfully disciplinary outlooks. Not only must the college office constantly view every issue from a college-wide perspective, but to the greatest extent possible the decanal staff should be able to step in and assist or even replace a colleague with a minimum of preparation. The more familiar an associate dean is with the full spectrum of the college, the easier this will be.

The principal disadvantage is that relatively few faculty have experience, or perhaps even much interest, in such issues as building maintenance schedules, policies for indirect cost recovery allocation, or legal requirements in student harassment cases. The learning curve can be very steep in these areas, and if the array of duties seems too technical and not academic, interest may soon wane. It is hard to predict this reaction. Faculty may think that the opportunity to work in the office of the college's chief academic officer means they will spend much of their time tackling academic issues. That should certainly be true for some part of every decanal's time, and if the balance tips toward management of things rather than advancement of programs, the staffing can be unstable.

Finally, some colleges build their team around constituencies: students, faculty, external relations. The advantage is that these various groups tend to have quite distinctive outlooks and requirements, and an associate or assistant dean who is immersed in student academic affairs, for example, quickly gains an appreciation for the special difficulties and needs of that population. Constantly adjusting one's mindset from faculty to students, from alumni to on-campus administrative offices, can be unproductive.

The potential disadvantage is redundancy of effort, with each office needing to tackle questions and contact people while trying to learn the same information already on someone else's desk. More serious is the risk of compartmentalizing the college's treatment of its constituencies so that faculty and students hear different interpretations of a question, or even hope that they are entitled to a "better" read on the matter than other groups. Again, problems can be avoided with good communication among the dean's staff and clearly developed positions and procedures.

In short, any of the models can work brilliantly with prudence and practice. Actually, however decanals are designated, most colleges show a hybrid of these three types. For a number of reasons, including personnel policies, budget restrictions, and institutional limitations on creating new staff positions, a new dean probably will neither want, nor be able, to sweep away the existing structure but rather will examine its workings and modify rather than demolish. The pattern of other colleges or schools on campus can be very helpful in suggesting what works in that culture. But it is important always to recognize that colleges come in all sizes, and an arrangement that works wonderfully for a small college of nursing or communications may be inadequate for arts and sciences or engineering.

Much will depend on the dean's own preferred style of communicating and delegating, as well as the areas she or he wants to promote as leader of the college: graduate programs, external funding, recruitment and retention of minorities, professional curricula, practicum experiences, public service. The choices will be influenced by the dean's goals for the college and its strengths, and the dean may want to be personally responsible and visible in these areas.

Yet another variable for the decanal team is whether an associate dean serves for a predetermined and temporary assignment or an indefinite tour of duty. For example, all but the very small colleges have associate deans who steer faculty development and academic programs. Sometimes these individuals step out of their regular faculty roles for fixed terms, usually three years; in other cases the college has what amounts to a stable civil service that remains unchanged for a decade or more, providing continuity from one dean to the next and a depth of institutional memory that no individual dean could hope to amass. These two types of appointments usually involve very different kinds of people.

The first category often includes leading faculty who have filled leadership roles in their departments, not infrequently as chair, and enjoy a high level of trust among the faculty, have a detailed knowledge of local issues, and are willing to devote hard work to a hard job precisely because it is a short-term commitment. This type is very close to the faculty citizen-dean described in Chapter One. Such faculty can be invaluable, for example, in giving fearless and compelling assessments of tenure and promotion cases, especially problematic or murky ones. Normally, if a senior faculty member agrees to spend three years in the dean's office, there must be agreements to protect his or her long-term research and other plans: a research associate, a postdoctoral sidekick, added travel money, one month away from the office in the summer for research. After all, the dean is borrowing a scholar from that person's main career, not coopting a permanent colleague. Sometimes a one-term associate dean from the senior faculty will find the tour of duty so interesting that the next step is a deanship somewhere (even in the same college, if a vacancy occurs!).

The second type of appointment, common both for assistant and associate deans, involves faculty who for whatever reason have become peripheral to their own departments but are interested and often very skilled in the workings of the academy. Often these are long-term associate professors who are (or were) strong teachers but have not kept up their research. Precisely because they are committed to the welfare of the college and do not have a strong research program commanding their attention, they can be invaluable in a second-tier role in the college administration. They know the place intimately, they care about it, and they are glad to play a role that is appreciated rather than run up against the realization that they have not kept up with their own colleagues. These associate deans may remain in the college office for many years and provide exemplary support to the dean with wisdom, cautionary tales, and academic savvy.

We must note the obvious: sometimes the situation can be unhealthy, with an incumbent there simply because he or she has always been there, far beyond the end of helpfulness or contribution. The dean will need to be aware of this possibility, without reaching any conclusions until taking the full measure of the person's gifts and record.

Last are the decanals who have never been on the tenure track. Most in this group are assistant deans rather than associates, although there are highly admired examples of associate deans without tenure affiliations. Lecturers will sometimes take up a staff role in the college office and by dint of their talents and work earn a place in the decanal team. In several universities large and small, the dean's staff includes faculty who had been on the tenure track but stepped back (recognizing that their dossier would not be compelling), came off the tenure track, and brought enthusiasm, local knowledge, and talent into the management of the college. Hiring such a candidate is a step that the dean should take only cautiously and with a broad base of support both in the college office and among the best faculty citizens, lest it appear that a "failed" faculty member has in some sense been placed over those who have earned their stripes in the faculty.

A mix of short- and long-term appointments among the assistant and associate deans is wise because it provides both stability and fresh faculty perspectives at regular intervals. It also allows the dean to mentor future administrators. The same caveats apply to prospective associate deans as to deans: all must recognize and accept ungrudgingly the changes that this move will require in faculty habits, especially for short-term shifts. The faculty member may believe that his or her research program can be held in place for three years but soon resent the pressures of the office and repent of the decision to interrupt a successful career for an ill-advised adventure. Accordingly, many a dean is chagrined to learn that an associate dean has unilaterally postponed critical work for the college while finishing a publication. Faculty accustomed to working independently may charge off to do an assignment on their own without the prior collaboration necessary for a successful outcome. Just as we often think of mentoring new faculty, a similar process is essential to allow new assistant or associate deans to learn their roles.

Collaboration

The way a dean delegates tasks and responsibilities will determine whether the office succeeds or fails. It is not enough that the staff understand what the dean is asking or how the dean wants it done. With delegated authority comes the obligation both to take charge of a function confidently and knowledgeably, and the ability to keep the dean informed. Conversely, if appeals come to the dean about decisions by staff members, the dean inquires about the situation but rarely second-guesses the person in charge.

A word about speech and silence. The two most delicate and important aspects of administration are the need to confer intelligently and discreetly before speaking about a topic and the ability to maintain confidentiality. These sometimes seem harder for academics than for most, because as mentioned earlier, information is the currency of the academic realm. Ground rules and occasional reminders to all—including the dean—will not be amiss (for example, what to tell and not to tell one's spouse or partner about office matters).

Regular staff meetings are vitally important for two reasons. One is obvious: keeping all staff current on the issues facing the college and ensuring that all are aware of the appropriate actions, positions, or plans in each case. Even in routine spheres of responsibility, a heads-up on new developments can forestall problems. If, for instance, the advising office reports student confusion about the new general education requirements at preregistration, the office will be alert to the prospect of calls from anxious parents or faculty advisers. Staff meetings ought to be relatively free-form, more like an animated conversation verging on argument than orderly staff reports. In short, academic habits are transferred to the administrative conference table.

The second reason follows closely on the first. Deans are the sounding boards for all kinds of topics, from the cast of the annual budget presentation to plans for faculty recruitment, new alumni initiatives, or priorities for renovating facilities. Collectively, the decanal staff understands the big picture in a way that no other individual or group can. That panoramic wisdom is precisely what the dean needs and cannot find elsewhere. Virtually all deans who have associates (or assistants) report that they have been spurred to important intentions and deterred from probable disaster by candid, unflinching commentary from these associates.

Likewise, all stages of strategic planning are refined in this crucible of commentary. An annual retreat for assessing the past year and setting plans for the coming season is now normal for most departments, and it is a virtual necessity for the college office where the variety and urgency of many competing topics makes reflection, acknowledgment of accomplishment, or even prudent planning seem like a luxury.

A final note on the sounding board function: associate academic deans frequently help the dean think through the merits and problems of promotion dossiers, whether by clarifying the nature of surface chemistry for a musician dean, for example, or helping to sift through departmental rhetoric and assess the true quality of a teaching record.

Staff Development

In concentrating on deans thus far, we do not want to ignore the importance of staff development at every level. Some deans invite consultants to make presentations and lead discussions at staff retreats, especially when they wish to stimulate new ideas about planning. Updates and training on new software programs are necessary for keeping pace. In-house experts on institutional research or public relations are another source of information to improve the work of the college. Beyond such group occasions, however, the dean must encourage individual staff members to advance their computing skills through short courses, seek professional accreditation where appropriate (for example, certified professional secretary, certified fundraising executive), become active in professional organizations, and attend workshops on current academic issues. Increasingly, colleges are providing staff with time off and funding to pursue such activities. And of course, the dean can set the example by participating in similar activities as well. When staff members return from these experiences, they should share what they have learned with their colleagues in whatever setting is most appropriate, whether with the academic leadership or the office management staff.

Staff Diversity

A related issue is staff diversity. An entire segment of the college staff—or indeed, the entire staff—may be without diversity in gender or ethnicity. This is often true of advising staff, who tend to be white and female. Often, if the issue of diversity remains unaddressed in the central administration of the college, it will be likewise—and thus a greater challenge—in the college as a whole. As part of a larger effort to address diversification of staff, faculty, and students with department chairs, the dean provides leadership by example. In particular, we must recognize that the traditional pathways to academic leadership—positions—department chair, dean, provost, or president—still favor white males. The selection process and qualifications traditionally sought work against candidates who do not fit the mold, no matter how great their preparation. In particular, without experience as department chair, a woman or minority candidate may find advancement very difficult.

To make a difference, the dean needs to understand the situation and find ways to overcome these barriers. Several large public universities and some private schools have developed internships in the college to allow faculty members to test their suitability for administrative positions before moving more deliberately in that direction. Another strategy is to appoint women and minority faculty members as acting chairs when vacancies occur. This allows their colleagues to assess and appreciate their work over a specified period of time before a regular appointment and allows these faculty members to test their own interest and aptitude.

The danger in this stratagem, of course, is twofold. First, acting chairs can find themselves in a tricky situation, often turbulent or risky; the very fact that the department has not made a regular appointment is a sign of an unusual state of affairs. This may not be anything like a fair test of a novice's ability to be chair under normal conditions and may have the opposite effect to what the dean intended by making it even harder for that person to continue in the role. Second, if this approach applies only to underrepresented groups it will feel and look like tokenism or even a way to undermine the prospects of these faculty: we will let you try out in a situation with a high probability of failure. Still, such appointments often have a positive outcome if the dean can find support among the faculty for them.

The best and simplest thing to do is to set an example with exemplary appointments in the dean's own staff and in faculty leadership roles without fanfare and without suggesting that they are risky appointments. The issue is one of access to opportunity for the candidate and broadening the talent pool for the college. All parties owe the necessary support to make it work. Above all, it is important to avoid making one or two appointments and leaving it at that—a monument to token gestures.

The challenge is somewhat different in diversifying the support staff in the college, where there is most likely to be a gender gap—traditionally these positions were filled mostly by women—whether or not there is also ethnic underrepresentation. The latter imbalance may well be easier to address than the former, with well-publicized encouragement of applications from protected classes of individuals, help from the personnel office about where to recruit a diverse pool of candidates, and help from current minority staff members in locating possible applicants. The greatest asset to recruitment, however, is a positive climate in the office where all staff feel comfortable and valued. Leadership for this rests squarely with the dean, who must ensure that all staff members at every level are treated with respect and considered for promotions and other recognition strictly on the basis of merit.

Faculty Governance

Nothing irritates the faculty more than the suggestion that the dean "runs the college." Indeed, deans come and go while faculty remain in their positions, and numerous responsibilities lie at the heart of the college enterprise that are their peculiar property. The dean provides an administrative context in which the faculty can pursue their shared academic duties. All colleges have some form of bylaws, all have a governance structure, and all have a set of standing committees.

The central formal event in the life of the faculty as college citizens is the faculty meeting, which all are entitled to attend though most decline to do so. Henry Rosovsky called the monthly meetings at Harvard "a well-choreographed ballet," filled with familiar and traditional moves and relatively infrequent surprises (1990, p. 51). Few colleges have monthly meetings, partly because that feels like too great a claim on the faculty's time—and truth be told also because there is rarely enough business requiring the participation of the faculty as a body to justify so many sessions each term. One or two meetings each year tend to draw larger attendance because they are devoted to popular rituals of arrival and departure: the introduction of the new faculty in the fall, together with the dean's observations on the state of the college, and the final meeting in the spring to honor those retiring and hand out other recognitions. In between, meetings may have minimal attendance or even be canceled for want of a quorum (or an agenda). If faculty meetings are nothing more than press conferences or sermons, they will wither, and deservedly so. As long as the bylaws of the college allow for the faculty meeting to address its business with the quorum at hand and the agenda is circulated so that faculty can attend if the issues are important to them, then most faculty are content to leave the legislation to whatever attendance a given meeting draws.

It may happen that a very large college becomes so impersonal that the faculty feel detached from the legislative function and thus disenfranchised in some way. Colleges have addressed this problem by creating representative bodies to conduct the business of the faculty, with widely published reports of all its deliberations and actions. A meeting of the full faculty can always be called on petition, and the ultimate authority rests with the full faculty. Even though the academy prides itself on being a hands-on, direct democracy, such elected bodies can work very well. The chosen members have a heightened awareness of their responsibilities for considering the issues, and the rest of the faculty are relieved not to feel, however dimly, that they are neglecting their civic duty.

Through the standing committees, the faculty exercise their responsibilities for the development, maintenance, and revision of the curriculum, promotion and tenure considerations, grievance hearings, student appeals, and other matters. The dean, or more often a designate, works ex officio with these groups. From time to time special opportunities—an emergency or the planning of larger ambitions, such as an instructional technology initiative or a capital project—may create the need for ad hoc committees or faculty task forces to advise the dean on issues not covered by the standing committees.

In all of these, the dean leads best from the sideline, fostering the work of the faculty but not presuming to predict—or appearing to dictate—its outcome. The college committees are not only the setting for both routine and special contributions by faculty to the commonweal but an important source of experience and contact with the administration. As we noted in Chapter Two, work in faculty governance frequently leads to other roles, such as department leadership, associate deanship, or a campus-level academic staff position. In short, this is one source from which future deans are derived.

Standing Committees

We have all endured college committee meetings with agendas too long and detailed for the members to participate in effectively or in which confusion reigns about the role and function of the group—and some would say those are the good committees! A new dean can contribute to the welfare of the college by standing back and surveying the college's standing committees with a critical and still-detached gaze.

First, is the current array of committees adequate to accomplish the tasks of the faculty? Too few committees means a daunting burden for each, and the result will probably be either a reluctance to accept so onerous an assignment— which means faculty who are not terribly busy with other academic work end up deciding the important questions facing the faculty—or insufficient attention to the committee's necessary tasks, or both.

The converse is equally bad: too many committees with vague and overlapping charges. Ironically, this situation arises from the first. Large and unwieldy committees split into several new entities that can in theory tackle a narrower agenda more effectively, but the parts of the old cluster do not separate neatly. A unified curriculum committee breaks out into one committee to review program changes, another to review proposals for new programs, a third to assess individual courses for general education—and none of these is now responsible for the overall health of the academic curriculum!

Faculty governance serves three primary functions: working with the administration, curriculum, and promotion and tenure. Depending on its size, a college may well map these functions to three distinct deliberative bodies (apart from the faculty as a whole). One is an executive committee, variously formed by direct election from segments of the faculty (such as academic divisions, graduate and undergraduate programs, or clusters of departments), or the chairs of the standing committees plus others with specific faculty governance responsibilities, or a mixture of these approaches. The executive committee meets regularly with the dean and provides a liaison between faculty governance and college administration. Dean and faculty can keep each other informed on the status of major issues, set agendas for faculty meetings, and discuss and shape plans or policies that will go out to the wider faculty for deliberation. Above all from the dean's perspective, the committee provides candid, confidential advice from a source that often feels out of reach to the dean simply because of the organizational gulf between "us" and "them." This group should be tapped for discussion of controversial matters, gauging reactions to possible initiatives, and bringing faculty concerns to the dean's attention. Along with the associate deans and the department chairs, the executive committee is a third collective voice that keeps the dean in touch with the needs and intentions of the college as a whole.

A second committee will review and make recommendations about curricular matters in the college. An associate dean or other dean's representative may serve as liaison to this committee, both to provide assistance with the administrative side of the committee's task—compliance with college and campus procedures and deadlines—and to make sure that the committee's work takes all relevant facts into account, thus avoiding subsequent confusion or frustration and a faculty view that the college does not support their efforts. The curriculum committee is always (or should be) elected, because it functions in an area that belongs unambiguously to the faculty.

The other crucial contribution to faculty governance consists in advising the dean on tenure and promotion recommendations. It is important to note that all stages of tenure or promotion reviews are advisory, up to the final responsible body of the institution, whether the trustees or the president. Thus the composition of promotion and tenure committees varies from place to place. Sometimes the members are elected because the faculty want trusted colleagues to make these most agonizing and important recommendations; sometimes the dean's need to know that the advice will be competent, dispassionate, and balanced leads to an appointed committee (often after discussion with the executive committee). In some colleges, the executive committee itself serves as the P&T committee. In any case, the body passing on recommendations should be made up mainly, if not exclusively, of full professors.

All committees charged with collegewide business should be representative, in some clearly defined manner, of the disciplines in the college. As we suggested earlier, it can be difficult to find good candidates willing to serve on these time-consuming and detail-oriented committees. The dean can encourage department chairs, or the committee on committees, to seek appropriate individuals and not simply nominate people who have nothing better to do. In the end, if faculty members believe that their service can make a difference, they are more likely to participate in college life. The dean's role is to ensure that the purpose and function of each college-level committee is clear and to provide regular reports of the accomplishments of these groups.

In addition to these basic committees, the range of possibilities is great. Some colleges will need a separate committee to deal with graduate matters, others a committee devoted to overseeing and enhancing externally funded research or issues such as human subjects review, animal care, teaching buyouts, and so forth. Interdisciplinary programs are a high priority and a massive challenge in both organizational and academic terms. Many colleges, especially large and comprehensive ones, have one or more coordinating committees. Undergraduate research support, study abroad in conjunction with on-campus requirements for the major—the list seems to grow in size and urgency each year. The dean can and should encourage periodic review of the college's standing committees in order to keep them up to date with evolving priorities.

Ad Hoc Committees and Task Forces

The same peril that attends standing committees lurks near the creation of any ad hoc committee: Is it necessary? Is its task clearly delimited? Will appropriate faculty be willing to take on another assignment at the cost of some present activity? But beyond these is the risk that a body created for legitimate but temporary purposes will linger, settle, and ossify into a new piece of permanent but needless administrative work. Ad hoc committees should be relatively rare and serve a specified purpose. (That is, after all, what *ad hoc* means: *for this!*)

Committees may be authorized by the faculty as a whole, by its executive committee, or by the dean. In the latter category the most frequent are search committees for positions that will report to the dean, such as assistant or associate dean, department chair, director, or college staff. Although most people readily admit that small groups work better than large ones, the academic urge to have all views represented (which is not the same as heeding them!) keeps pushing for unwieldy committees; search committees for a dean or provost commonly have close to twenty members. For a department chair or an assistant dean, little or nothing is gained by a committee larger than five. The dean should handpick the chair to ensure effective work and an understanding of what he or she regards as the key issues in the selection process. Oddly, despite the number of committees on which faculty serve, appreciation of procedure is not widespread. Again, the academic temperament fully appreciates the value of vigorous discussion and argument and respects the conclusion reached in this way, but feels frustrated, even offended, by regulations that seem to aim at dampening freedom of action. Thus the dean needs to spell out the controls or regulations—affirmative action, resource limits, time lines, other considerations—and emphasize their relevance and necessity. Once that is done, the faculty approach to committee work, though not always efficient, is surprisingly effective, but the dean or a designee should keep in close touch with the committee chair to ensure that the process stays on track. If there are procedural missteps—for example, a dominant committee member sets up a ranking system that favors one candidate—it will be far harder to reverse the damage and rescue the search than to raise pointed questions early on.

Ad hoc committees can also be good ways to respond to special opportunities or challenges facing the college where faculty input is desirable. If, for example, the college were fortunate enough to receive a large bequest to implement along guidelines suggested by the donor, an ad hoc committee could be charged to develop a specific proposal for using the funds. Or if the provost called for a procedure to equalize faculty workloads, the project would be dead at the start without input from a faculty group appointed for the purpose. Finally, the executive committee itself can serve as an ad hoc body on behalf of either the faculty or the dean.

When the committee completes its appointed task and deadlines have been met, the dean should not merely receive a report but make a point of dismissing the committee with sincere thanks and indicate what the follow-up will be. This last step is essential to overcome the persistent skepticism of faculty members regarding the results of committee work.

A task force, as distinct from an ad hoc committee, usually has a larger membership, a less specific charge, and a longer time line. For all these reasons, deans should create task forces far more sparingly than ad hoc committees, but when doing so give them the prominence they deserve. Task forces can focus attention on issues of central importance to the college—for example, examine the state of interdisciplinary study in the college and make recommendations for improvement. A wise dean will form a task force with faculty advice and make ample room for its members to shape the issues, especially because they will likely have a stake in the outcomes.

Faculty Unions

Faculty unions are found only on a minority of campuses (how tempting it is to say instead that most campuses do not have organized faculty!), but where they exist they introduce a very important new feature in the professional terrain. Moreover, unions take a variety of forms, and the bargaining agreements are equally varied. Accordingly, we must be careful in predicting the dean's role in relationship to them. Some features, however, are fairly constant.

First, a dean normally is considered part of management; hence, some union agreements preclude the dean from holding a tenured faculty position. In view of the importance that tenure has for academic life, a candidate should learn how the union agreement touches the academic appointment of administrators before applying for a position at a unionized institution. Next, the union perspective will in all probability be represented on the search committee, and so the candidate should ask to see the bargaining agreement and perhaps consult with a colleague from a unionized campus. Not doing so invites confusion about a basic feature of the institution that will be puzzling to the uninitiated and may be unwelcome to some decanal candidates.

Finally, after accepting a position, the new dean will want a careful tutorial in the campus contract at the earliest opportunity. The contract will affect all vital aspects of the dean's role and authority, and in this case it would be most unwise to indulge in on-the-job training. The best procedure is to review the agreement with the contract administrator, who can clarify his or her role in working with the union and alert the dean to potential problems. The contract administrator can advise about the nature and extent of direct contacts that the dean should have with union officers. At the very least, the dean will need to play a role in the faculty grievance procedure and oversee the implementation of the nondiscrimination, workload, promotion and tenure, and personnel policies in the college. We also advise an early meeting with the union president and other key individuals, such as grievance officers, to establish lines of communication before cases inevitably arise.

Some typical issues the dean may face include disgruntled faculty members who wish to change departments or otherwise believe they have been treated unfairly, committees that have ignored certain aspects of the procedures for tenure and promotion, and department chairs who have not followed appropriate termination procedures for part-time or temporary faculty members. A number of faculty members will have workplace environment complaints, such as mold in the ceilings or air ducts, smokers outside the window, and so forth; solutions to these problems can be costly and must not be undertaken lightly. Often the dean is most valuable as a mediator in search of solutions before problems become larger but must be prepared to follow the formal process in the contract if no resolution is achieved. At all stages of these dealings, the best advice is to be straightforward with union representatives and refuse to be defensive in the face of criticism or even hostility.

Two areas of conflict pose the most difficult challenges: sexual harassment cases and budget reduction mandates. Whereas all deans must deal with sexual harassment incidents that emerge in their colleges, those at unionized campuses will have strict procedures to follow that can keep a case alive for years. The procedures laid out to protect the rights of accuser and accused have the advantage of being clearly spelled out, but following them can be a maddening object lesson in bureaucracy.

In budget reductions, the problem is one of constraint, because contract provisions may directly impede the dean's flexibility in making the cuts that a prudent administrative analysis demands. For example, personnel policies can make it very difficult to eliminate positions, even temporary ones, although personnel expenditures, of course, constitute the largest part of the budget. In such circumstances, the contract administrator becomes a crucial figure not only in the welfare of college personnel but in all other aspects of the college's operations and plans. Because the terms of the bargaining agreement are in force, the dean's only course, when in doubt, is to consult with the contract administrator.

We must not leave the impression that working with a unionized faculty is simply a negative experience. On the contrary, there are many advantages to such an arrangement. Having a set of clear policies and procedures for handling complaints, grievances, salaries, and other personnel issues leads to fair treatment of difficult and delicate matters. Moreover, there is usually a third party working on problems: the union grievance officer, who is fully as interested as the dean in reaching a quick and acceptable resolution. After all, unresolved matters may go to arbitration, which does indeed provide an end to the situation but not necessarily along the lines that either party wants. More personally, the dean receives the same health and retirement benefits as members of the bargaining unit, and in general those are often superior to what is available at nonunionized institutions.

In the end, good working relations with the union will depend on qualities that a dean should have in any case: willingness to express appreciation for aspects of the relationship that are going well and readiness to work with union representatives to help the faculty with serious problems.

Suggestions for Further Reading

Bérubé, Michael, and Cary Nelson (eds.). *Higher Education under Fire: Politics, Economics, and the Crisis of the Humanities.* New York: Routledge, 1995.

Birnbaum, Robert. *How Colleges Work: The Cybernetics of Academic Organization and Leadership.* San Francisco: Jossey-Bass, 1988.

Chafee, Ellen Earle, and William G. Tierney. *Collegiate Culture and Leadership Strategies.* New York: ACE/Macmillan, 1988.

Keeton, Morris. *Shared Authority on Campus.* Washington, D.C.: American Association for Higher Education, 1971.

Keller, George. *Academic Strategy: The Management Revolution in Higher Education.* Baltimore: Johns Hopkins University Press, 1983.

Rosovsky, Henry. *The University: An Owner's Manual.* New York: Norton, 1990.

Schuster, Jack H., Daryl G. Smith, Kathleen A. Corak, and Myrtle M. Yamada. *Strategic Governance: How to Make Big Decisions Better.* Phoenix: American Council on Education/Oryx Press, 1994.

CHAPTER SIX

DEPARTMENTS, PROGRAMS, AND THEIR LEADERS

M ost colleges, whether freestanding or part of a larger institution, include a federation of departments and programs. This is certainly true at colleges with wide and varied intellectual responsibilities, including arts and sciences, engineering, agriculture, medicine, and (usually) business. The size, traditional power, and specific roles of departments vary from one college to another. Departments in medical schools, for example, are extraordinarily stable and the headship is a very powerful position that a vigorous and skilled leader may hold for many years, whereas in arts and sciences the chair or even head is less powerful and less durable. (See the following section on the difference between chairs and heads; we will also occasionally use the neutral term departmental executive officer [DEO].) Agriculture tends toward the medical model, business more toward the federation model of arts and sciences. In other single-discipline schools with more sharply defined missions, such as law and theology, or special missions such as graduate schools, there is usually no formal departmental structure but a flexible array of programs or divisions lacking the autonomy that characterizes the department. Our concern here is with colleges that do use a departmental structure. For them, departments constitute the political and curricular framework for all concerned. In some senses, the college would not need to exist if not for the complex of disciplinary entities that it unites and steers.

Dealing with the Multiple Identities of Departments

Whether as faculty or administrators, we take for granted the existence of the college and the presence of departments, and perhaps their current configuration may seem inevitable and immutable (though not ideal). As obvious and familiar as these units are, however, deans should consider what they signify, what they do, and how best to work with their DEOs.

Academic Constituencies

Departments and programs offer all the courses of study and house the faculty of the institution. They tend to be organized very conservatively following the historic establishment of the disciplines in a given area (it used to be said of the arts and sciences that departments were all named for books by Aristotle). Their names and configuration collectively bestow identity on the college. As handy as tradition may be in sustaining the identity and place of the individual disciplines, however, it also presents colossal challenges for the dean.

First, for reasons deriving more from history and anxiety than from present reality or academic justification, departmental barriers frequently seem insurmountable to those inside them. This silo mentality impedes progress both internal and external. For example, the evolution of a disciplinary major to include cognate study in other departments often bogs down if it seems too much like dependence on another unit to prepare "our" students, and cross-listing courses or team teaching across unit lines can make international peace talks look like consensus politics.

Second, even when disciplines have manifestly changed in orientation or overlapped extensively with their intellectual neighbors, any suggestion of merging or reorganizing the departments (much less the college) can meet with cries of alarm, most commonly, "We cannot surrender our identity, autonomy, and place in the intellectual universe," or "Nobody will hire a graduate of such a program. It is a formula for decline into oblivion."

Conversely, the directors of programs often seek departmental status for the prestige, independence, and name recognition that they believe will accompany such a move. Many fields now commonly enjoying departmental status began their lives as subunits of other departments or as programs—for example, environmental studies, nuclear engineering, biostatistics and epidemiology, women's studies, and a host of others. In their days as programs, these fields relied on the larger, more permanent departments for faculty time, visibility, and even lab space or library acquisition budgets. The considerable benefits of flexibility in building new, evolving, and distinctive academic programs, especially at the doctoral level, and the chance to bring together faculty with wide-ranging interests, is offset if a program cannot count on the home departments to release faculty for teaching away from their home base or if the faculty member cannot carve out the time and effort to provide all the other support—advising students, directing dissertations, and serving on examination committees, not to mention the normal gamut of faculty governance committees—that is already being demanded back home in the department.

Administrative Components

Departments have the administrative challenge of attracting and serving students, providing a supportive atmosphere for faculty development and scholarship, and fostering a culture of participation in the civic life (committees, policies, procedures) that allows their work to proceed smoothly. Of these three, civic life is most likely to be problematic, or—to put it the other way around—if a department is struggling with its mission, the source of the problem is probably in its shared administrative tasks. However much we may hear about students being slighted or ignored by reclusive and self-absorbed faculty, most faculty enjoy teaching and want their students to do well (even if the motive is ego, the effort is still there!). Thus they want to foster a setting in which students can succeed. And most assuredly, the faculty will put in the effort to make their own professional work convenient and appreciated; that is human nature, and certainly for the over-achieving type that is attracted to academic life! But administrative work—the speakers committee, representative to the campus senate, the human subjects review panel, chemical safety officer—holds little charm and receives little reward. This is the aspect of academic life that faculty participate in least willingly, and on the whole, least effectively. It is quite simply not why they are in the academy. But in addition to issues of reluctance and talent there are further potential difficulties of division: faculty are divided by subdisciplinary perspectives (for instance, physical versus cultural geography), age, research productivity, theoretical approaches, or personal grudges. Recent work (Massy, Wilger, and Colbeck, 1994) shows that the best departments are those in which members share goals in accomplishing such tasks and understand the role that each one plays in the overall success of the unit. The dean, though perhaps not able to achieve this ideal directly, can help DEOs to do so partly by sharing this research and presenting an example at the college level by involving them in planning and evaluation (see more on this in Chapter Seven).

Much of the administrative work of the college is actually done at the departmental level, especially in the areas of planning, budgeting, personnel evaluation, grants accounting, and preparing reports. Indeed, this reflects one of the most difficult facts of campus administration: although the amount and complexity of administrative work achieved in a college office has grown considerably, the impact of sending each of these new functions down to every department has felt like a disproportionate burden on departmental staff. The dean must try to ensure that all units have the support they need for these tasks, simply because the effectiveness of the college depends on it. One form of protection for the department is to ascertain, before sending a new function or complication down, that it really has to be done and can only be done there.

For example, new staff members should be provided with training to help them adjust to the requirements of their roles. When the system introduces changes such as new software, workshops will help departmental personnel with implementation. All units must appreciate that there is a real link between the college and departments, one that comprises information as well as the recognition that a single department's actions can have consequences for many other departments. One big surprise—such as an unauthorized budget overrun by an ambitious theater department because of an expensive guest artist—can harm the entire college. Departmental staff must be unequivocally clear about the college's expectations in budget management and reporting. Carrots are as good as sticks. Special awards for departmental staff who have been especially effective from the college's perspective (with the accord of the DEO, of course) send a strong message of appreciation.

The strength of a department is measured by the reputation of the faculty, the achievements of its students, its size, its effectiveness in working together, and its contributions to the welfare of the institution. These factors taken together will directly affect a unit's power in the college. The dean must consider the interests of the best departments when making decisions and allocating or withdrawing resources. Most good departments are savvy enough to understand this and act accordingly; sometimes a department will rely on its perceived quality too much and claim undue consideration. For example, a department at a large research university believed it had been granted special status in perpetuity some years earlier and expected to get a 50 percent bigger increase in money than any other department, year after year, no matter what other factors arose! If special support does not materialize, this leads such a department to the conclusion that the dean does not support quality. Admittedly, no dean can give in to this kind of extortion. But a dean who, while understanding the political realities, can honestly promote most decisions as ways to improve quality may gain the support of the best department for collegewide goals. If unfounded expectations fuel a power play on the part of a strong department, the dean can point out that keeping a weak unit weak will only drain energy and resources from the college, that no department however good can be self-sufficient, and that few departments can remain strong with isolationist attitudes.

This is not to urge peremptory treatment of the college's star programs. The dean needs to deal with strong departments very carefully because their voices can be important outside college bounds. Widely respected departments have earned their position and have received support to get there. It is fair to point this out when discussing current efforts to advance other units in their turn (see Chapters Eight and Ten).

Faculty Homes

Departments also serve as professional homes for faculty; offices, research labs, reporting lines, disciplinary colleagues, and the day-to-day realities of careers embody professional identity and achievement. In that context, few matters are more important than space, and particularly contiguity. A department that is physically scattered, or even divided into two locations, generally does not thrive. Colleagues who are in separate buildings see less of each other, communicate less with each other, and eventually may think less of each other in both senses. Projects are harder to get under way and to staff, the spark of creativity just does not travel as easily between buildings, and collegial responsibility seems more abstract. Meanwhile, those who wish to withdraw from the life of the department, or even hide from common responsibilities, can do so. When space is tight, it may seem sensible to put clinical psychology in one location and cognitive psychology in another as long as all faculty in each division are together, but that is the beginning of the end for a department with strongly distinguished subdisciplines.

By the same token, departments that have an entire building to themselves (which is the dream of every department) can stagnate both as disciplinary units and as clusters of college citizens by interacting only with each other. This is particularly true if they are at some distance from other college buildings. To many departments, "quality space" eventually means "our own building, very near the library, regularly remodeled and expanded as we hire new faculty." In fact, a strong and growing department may need to move in order to accommodate its prosperity. It is no small irony, then, when a department that has lamented its quarters for years and is finally offered more and better space reads and resents the offer as an eviction notice. There are many tales of public demonstrations, letters to the campus newspaper, complaints of abuse, overwrought rhetoric in faculty meetings and deans' offices, even barricades! The most common allegation is that this move is a complete surprise. Departments need a voice in the planning process, both to tap into their wisdom (after all, it is their space!) and to give an outlet for their concerns. Although airing generalized anxieties and concerns is an important part of the process, it should be restricted to initial stages.

Faculty in all fields now rely just as much on powerful and up-to-the-minute equipment for teaching and research as on a good physical environment. Teaching is hardly less dependent on technology than is research, and state-of-the-art classrooms are an investment that pays off across the board with new technologies, better student performance, and far greater flexibility in course content. An office with a computer that cannot support such necessities as Internet access or advanced e-mail is little better than a pencil with no paper. The department and the college will soon pay the price in the productivity, the reputation, and the quality of students and faculty alike. The same is true of laboratory space and equipment. The college has the obligation to provide these necessities according to disciplinary need, equitably within the limits of available resources, and to upgrade them as aggressively as possible. It is like maintaining a home—the alternative is disrepair followed by expensive losses (see further on faculty development in Chapter Nine).

Student Identity

Students likewise think in terms of departments for their identification with the institution. Graduate students identify with specific departments or programs from the time of their arrival, and undergraduates are encouraged to choose a major as soon as possible so as to have an academic home. Because most advising takes place in departments—for courses, theses, and careers—students feel a sense of belonging to a single academic unit, often without reference to the college. In a small college, the dean may advise individual students as well as be directly involved in academic appeals. Contact with "the dean" in a medium or large college probably means the associate dean for student affairs, whom a student may encounter for special problems; the dean is a ceremonial figure whom they meet only on formal occasions. Thus students' academic success and potential allegiance as alumni are often tied intimately to the quality of their departmental experiences with advising, curriculum, instruction, internships, clubs for majors, and more. That is a huge part of the college's relationship to its largest and most far-flung population. Clearly, departmental relations with students are of crucial interest to the dean.

The college office plays a vital role as well in providing support for advisers, including easy access to records and clear, reliably updated information about academic requirements and institutional services for students. Once again, recognition of superior work with students by faculty and staff is important and puzzlingly rare. Teaching awards have become far more numerous over the past decade, but time-consuming roles such as advising or other kinds of effort outside the classroom are all too frequently regarded as uncomplicated, unimportant, or even a distraction from "real" work. Here the powerhouse departments are at no advantage. Deans are constantly startled to find that graduates of the humblest departments have as fierce a loyalty to them as graduates of the academically more distinguished programs if they have memories of being noticed, well taught, and well treated. In making phone calls to donor alumni in a faraway state, for example, one dean was astounded to hear successful physicians praise the biology department—which had been in the college cellar for as long as anyone could remember—and single out for special praise the very faculty members who had been written off as scientists.

Working with Departments and DEOs

As colleges are gatherings of departments and programs, the internal management of those units is the key to a successful (or unsuccessful) college. The dean's role in appointing department executive officers, mentoring, and evaluating them, and in setting clear, equitable, and effective standards for departmental leadership, can make or break the college.

DEOs as College Administrators

DEOs play a role in their departments that is analogous to the dean's for the college, and just as vital. As the line officers who have constant direct contact with faculty and students, oversee the departmental curriculum and scheduling of classes, recruit new faculty and students, establish relationships with external entities in business and industry, meet with alumni and donors, and interact with numerous administrative colleagues, DEOs do a great deal of the work of the college. Moreover, the quality of their results taken together will substantially define the quality of the college on and off campus.

Recruiting Faculty. Consider, for instance, the DEO's role in faculty recruitment: it is an unceasing exercise in diplomacy and practical efficiency. The first challenge is to convince the department to agree on what is needed, then to persuade the dean to endorse and fund that plan. The selection of a search committee is probably the most delicate moment. The colleagues will place huge significance on every choice—and omission—of members. In fact, departments can be more distressed by the composition of a search committee than by the results of the search itself. The committee normally has considerable latitude once it begins its task, but the DEO must charge the committee, lay out the rules and expectations at the outset, and follow the progress of the search. When the committee is ready to interview finalists, it is again the DEO who takes the proposed short list to the dean and any other reviewing office, such as affirmative action. Obviously the DEO plays a crucial part in the interview process, and when the committee or the full department settles on its choice, takes that recommendation to the dean. Valuable as all the committee members may be—faculty and students alike—the DEO carries out their recommendation, whether to make the offer or to convince the dean to do so.

Given the scarcity of faculty positions and the needs of the department (developed in concert with the college), the DEO's role is of critical importance for the health of the unit. A successful recruitment benefits all: students get good teaching, faculty members gain an energetic new colleague, and the departmental-college budgets are strengthened by increased enrollments and possibly grant funds (see further in Chapter Nine).

Achieving Diversity. Leading the college to achieving diversity in the faculty, staff, and student populations constitutes one of the dean's chief responsibilities. The dean has relatively few new positions with which to alter the composition or balance of any department, and for well-rehearsed historical reasons most departments show some significant demographic imbalance, whether the engineering department that is almost entirely male, the foreign language department that is disproportionately female, or the department in any field that has never achieved any meaningful level of racial or ethnic diversity. In short, if no sensible DEO (or dean) will use every recruitment to impose an alteration in the demographics of a department, it is equally true that every recruitment represents an important opportunity to make as many kinds of progress as possible: intellectual quality, coverage or specialization, and diversity. In this setting, with the dean's support—but never coercion—an effective DEO can engage the faculty in finding qualified minority candidates for positions and to offer programs and lectures that attract a diverse body of students.

Collegiality. A department is a close community—close at least in the sense that the faculty have their offices and labs near one another, and ideally also in the sense of being congenial in their dealings as colleagues. Some departments manage to place a very high premium on collegiality and can work through even the most taxing decisions on recruitment, tenure, curriculum, or budget without adverse effects on the community. Others seem to thrive on internecine battling over trivial issues. For example, one dean reports that some years ago a faculty member filed a formal grievance with the institution because when a corner office was vacated, it was assigned to someone with one year less service than himself. When he lost that complaint, he filed again because he was assigned to teach at 9:00 A.M. instead of 10:00! The department remained mired in mediocrity as the faculty focused on such issues, and it never could attract a leader who could reorient the faculty's energies from squabbling and resentment to teaching, scholarship, and citizenship.

Academic memories are as long as any, and what department has not had crises that left all parties resentful of the outcome—sometimes for years? But a DEO who can work well with widely varying personalities can harness the energy of almost any group of faculty and create an ethos in the department that enables members to get past such treasured scars and agree on new goals. Keeping the most emphatic egos in check is no small task, and may require the dean's involvement in diplomatic, or even decisive ways, but a DEO who cannot make room for the especially developed ego when feasible, and stand up to it when necessary, will ultimately fail as DEO and leave a political mess that may take a decade to clean up.

A department that settles on worthwhile plans and then delivers under the leadership of a strong DEO brings benefits at all levels. For example, if a foreign languages department agrees that it needs an enhanced language laboratory and a respected DEO takes the proposal to the dean with the assurance that the department can find half the funds for itself, the dean can feel confident in providing the rest. The department will gain not only a valuable facility but enhanced standing as a creative component of the college. The dean will have an accomplishment to point to when appealing for external gifts, and the college will grow in public esteem as energetic and innovative. Conversely, troubled departments are equally well noticed, and a distraction for the dean. Their proposals, especially when couched as demands, may strike the dean as outrageous because they are unrealistic. The dean's best response may be to counsel the DEO about the kinds of proposals that would be acceptable, perhaps involving measurable achievements by the faculty. Unfortunately, if the DEO is unable to resolve the problems, they will come next to the dean's office. By that time, more drastic measures will be necessary, and the DEO is often a victim of the solution. The department has lost leadership, and all who see this upheaval are ready to assume that the college likewise is in disarray.

Budgeting. DEOs make or break the budget for the college. They are the main allocators of resources because they deal with so many individuals. Thus their financial wizardry, or lack of it, directly affects the state of the college. The entrepreneurial types, if they have good judgment, can accomplish such miracles as changing the fee basis for a clinical operation and transforming it from a drain to a resource generator. Departments that develop placement tests (in languages or math in particular), so that students who are inclined to take the lowest level courses must enroll in classes commensurate with their preparation, can bring real relief to the instructional budget: fewer introductory courses to staff, fuller enrollments in the more advanced courses—and a better education for students. DEOs who whine at the status quo, rather than use the budget better, take their toll on the welfare of the whole college.

Fundraising. Fundraising is more and more a fact of administration at every level (see Chapter Fifteen). Although the dean clearly plays the lead role, the DEO has a very significant part to play as well, which we may introduce briefly here. Many external gifts and grants are prompted by a need in a specific department, or by a donor's admiration for that unit, even though the gift may formally be awarded to the college, as with endowed professorships, new or renovated facilities, labs, and library collections. DEOs are key members of the college fundraising team for the simple reason that they are closer to the operations and opportunities that may be put before prospective donors. The university's development officers are more likely to know of persons to cultivate but often have no clear idea of what will fire that donor's imagination; the DEO will know the unfunded program dream, the stellar faculty member who can transform the lab or the classroom, the kind of special support that will capture the very best students who are now lured elsewhere. Once the idea and the potential donor are identified, the DEO, together with the relevant individual faculty member, will be essential to follow up and help secure the donation, and then invite the donor in to witness the results.

Pursuing Grants. All sciences and many other disciplines live or die by the relentless pursuit of external grants and contracts. The DEO can greatly facilitate that pursuit by taking an active role in promoting applications and providing a context for the successful applicant to conduct research, such as by providing support staff and striking deals for equipment. Equally important, the DEO will search for grant programs in support of curricular revision-innovation and instructional improvement. All these activities help the college profile even as they accomplish indispensable goals.

DEOs as a College Cabinet

It would scarcely be exaggerating to say that a dean is only as effective as the collective achievements of the DEOs. Astute deans, therefore, appreciate good DEOs. They praise and reward those whose performance is outstanding and mentor those who need help. This brings us to the twofold challenge for deans in their relationships with DEOs: to achieve individual rapport while facilitating a positive working relationship among the DEOs collectively.

Achieving Personal Rapport. The dean must know each DEO well—administrative strengths and weaknesses as well as personal qualities. This is more than just good manners, although as one dean put it, basic courtesy toward the chairs goes a long way. Most DEOs have more (and probably more appealing) things to do than request unnecessary appointments with the dean, and so such requests should be answered speedily. A dean who becomes inaccessible to the college's DEOs sends a terrible signal of indifference to key administrative officers and is also letting small issues that could be solved with a simple conversation turn into problems or even emergencies. No dean can have a completely open-door policy, but it should be as close to that arrangement as possible for the chairs. This means listening to their concerns and following through on commitments promptly and conscientiously. It means giving undivided attention when they visit or call, and it means taking the initiative in staying in touch, not waiting for the next problem to develop before talking to them again.

Having lunch away from campus and the distractions of the day, a casual time when the chair can talk about her or his academic interests, can build a personal rapport and give the dean insight into the DEO's style and outlook. It is imperative that the chairs trust the dean, and vice versa. But beyond that, what are the DEO's aspirations, personally and on behalf of the department? What directions does the DEO believe are the best for the department in the coming years? Does he or she like the job, perhaps hope to become a dean, or is this time served with gritted teeth and hopes of quick parole? What led this person to become a chair in the first place? Does he or she attend professional meetings to keep abreast of the field, or receive invitations to speak or consult? Conversely and equally important, is he or she around enough to lead the department effectively? There is no need for close friendship; some want to have a social relationship with the dean, others keep personal aspects to a minimum. As long as the DEO feels individually valued and respected on the job, and the dean knows that the person is up to the task, the rapport will suffice on both sides.

Encouraging DEOs to Work Together. Persuading the DEOs to work together as a unit is more challenging. The question almost invariably crystallizes around resources. All chairs know they are competing with each other for finite resources—money, students, space, staff—and their constituents are looking to them to deliver. This is unfortunate, because the dean really wants the DEOs as a group to work on curricular, intellectual, and institutional goals as reflected in the college plan, as well as fiscal ambitions. All coherence is lost if the DEOs share only the gloomy reflection that not all proposals can have top priority.

To the extent that the dean can focus the DEOs on goals and programs as a shared responsibility, rather than as an arena of competition for insufficient resources, they can function as an invaluable source of practical help and collective wisdom for the more specific questions that will then take shape as resource allocation. The greatest anxiety among chairs always seems to spring from a suspicion that they have not been given the full picture. Thus if the dean lays out the college budget (not the specifics of any departmental budget, of course!) in candid detail, the DEOs will have greater confidence in the overall situation and tackle the issues affecting the whole college rather than starting from provincial concerns.

Ironically, the twin fears of being left out of the budgetary debate and of having individual departmental issues inappropriately opened up for discussion by other DEOs cause some to shy away from the dean's invitation to tackle the collegewide questions. They must be confident that their advice will be taken seriously and that they are not risking their own unit's status. In discussions about resource allocation (or more probably, reallocation), reasonable and objective criteria such as enrollments, cost per credit hour, or total generated income make the picture clearer and focus on issues rather than winners and losers; there will be ample opportunity for that conversation once the dean takes any action! But touting objective criteria is worse than doing nothing if they are inconsistently applied. In financial matters especially, one of the worst things a new dean can do is to promise a pool of resources and then deploy only a portion of what was under discussion and keep the rest for unspecified later uses. If the dean needs a reserve fund for new initiatives, that should be made clear to the DEOs from the beginning.

All deans and all DEOs lament that there are too many meetings. True enough, but the college leadership needs to meet regularly for two reasons. The most obvious is to work with the dean, as already suggested, and the other is even more basic. Most DEOs, with the notable exceptions of the agricultural and health sciences, serve for relatively brief periods—three or four years—and so about a third of the executive officers will be new each year. In a large A&S college, this may mean ten or more newcomers at the table each fall. Not all will even know each other at the start, and the newly constituted group will need to sit together and work together in order to be effective as DEOs and as an advisory group. The size of the group also affects what it can and should try to accomplish. Small meetings (a dozen or less) are usually more substantive, more like the dynamic of the college staff, and some deans of smaller colleges meet every week. With this frequency, the group is abreast of the issues and can work efficiently in brief sessions. With larger groups of DEOs, as one often finds in arts and sciences colleges, meetings are less frequent (scheduling problems alone will ensure this), but longer, more wide-ranging, and more contentious. In large colleges, chiefly A&S, the chairs may meet in subsets (humanities, sciences, and so forth) for more substantive meetings, with plenary sessions perhaps once a term. In any case, all members should be able to contribute items for the agenda.

Overworked though the retreat is by corporation and campus, it is still a valuable activity if used sparingly and with a clear focus. Some deans assign readings and bring in speakers on topics such as diversity or technology in higher education, or devote a portion of the time to practical training on issues such as conflict resolution or working with probationary faculty members, and perhaps use more experienced chairs as resource persons. Here the DEOs and the dean can begin the planning process in a format that encourages brainstorming and creative thinking. Few deans have the energy (and few DEOs the stomach) for more than one retreat a year, either in the fall to welcome newcomers, build a group dynamic, and set the year's agenda, or in the spring to assess the results of the year's labors and acknowledge those chairs at the end of their terms. These acknowledgments are also keenly appreciated if they occur at the dean's home and include spouses or partners. The fact that the dean (and family) invests the energy to bring everyone together for a social evening conveys a strong message to the chairs.

Every dean has to discover by personal experience how much communication of details to the DEOs is needed or appropriate, especially about tentative matters. Raising baseless hopes of a bonanza—new funds, for instance—is no better than raising groundless concerns about perils that may never materialize, but if the dean keeps the DEOs abreast of current issues they can bring the full weight of the college community to bear in very short order, whether to bolster or to oppose. Yet what to do about rumors of an impending budget cut, when the dean knows that it is coming but perhaps not of the rumored magnitude? Some questions to consider are these: Can the DEOs actually help? If not, is this simply scattering information for its own sake and perhaps causing needless flurries? What is the timing of the issue? A proposed policy that is at best some months away and may evolve considerably before the college can have any impact on its final form is best left aside for now. Is the matter confidential? That must be made clear, because the natural impulse is to share information with the department in hopes of affecting the outcome.

A special form of this question lies in reporting the dean's discussions with the chief academic officer (or provost). Whether or not the dean reports anything,

DEOs will freely surmise about all the topics that might or should have been under review. Thus when they ask questions, as they certainly will, the dean needs to be ready to answer frankly but diplomatically (see also Chapter Thirteen). One extreme situation that some deans have faced is knowing that the provost is contemplating a reorganization of the institution that could drastically affect the college, possibly even moving several departments or programs to another college or breaking up the college completely. If there is no impediment to discussing such a move with the chairs, it is important to try to raise it without panic, and thus make possible a substantive discussion. If, however, the provost regards it as confidential, then the best course is to elicit wisdom from the chairs on organizational alternatives without breaking that confidentiality.

Every college has a mix of new, experienced, and departing DEOs, and each type presents different challenges. Those who have been in office for at least two years probably have as good a grasp on their job as they ever will. If they are old-timers, they have probably seen several deans come and go while their role has remained essentially the same (everyone knows that deans come and go faster than faculty). Although they may be slow to adapt to innovations, these faculty leaders are a source of stability for the college. They can be invaluable in mentoring newer DEOs, as well a new dean. Longtime DEOs are probably even longer-time faculty members in the department—it is time well spent, then, to make their acquaintance, acknowledge their achievements, and seek their reactions to plans for change or growth. Inevitably, as with college staff, a few of these DEOs will decide during the first year or so that it is time to step down. In most cases, both parties come to that conclusion.

Recently appointed DEOs, in contrast, may well be uneasy about the arrival of a new dean. They are already facing a new role in their own bailiwick and realize that they now serve under someone who did not appoint them. Yet for precisely that reason, new DEOs are probably more open to suggestion and reorientation than the old-timers. The dean might recommend training workshops, such as those offered by AAHE and CCAS, and arrange for veterans to offer orientation sessions for newcomers. Some institutions provide seminars to orient new administrators both to campus practices and to the college's expectations.

Faced with an annual turnover rate of 25 to 35 percent, the dean is always preparing the next cadre of leaders—not only DEOs but also associate DEOs and committee chairs. As a general rule, there will be a considerable number of faculty who would perform splendidly in any of these capacities but have been either bashful, overworked, or overlooked, and at least an equal number who believe this describes them but do not qualify on any count. Suggestions from current DEOs about prospects among the faculty will be more informed but probably no less biased than the faculty population at large. Encouraging the appointment of associate chairs is another way to provide apprenticeships at the departmental level. When the opportunity presents itself, the dean can also encourage promising individuals to think about service as DEOs. Reverting to the category of overlooked faculty members, many deans have been able to increase diversity among the chairs by appointing a female or minority faculty member to an acting position for a term of (ideally) two years, and providing mentoring. If that stint goes well, the faculty are often quite ready to endorse a regular appointment.

Selecting DEOs

This introduces one of the most important and delicate decisions a dean makes: selecting a new DEO for a department or program. Practices vary greatly from one campus to another, and even from one college or school to another on the same campus. In the weakest system, the unit's faculty elect a chair for a short term, not more than three years, often not renewable. As a result, almost all tenured faculty face this role at some point in their careers, and the department is virtually rolling the dice every three years and hoping for the best (or praying to avoid the worst). In these situations, the dean has little say in the outcome.

At the other end of the spectrum are heads, appointed by the dean without fixed terms. Major research universities have made extensive use of this position, and many of the great departments in the country, especially in the sciences, were built up by brilliant, powerful heads in the early to middle years of the twentieth century who held office for two decades or more and had nearly unfettered authority. The trend nowadays is towards more uniform use of the title chair, but in areas that have a tradition of durable, powerful executive officers, it seems a change in title more than in role.

The most common arrangement is for a chair to be appointed after some form of search initiated by the dean (internal or open), for a fixed term that generally ranges between three and five years with the possibility of renewal after formal review. Not all deans have a choice in how DEOs are selected (especially on unionized campuses and in disciplines with traditions of powerful faculty prerogative), but most deans would agree that all parties are best served by this arrangement. The faculty can express their views privately and at length, but the dean makes the final selection of a chair with whom he or she—and the other DEOs— can work effectively, and also provides a graceful way to discontinue the arrangement if any affected party sees a need for change. Because the selection of a DEO is so critical to both the college and the department, it is worth considering the search process in some detail.

Where to Search

The first question is whether to search internally, externally, or both for new departmental leadership. The departmental faculty will have their opinions (usually divided), but because an external search requires the commitment of a line that would otherwise have gone for other purposes, the dean must decide whether the situation justifies the commitment. Recruiting a DEO from outside is always an expensive proposition, but doing so may be both necessary and desirable. Here are some of the considerations, not in order of importance:

Is there a vacant position in the department that could be used for a new DEO? This is not essential, but it helps. If so, the field of specialty will be at most a secondary consideration in recruiting, and if the vacancy is in a crucial area the department may suffer some distortion or reduction in its coverage of the discipline, especially in smaller departments. Conversely, this may be a chance to add a new area of emphasis.

Are there qualified candidates in the department who could work well with both colleagues and college? A stable, mature department ought to be able to provide leadership from its ranks, but there are a score of reasons why this might break down from time to time—and not all departments are both stable and mature. In general, the appointment of a chair from current ranks signals that the dean has confidence in the department as a self-governing community. This is also an opportunity, as we suggested earlier, to engage colleagues who have not previously occupied such responsible positions but have the qualities of character, temperament, and judgment to be good executive officers.

What would be gained, solved, or avoided by an external recruitment? What do the faculty want, and what factors are shaping that preference? These last two questions are closely related. Faculty are often very astute judges of the department's condition but can tolerate an amazing degree of internal stress or discomfort. Actually, most of the time a department lacks the means to take best advantage of its good side or to remedy its troublesome aspects. In nearly all cases, this would mean hiring someone, inducing a departure, or gaining new resources for programs, space, and equipment. Appointing a new DEO is a precious opportunity, occurring at predictable intervals, to tackle some of these concerns. If there is no open position, then hiring an external chair will swell the ranks of the senior faculty, and surely the new leader will get some funds for new programs, additional lines, staff, and so on, which have not been forthcoming in the normal budget cycles. So alluring are these prospects that a dean's insistence on an internal search can be read as meaning the department is not well regarded.

Although these assumptions may be partly correct, the situation is usually far more complicated. As we just mentioned, a thriving department may have several good candidates to choose among, whereas a weaker or smaller outfit may have no one ready for leadership. In contrast, a sound department may hope to attract a DEO not for administrative leadership but to take it to the next level of academic visibility and excellence. This ambition will cost the dean dearly but would be a far better investment than appointing a leader for a mediocre group that has not accomplished much on its own.

The dean meanwhile may wish not merely to strengthen the academic fiber of the department but to change its tenor, perhaps by a greater commitment to diversity or funded research or interdisciplinary cooperation, realizing that those who have been part of the problem will not likely be able to find the solution. These are often the very departments, however, that would prefer an internal search in order to preserve the status quo. Thus, insisting on an external search can spark resentment because of the obvious message the dean is sending, but the faculty will be participating in the selection process, and having a meaningful voice in the process wins over all but the angriest.

Finally, the dean takes into account the larger goals of the college, which may duplicate departmental factors on the broader canvas.

Choosing a chair for the search committee is one of the most important steps to finding the right leader for the department. One shrewd option is a current or former executive officer from a related discipline. Such a person understands the needs of the discipline and the role of the DEO, and can address the concerns of the faculty with some detachment. Moreover, such a chair can steer the committee away from valuing scholarly credentials above all else. The search committee should be no larger than five, including at least one senior faculty member and a diverse group representative of the department.

Assuming that the chair of the search committee understands procedures, the dean need only meet with the group at the outset to deliver its charge. This is the time to stress the qualities most needed in a DEO (they are the familiar ones, as for any leadership position, including useful experience, an outgoing optimistic personality, evidence of success as a potential role model for faculty, and so on). But the progress of a search is seldom uneventful, and the dean should confer with the committee chair regularly to be sure that good candidates are being identified and recruited. In an internal search, the dean may take a stronger role by encouraging promising individuals to apply. In an external one, the dean usually waits until there is a short list of candidates for on-campus interviews before getting directly involved.

At this point, the dean might call the candidates before they come to campus, talk with them about their interest in the position, and ask permission to speak with their own chairs, deans, and other appropriate people. This allows the candidates to come to campus with some sense of the situation, and the dean may learn about issues to pursue in greater detail beforehand. Either way, the call opens a relationship for future interaction.

Here emerges one of the benefits of involvement in national organizations for deans: knowing colleagues to call. A professional acquaintance is more likely to speak frankly about the candidate than a stranger. Calls about candidates are a critical part of the dean's role in the search; many a dean has unloaded an undesirable faculty member into a position elsewhere because no one bothered to call. Standard questions probe the evaluators' overall impression of the candidate as DEO material, including evidence of leadership, performance of administrative tasks, ability to work with colleagues, general temperament and energy level, sensitivity to diversity, and motivations. Careful notes of these conversations can help a dean justify a decision not to pursue certain candidates further while still protecting the evaluators' confidentiality.

Dynamics of the Search

Now the usual dynamics of any faculty search assert themselves. Although committees often push for as many as five on-campus finalists, three will suffice if dean and committee have done their work. With more than three, impressions of the first candidate begin to fade; the schedule stretches out until a hot candidate takes another offer, feels neglected, or loses interest; fewer people are able to interact with all of the candidates to make useful comparisons; and so forth. Happy the committee that can keep a few strong candidates in reserve to interview if the first group does not result in a hire; better to plan on closing the deal with the first string!

The interview itself includes faculty and administrative components, such as for the dean (Chapter Three). There are standard items on every campus—meetings with faculty, a presentation to the department, talking with the search committee, meetings with other department chairs—but the dean plays a far more active role than in a simple faculty recruitment. The dean holds a meeting with the candidate at the beginning of the schedule, to brief her or him on the college and offer information about the plans for the interview, and also holds an exit interview, to hear how the candidate now views the job, answer questions, and provide information about the next steps in the search. The exit meeting is particularly important for gauging the candidate's savvy, energy level, and interest in the position. Sometimes candidates arrive at the exit meeting too exhausted to talk and are judged to be lacking the energy or staying power to do the job (again, as with decanal candidates, stamina is almost as important as content!).

The committee's final recommendations should include notations of strengths and weaknesses on each candidate, but the dean often wants to make follow-up calls and have a final discussion with the committee before extending an offer. If there is substantial disagreement in the department, it is wise to talk with members individually and possibly as a group. If the divisions are deep and reflect serious concerns, it is far better to abort the search than bring a DEO into a negative situation that will at best be turbulent and at worst damage the department. This is the dean's call. If the differences of opinion will not finally prevent the department from uniting behind a DEO, proceed. In other cases the faculty rally strongly behind a candidate whom the dean or CAO thought was a bad choice: the dean probably should not proceed with the appointment, as painful as the decision may be, on the admittedly questionable premise that the instincts of experienced administrators trump faculty sentiment in matters of leadership. Negotiations can be tricky. It helps to begin with the attitude that if the candidate is truly interested in the position, a deal is possible. Some of the most common issues are these:

The Candidate's Salary Expectations Are Too High. In this case, the range of current DEO salaries as related to length of time in office, academic rank, and other relevant criteria should be discussed.

The Candidate Assumes the Position Will Carry Tenure Immediately. For many schools this is no problem, but there are institutions that simply do not give tenure the first year of any appointment. Candidates must be fully informed about the policy, and how it normally works. Likewise, a few campuses do not contribute to faculty or staff retirement plans during the first year, and no faculty member wants to discover that on the job.

The Candidate Wants a Position for a Spouse or Partner. This is what used to be called the "trailing spouse problem." This topic always seems to pop up in the latest possible stages of amicable negotiation—as when Lieutenant Columbo turns at the door with "just one more question" for the murderer. At this point, however remarkable the additional person may be, the cost of recruitment has risen sharply, and the question abruptly becomes: How much do we really want this candidate? What are reasonable efforts to make in this regard? Would the partner's appointment even fall within the college's purview? Will an appointment generate a potential conflict of interest or supervisory dilemma? Will it create problems elsewhere in the college or institution? And, perhaps most importantly, is the work of the companion up to the standards of the institution? If all these issues come out right and something appropriate can be found, wonderful! If not, there is great potential for widespread, long-term damage.

The Candidate Wants Greater Resources Than Anticipated. This may be salary or funding for the department. As with the previous issue, the question is how far the dean and the college should go without doing injustice to college priorities. If a candidate cannot work with the dean toward a mutually agreeable package, it is very likely that there will be a rocky working relationship as DEO, and the dean should be hesitant to appoint.

The Candidate Seems Unable to Decide. Lengthy negotiations, especially with frequent changes of subject, are a bad sign. The candidate is quite probably waiting for another offer, working on a counteroffer back home, or trying to fight off a gut feeling that this move is wrong. Eventually, time must run out and lack of decisiveness becomes a decision by default.

Orienting New DEOs

Once the new DEO, internal or external, is on board, the fun really begins. As mentioned earlier, orientation is extremely important. It is best to have several staff members cover topics ranging from budget management, curriculum changes, and faculty evaluation to student complaints and conflict resolution. The outgoing executive officer (if still around) or administrative assistant provides indispensable information about departmental operations. With new DEOs and other new faculty arriving close to the start of the new year, the on-ramp is very short and the traffic very swift!

Supporting the DEOs

From there the dean's role, as with all DEOs, is to support their work, provide constructive feedback, and recognize good performance. First, the dean should be forthright about workload expectations. In most colleges, including professional schools, chairs teach on a reduced schedule (typically half the normal load), but in a few cases the range of responsibilities may make regular teaching problematic. Because DEOs are role models for the faculty, involvement in instruction and scholarship is very desirable. The mix of responsibilities ought to be part of a yearly discussion based on the variable demands for that period. Second, the dean must make clear the basis for annual evaluations. One approach is a goal-setting session with chairs early each fall, with assessment at the close of the academic year of the activities accomplished. Another is to fold goal setting into the spring evaluation conference, to sum up the current year and look forward to the next. The first alternative is more formal and allows for a fuller discussion and record of proposed activities; therefore, it is preferable if the dean can manage the time.

The reason why being a DEO is good preparation for deaning is that both persons frequently feel isolated, wonder how the job's going, and are not sure how to tell. Support from the dean takes a variety of forms. When there are concerns, the dean should counsel with the chair promptly, candidly, confidentially, and humanely, without any possibility of rumor-mongering among the faculty. When the DEO invites the dean to speak to the department, the dean should take the potshots that the chair has been unable to handle (for example, when the faculty is upset by a decision the dean has made and will not accept the explanations offered by the chair). When DEOs bring the dean proposals that are a high priority for their faculty members and have merit, the dean should try to make a response, no matter how minimal. In recent years, for example, emerging departments of environmental studies have been compelled to add faculty and courses, and such programs depend on technology in geographic information systems. This has been a very expensive development, where even the cost of software would break many a department's budget. Although deans can understand the importance of such projects and the department's desire to offer students an up-to-date education, there has been little choice but to move incrementally. In this as in some other technical areas, the field advances faster than the college can ever respond, but to ignore the need would be irresponsible. Even the most compelling projects usually cannot receive full support immediately, but offering a way to begin recognizes the DEO's leadership. If a chair or department insists on all or nothing, the answer is far easier.

Some chairs want to use the dean as a sounding board, so it pays to think about this matter in advance and decide how to deal with it. New DEOs may need the dean's ear more often, not a bad idea when the goal is to get them used to the job and the college as quickly as possible. But they should also be encouraged to appoint a knowledgeable associate chair with whom they can discuss routine operations of the department and interpersonal matters. It is not a good idea to encourage dependency, nor should the dean offer a solution to each problem discussed. It is better to suggest alternatives or something that has worked in the past, or probe the issue with questions that might suggest a resolution. Because not all chairs will be interested in sharing their tentative ideas with their dean, in the interests of good communication it is probably wise not to announce a policy on such consultation.

How closely should the dean follow the day-to-day workings of the departments? At a respectful distance! DEOs are responsible for those activities, and deans presumably have basic confidence in their DEOs—or else they have a different problem entirely. A dean's life is full enough without micromanaging numerous departments, but at the same time good and regular communication with the DEOs both creates and maintains confidence that they are abreast of things. Naturally, any DEO needs to report news of the unexpected—particularly if it is unwelcome news—without delay. Anticipated budget shortfalls or personnel problems, for example, and lesser but hampering problems such as the environment or equipment, can probably go to other offices for resolution, with a timely report to the dean's office (not necessarily to the dean). Some DEOs and departments prefer to handle problems in-house and only inform the dean in emergencies. This is fine as long as it does not suppress situations that *must* be reported through formal channels—a sexual harassment complaint, for example. At a minimum, any matter with potential legal implications—personnel problems, accidents, or unusual behavior, including alcoholism—needs to come to the dean immediately.

And problems there are in abundance! At the risk of sounding like Gilbert and Sullivan's Koko, there is the chair who asks for everything and refuses to prioritize—but no funds go to a department that can only survive on everything. There is also the chair who asks for nothing even when resources are available. When there are funds for extra merit raises, for example, this DEO submits no names, either because of an inability to recognize achievement or a dread of resentment from colleagues. If the DEO will not make recommendations the dean should indicate that he will, because deserving faculty should not suffer from sluggish management.

Then there is the whiner who, no matter how generously the department is treated, complains about being overlooked. A short statement of the facts, followed by silence, is appropriate. And last, there is the chair who is always bringing in the opportunity of a lifetime—to buy a "bargain" piece of equipment, hire the perfect researcher, or obtain matching funds, always with an absurdly short response time. As in other settings, offers that sound too good to be true generally are.

Should the dean meet with individual faculty members? Yes, certainly. A dean who categorically declines to sit down with faculty on the simple bureaucratic principle that they must talk only to their DEO will miss the opportunity to meet interesting people who have no alarming agenda, shut off persons with legitimate concerns about their dealings with the DEO, and quickly gain a general reputation as aloof, arrogant, and ill-informed. Here is another example about salaries. Suppose the dean is assigning merit raises in addition to the department's allocation but based on recommendations from the DEO. A faculty member who failed to get such a raise might appropriately come to the dean to ask why not; another might wish to appeal a DEO's decision to the dean or come to complain about unfair treatment. All of these might start and end with e-mail, but the more delicate topics surely deserve a visit.

Whether the dean or an associate dean meets and listens, no action should be taken before conferring with the DEO. Sometimes, of course, exasperated DEOs will ask the dean to see a faculty member whom they have been unable to satisfy. All this being said, the dean should make it plain that faculty members ought to start with the DEO, both as a matter of protocol and because that is who is in the best position to address most local problems.

Finally, we return to evaluation of DEOs. The annual review that faculty members receive in the department now comes from the college office—for both administrative performance and as a faculty member. This means the dean must weigh the annual academic merit of faculty in many different fields. In theory this is quite reasonable, because deans read promotion dossiers across the spectrum of the school each year, but a chemist-dean assessing the year's work of the DEO of classics (or vice versa) will inevitably render a less fine judgment than departmental colleagues. Some deans of large colleges—again, mostly but not exclusively A&S—draw on the broader expertise of a small advisory group usually drawn from current or former members of the college promotion and tenure committee in relevant fields.

Comment and criticism need not wait until the end of the year. Constructive criticism presented diplomatically and balanced with observations about positive accomplishments will often be appreciated, perhaps even more than recognition of what has gone well, crucial as that is, if the DEO is struggling and needs help. This is very difficult to do without distressing or alienating someone who is after all playing a role with little formal preparation, one that is not a permanent part of the job description. Long experience has shown that, unfortunately, problematic chairs do not derive any real benefit from a largely positive evaluation even if they have made some progress. Even worse, when they stumble again, they have a written record that is more optimistic than circumstances warranted. It is essential that any written evaluation of a problem DEO state areas of concerns at least as explicitly as any partial approbation.

To be sure, the annual increase is the only durable reward for a DEO. Promotion to full professor, if it comes during this time, will depend on the usual scholarly criteria, and any administrative supplement is temporary. Nevertheless, other nonrecurring forms of support can make a difference both practical and psychological: a research assistant, support for attendance at an international meeting, special help with fundraising, or even opportunities to represent the college on important occasions.

Not all DEOs succeed. Fortunately, most of these are tolerable nonsuccesses, and most of the time, a mediocre or poor performance will be unrewarding enough for all concerned that one term will suffice and the department will move on to another leader by general consent. A few are more obtuse about their performance and only realize the problem when they are denied renewal. The worst case, mercifully rare, is the spectacularly inadequate DEO whom the dean has to remove from office. How to know when to replace a DEO? If despite the dean's best efforts the chair has not made meaningful progress toward addressing problems in personal performance and in the department, or if a faculty insurrection is brewing, it is time to act.

The difficulty may be nothing worse than a very bad fit with the job. An outstanding fundraiser can be a feckless manager of people, and someone who works well with faculty and staff members can find it impossible to make hard decisions or deliver needed criticism. Finally, the problem may just stem from staying on too long as DEO, until the problems become permanent and the lost opportunities read like an alternative history of a more successful department. Grudges and resentments take root, and simple job fatigue diminishes the person's effectiveness as a faculty colleague (not to mention the long-term reduction in research productivity). This is the strongest argument for fixed terms as DEO. Changes can be made without loss of face or needless acrimony. In discussing the need for change with the DEO, the dean does not want to get into specifics beyond what has been recorded in the written evaluations. A fair and gentler statement is that the department now needs a different kind of leadership (this is also a diplomatic formulation when questioned by faculty or the media).

In the last analysis, the most likely source of wisdom for a dean in dealing with DEOs is the golden rule based on personal experience: most deans have served as departmental executive officers and know full well how they were treated—or wish they had been.

Suggestions for Further Reading

Bennett, John B., and David J. Figuli (eds.). *Enhancing Departmental Leadership: The Roles of the Chairperson.* New York: American Council on Education, 1990.

Higgerson, Mary Lou, and Susan S. Rehwaldt. *Complexities of Higher Education Administration. Case Studies and Issues.* Bolton, Mass.: Anker, 1993.

—. "Ideas for Planning a Department Chairs Retreat." [http://www.calpress.com/Retreat/]

Leaming, Deryl R. *Academic Leadership: A Practical Guide to Chairing the Department.* Bolton, Mass.: Anker, 1998.

Lucas, Ann F. *Strengthening Departmental Leadership: A Team-Building Guide for Chairs in Colleges and Universities.* San Francisco: Jossey-Bass, 1994.

Lucas, Ann F., and Associates. *Leading Academic Change: Essential Roles for Department Chairs.* San Francisco: Jossey-Bass, 2000.

Massy, William F., Andrea K. Wilger, and Carol Colbeck. "Overcoming 'Hollowed' Collegiality." *Change,* 1994, *26* (4), 11–20.

Smith, Holly M. "Getting and Keeping Good Department Chairs." Paper presented at the annual meeting of the Council of Colleges of Arts and Sciences, Seattle, Nov. 1999.

Tucker, Allan. *Chairing the Academic Department: Leadership Among Peers* (3rd ed.). New York: American Council on Education, 1992.

Warren, Charles O. "Chairperson and Dean: The Essential Partnership." In John B. Bennett and David J. Figuli (eds.), *Enhancing Departmental Leadership: The Roles of the Chairperson.* New York: American Council on Education, 1990.

PART THREE

THE WORK OF THE DEAN

CHAPTER SEVEN

PLANNING

Planning is a perennial hot topic for deans, the subject of sessions at national meetings and workshops, electronic discussion groups, and informal conversation wherever deans happen to collide. Because of the fluid state of the academic environment—institution-level planning or the lack thereof, turnover in deanship, incomplete or ineffective inherited plans for the college, and above all, changing conditions on the ground—new deans almost always face a planning challenge, and longer-term deans often do. Just as much as in business, the internal and external environments change quickly in higher education. But although deans appreciate the need for planning, finding the time to do it well means making frustrating trade-offs with some other valuable function. Furthermore, they often lack the expertise to develop a plan that will work and show results.

This chapter aims to provide practical advice on planning and tools to use in the process. We stress that there is no one approach that works for every situation. Where to begin, what kind of goals are appropriate, the length of the time line, whom to involve, and a host of other variables may be different. However, certain broadly applicable principles help outline a workable approach to the needs of colleges. We will focus on these, as well as on the critical issue of implementation (together with potential pitfalls of turning a plan into practice).

Preliminaries

Two issues arise before actual planning begins.

Why Plan?

No sensible dean would wade through the conflicting claims, fiscal strains, and shifting political realities of a college without a plan to address the needs of students and faculty, programs and facilities. But there is endless variety in the ways to construct plans, and almost as much in the forces that impel their creation. The call for planning may come with eagerness, dread, anger, resentment, or even touching, unattainable hope. For example, the need to develop a strategic plan may not arise directly from conditions in the college or the mind of the dean, but rather from the current state of the institution. In other words, it may come not from an ailing college that must get attuned to a healthy campus, but from a campus with problems or aspirations that the college shares.

When asked about the biggest challenge they faced in planning, many deans mention the central administration of their institutions. Their concerns arise from two opposite situations. In one, the planning process is controlled from the top and is so restricted that the results are of little utility. Under this scenario, some deans even write the plans themselves with little or no consultation, because they assume that broad input will not matter. At the opposite pole is the dean who wants to plan but is in an environment where no overt planning takes place at the institutional level. When institutional mission, vision, and priorities are not clear, the dean ends up planning in a vacuum and wondering whether, and to what degree, institutional support might be forthcoming. Although these scenarios are different, our advice for each is the same: Just do it! Deans who are committed to planning do not allow constraints to get in the way. A plan can be made to order based on a truly useful plan generated by the college. At the other end of the spectrum, the dean and college can focus on goals that are achievable with a minimum of help from the institution. If the institutional leadership changes in the middle of college planning and the dean discovers that some goals no longer fit the new administration's attitudes, they can be revisited. But the dean needs something to work with, to guide daily, weekly, and monthly decisions—and there is no substitute for a good plan.

The worst case is the process mandated from the board of trustees or the legislature. It is worst because significant decisions are made at the greatest distance from on-campus realities, and are commensurately more likely to arise from ulterior motives, such as placating voters or importing corporate perspectives into academic management. Because of the distance between the external body and the internal details, the mandating group often wants more details than anyone can possibly provide (What will be the total increase or decrease in undergraduate enrollments over the next five years? How many of these will be in business and how many in chemical engineering?), and more finality (The plan should lead to the establishment within four years of new thresholds for graduate enrollment and externally funded grants that will sustain all graduate programs in the college for the next seven to ten years).

In many cases, the call for planning comes from the central administration, and has a strong top-down tone. And here a word in favor of rhetorical modesty. Over and over again, deans report that institutional documents setting a strategic planning process in motion tend to fall into two types:

- *Unrealistically cheerful.* "We are in very good shape and have no reason to anticipate specific adverse conditions in the near future, but believe it is prudent now to consolidate the remarkable gains of the past decade, consider how we can advance even further with the improvements we have already achieved, and take sensible, available precautions against harm from the unexpected."
- *Needlessly threatening.* "We have for too long been content to operate with priorities and policies handed down from a very different time in the history of this state and this university. Clearly, adverse winds of change are blowing through the public landscape, and education cannot expect to avoid the consequences. Accordingly, the university is initiating a planning process to allow us to sustain significant cutbacks with only the minimum long-term devastating impact on most colleges. Your college will be expected to contribute at least its fair share."

In contrast, the decision to undertake a new planning process may be the dean's, in response to appeals from the college community on an array of concerns that, taken together, show the timeliness of doing so. Perhaps a faculty body such as the executive committee gathers scattered opinions, considers their implications, and raises with the dean the idea of a more systemic review of the college. Otherwise, faculty are unlikely to express an overt desire for strategic planning, but rather will fret over real, definable problems affecting one or more specific departments, particular groups of faculty or students, and so forth. In other words, a growing number of local concerns can raise the need for planning. By the same token, however, some faculty will hope for a solution to their local issues and not a large-scale plan that alters other familiar practices.

The permanent campus community is probably even more concerned that the process will focus more on financial information than anything programmatic or academic, and new ways of managing dollars do not excite the faculty's participation. Ironically, however, the best and surest incentive for their involvement in such a case is the clear prospect of new resources that can be applied (or creatively diverted) to program opportunities. In the end, both parties are looking for the same things: better use of resources to provide stronger programs even under adverse conditions. It is a question of framing the plan's goals and methods.

Thus, the first step is to define as clearly as possible the reason for planning. Is the aim to create a new way of doing things, significantly different from present conditions, or to modulate in particular areas toward limited, definite goals? The more specific the conditions that prompt a call for strategic planning, the stronger the reason not to use current reality as the premise for the eventual plan. In fact, the directive to plan may not be cast in reference to the exigencies that are actually driving the process.

For example, a dean may be asked to develop a plan emphasizing new fiscal constraints. Although some pruning and better resource management could make the numbers work, the resulting organization might be unable to adapt to further changes. Instead, organizational restructuring, though a larger undertaking, would allow the college to thrive under the new realities. Similarly, some plans face the prospect of modest growth that must be used but cannot address more than a fraction of the top institutional priorities. Others reflect the ambition to seek a higher academic profile through costly recruitment of faculty or additions to facilities. Realizing these ambitions would certainly mean careful management and fiscal constraints in other areas, but to cast the process as fiscal rather than programmatic seriously misleads all concerned. It is important to be clear about the purposes of planning before discussing the process.

What Is a Plan (and What Is It Not)?

In light of these possible reasons for planning, we should recognize a few crucial facts about plans. First and foremost, strategic plans are at least as much process as product. If they do not engage enough people—enough different constituencies or enough in simple numerical terms—in gathering and interpreting information and contributing ideas, they will be narrow and shortsighted, and their appropriate fate is to gather dust on the shelf. It is precisely in compelling the community's attention, acknowledging its concerns, respecting its wisdom, and winning acceptance or even enthusiasm for new developments that planning has its greatest effect. More people will be thinking about similar topics than under any other circumstances except a major calamity (and even the harshest critics of planning would not prefer that alternative!).

Inclusive strategic planning also affects the nature of the questions being considered. Faculty, staff, and students bring very different perspectives to the table, and prioritizing will become more complex but more useful when questions that are usually considered administrative are put to a more heterogeneous panel, or when academic issues are presented for comment from business officers for the health of the institution. This is extremely important because in an operation so complex and so tolerant of independent action, there is much divergence not only in perspectives but even in attention to admissions or promotion of standards campuswide, let alone central nonacademic issues such as the campus environment, benefits, or facilities. Fuller participation in the planning process yields more information and participants who become part of a campus rather than a department. However distasteful they may have found past decisions, now they are participants in making decisions for the future.

Moreover, because the plan ought to guide action over a period of years, not simply mandate decisive action on a current situation, the plan is not a finished product. It will never be finished because the planners cannot pretend to know *how* the circumstances that guide them will change, but only that they *will* change. Thus the plan must be sensitive to what is more permanent (such as program quality or library resources) and what is transitory (such as enrollment surges or maintenance problems), and supple enough to incorporate changes after it has been approved and implemented. In short, although the process is real and has measurable effects, the product is illusory and of uncertain impact beyond a very short horizon. That is no argument against planning—quite the contrary, it is the best reason for engaging in it on a regular basis.

A plan is an integrated document, not a mosaic. In other words, it must be a plan for the highest included unit, not a gathering of plans for all the smaller units encompassed. This is a classic case of the whole being greater than the sum of its parts; a ring binder with thirty department plans in it can never serve as a college plan, and the same is true at the campus level. The college plan should observe from the highest perch, seeing the terrain—and drawing the map—of the college as a whole rather than accumulating and juxtaposing local plans. This is true whether the process of building the plan is top-down or bottom-up (see the following section). But the college is probably not the only unit on campus that is planning. The college plan is constrained by decisions made at the campus level, and it cannot pursue intentions that are incompatible with those of the central administration.

Finally, a plan needs to be driven by standards of quality and by clearly articulated purposes. This seems obvious enough, but many, many deans report that they had to endure planning processes on their campuses that were simply predicated on current resources and practices despite the evident need to do otherwise, or on a resource base that was apparently the figment of the president's hopeful imagination. Even worse is to begin by tacitly accepting any inherited inequities, grudging treaties, or long-term animosities as ongoing parts of the new design. A planning exercise that spends a lot of time explaining the present or escaping the past will never find time or energy to cast the future. In the end, planning is one part divination, one part common sense, and one part peace talks.

In the optimal planning environment, the dean begins by crafting an agenda to persuade the faculty and staff that a well-developed and executed plan is crucial for the continued viability of the college (see Keller, 1997). Such a document can point out new opportunities and present (without undue detail) the necessity to reallocate resources to meet changing demands, the desire to stay competitive, or the changing mission of the college inside and outside the institution (see Feiss, 2000). In a less favorable environment, the dean may have to invoke darker forces to justify more urgent action: planning as a necessity to deal with financial pressures or exigencies, to implement external accountability measures, or to respond to a request from the central administration. In all cases, however, the wise dean, with advice from a few knowledgeable colleagues, works out a process to involve the key stakeholders and maintain a high level of communication with them even as a schedule is established and met.

A well-crafted plan includes the college's mission and vision statements, an articulation of specific goals, objectives to meet those goals, and a reasonable timetable. Follow-up is built into the process. Parts or all of this may carry fancier names—strategic, contextual, TQM (Total Quality Management)—but the basic elements of planning remain obvious: what you have now, what you need and want, what is attainable, how and when. The picture that emerges from this process allows the dean to make decisions and manage resources for specific purposes and keep colleagues on track as they raise issues and develop proposals.

Where and How to Begin: Top-Down or Bottom-Up?

In which direction should ideas and decisions about the details of the plan flow? This is probably the planning issue that deans debate most frequently. The short answer is that the process can never move entirely in one direction, and for political reasons it should never be perceived as doing so; nevertheless, one direction will dominate from the outset depending on who decided to plan in the first place. That impulse will immediately establish whose perspectives are going to prevail in close calls.

Many planning experts advise bottom-up planning as the only way to ensure support for the final product. The thinking is that if faculty, staff, and students are asked to contribute their ideas early and are taken seriously from the beginning, they will reciprocate and understand that they have a role in the outcome. But on what topics are they to provide ideas? Already the arrow points downward as the college itself casts the questions. Faculty and student groups—the executive committee, for instance, or an ad hoc task force of its creation—can be the leaders in getting faculty concerns and aspirations before the college at the outset, even before the formal planning work begins.

Then in light of whatever instructions have come from above, or from the dean and the executive committee, all units of the college develop their own plans. More exactly, they present their own hopes and opportunities, concerns and needs, both as individual units and as components of the college. Mathematics, for example, needs to take into account not only its disciplinary, departmental concerns but also its role in teaching students at all levels in all parts of the campus. The college plan draws from these documents in defining the mission, articulating the vision, and specifying the goals for the entire college. Students could contribute in several ways—for example, as part of departmental committees or members of college organizations. Obviously no college plan can accommodate the full panoply of departmental hopes, but the very act of soliciting ideas from all units makes them partners in the process, and many goals that do not find a place in the current plan are still appropriate to work on, provided they are consonant with the college's goals.

The main objection to bottom-up planning is that the dean will inevitably have to say no—or at least, not yet—to a host of suggestions. Presumably all faculty and staff realize that unlimited ambition is unrealistic and a plan without limits is doomed. Still, being asked what one would like inevitably seems the best or even the only chance to have one's ambitions heard and recorded. For those who mistrust the system, or know there will not be many chances to ask for new resources or programs, the planning process is actually a logical time to be excessive. The resulting materials can be very uneven in usefulness even assuming all departments follow an outline.

To address this problem of deliberate excessive hope, some deans ask the departments to respond to a skeleton plan from the college—perhaps just the mission and vision statements—and explain how they could support college goals at the unit level and what they would need to do so. This approach engages departments in the overall planning process but directs their responses to particular identified themes. It is therefore tidier than a general invitation to plan, but it is also a partial inversion of the bottom-up approach and understandably generates

less enthusiasm from the key stakeholders because it limits their dreams. To overcome this problem, the dean might make clear what is surely true in any case,
which is that the eventual college plan will give priority to those units that find the
most effective ways to support the college goals.

The decision about the mode of planning may be a function of time, in that
the dean's deadline for submitting the college plan may be very tight or the bottom-up process may require more time than the dean wishes to allow. We counsel working immediately with chairs and directors of the various units to
determine the best approach, because they will be the ones to implement it. If the
DEOs have had a lot of experience with planning, they may know how to ham-
mer out a useful document in a relatively short time. It is unwise to take a bottom-
up method if key DEOs are novices and require elaborate direction.

The Planning Committee

Planning often seems to constitute a proof of perpetual motion: at any given
time, some part of the institution is laying the groundwork for the next grand
phase of its life. Accordingly, the sitting dean quickly comes to regard participation in some sort of planning as a central part of the job. A new dean may find
the college in the middle of an institutionwide planning process, adrift without a
plan, or somewhere in between. No matter which is the case, the college must
gain a clear sense of what it does and where it wants to go. For these decisions,
which will shape the mission and vision statements, the dean needs the best thinking available. Assuming the dean has a free hand in selecting a committee for the
task (that is, without constraining directives from the campus), the criteria for
members should be a solid grasp of the college's current situation; the wisdom to
see where weakness, peril, opportunity, and above all, quality lie; and the fortitude
to make recommendations free of parochial or personal bias. The obvious place to
look first is among the DEOs who are engaged in the issues on a daily basis, are
likely to be among the college's best citizens, and are indispensable in selling and
implementing the plan. Some deans prefer also to include distinguished members
of the faculty and even individuals from outside the college—for example, from
business or industry—whose perspectives they deem to have special relevance to
the process. The final mix will be determined by the constraints under which the
dean is working—such as the need to meet a quick deadline or to prepare for a
capital campaign. But even with an unlimited time frame, a badly formed committee will produce a badly formed plan. Selection of strong members is crucial
to every subsequent action.

Who should lead this planning group? Here the key qualification is experience in helping organizations to plan. There may well be a faculty member in the college who has these skills, or the dean may need to look outside for a neutral leader—someone who does not necessarily know the college in depth but can facilitate the process effectively. Both alternatives have advantages: the outside expert may be more effective at keeping the process on track and may even lend cachet in the eyes of a central administration that has a hefty regard for organizational gurus. But the faculty themselves are likely to see this choice as a slap in the face of their own abilities and a diminution of their power at a crucial moment. An insider will obviously know the institution better, and if able to maintain the distance necessary to be an effective facilitator, can ask more penetrating questions and elicit more useful information. Fellow deans in the institution may have suggestions for a facilitator from their own ranks, as may other administrators. If the main goal of the plan is to enhance fundraising rather than address programmatic priorities, the local chapter of the National Society of Fund Raising Executives (NSFRE) may be helpful. Its members often serve as consultants to nonprofit organizations for planning in advance of fundraising.

Whoever the chair may be, the dean works with him or her before convening the committee to establish the style, tone, and objectives for the process and set an agenda for the first planning meeting. This step is vital, because if there is any gap between the dean's purposes and the committee's impression of its task, all will be downhill from the start. A more mundane but also vital reason is to ensure that any information necessary for launching the committee is gathered and made ready before the group first meets. The distribution of relevant materials does as much to establish the agenda as any sermon from dean or chair.

Developing the Plan

There are several important steps to take in developing the plan.

Creating Mission and Vision Statements

The usual first step is to agree on a mission statement for the organization. If one already exists, it should be revisited, because there have surely been important changes in the environment since it was last considered. A mission statement describes the purpose of the college and what it does while distinguishing it from others of its kind (some would say "its competitors"). The latter could include other colleges in the institution or other similar entities in the state or region. The mission statement sometimes includes a formulation of key values and beliefs. The elements should reflect the group's best thinking about the nature and function of the college for the future. Two illustrations follow, modified from planning documents of Emory and the University of Delaware:

A concise statement: "The mission of the School of Public Health is to improve health and prevent disease in human populations around the world by acquiring, disseminating, and applying knowledge."

A fuller statement, including philosophy: "The mission of the College of Arts and Sciences is the teaching and dissemination of new and established knowledge and the creation of new knowledge within four broad disciplinary areas: the arts; the humanities; the behavioral and social sciences; and mathematics and the natural sciences. Fundamental to the mission of the College is the belief in the value of a liberal education, one that develops a breadth of understanding and capabilities in students as the foundation for their lives beyond the University. The College seeks to provide an intellectual and cultural environment for undergraduates similar to that found in the best liberal arts colleges. At the same time, the College aspires to the characteristics of a research institution. These dual objectives serve us well. Both undergraduate and graduate students throughout the University benefit from the faculty's commitment to teaching and scholarship. As a college embedded in a state-assisted land grant university, resources and expertise are also directed toward service to constituencies in the broader community."

The mission statement (who we are) naturally precedes the vision statement (where we want to go). More specifically, the vision describes what success will look like, assuming the necessary resources. The vision may be a stretch, but it cannot depend on miracles. Developing such a vision statement is considerably more difficult than defining the mission of the college. It goes to the heart of the planning process, which involves setting goals to achieve the vision. Fundamentally, however, the vision encompasses the same elements the dean considered when deciding to accept the position of dean. Based on its current state and future challenges that can be anticipated, what can and should the college look like in five years? What kinds of support might be available from internal and external sources? What is the overall direction of the institution, and what are its values?

A vision statement, then, is a description of the college at some point in the future. The statement should be forward-thinking in the sense that it projects what the college can become, inspirational in that it will elicit a commitment to action from constituents, and grounded in reality in that it sets out an agenda that requires stretching, but is achievable. Two composite illustrations are as follows:

- "Within five years the College of Business will reach the top quartile of comprehensive, accredited colleges of business in the United States, as ranked by *Business Week,* in recognition of the quality of its academic programs, the achievements of its faculty and graduates, and its service to business and industry."
- "Within four years the School of Nursing will be one of the top five nationally ranked schools of nursing with an exceptional reputation in three to four key areas. It will achieve a balanced budget through increased revenue from tuition, research and training grants, and development efforts, as well as through improved efficiencies and stewardship."

How should the planning group develop such a vision for the college? Each situation will be unique, but there are some significant steps to consider in the process so that the vision truly can be founded on reality.

Gathering Information

A brainstorming session at the beginning can determine what data and other information in addition to that provided ahead of the first session will be needed for planning. Budget histories of the college and its constituent units are vital, of course, but if possible the group should also have a budget history and projection for the institution. Enrollment trends, credit hours generated by faculty member and unit, and cost per credit hour data are also helpful. All such figures will be useful not only in determining how funds have been spent but also where funds for new initiatives can be found. Also important are planning documents for the college from the past ten years, along with an analysis of their effectiveness. In writing a mission statement, for example, it is always helpful to look at an earlier version and consider how the organization has changed. If the current method is bottom-up, the committee will review unit plans and draw out the most important ideas for the college plan.

Formulating Questions

A key part of gathering useful information is to ask questions of a wide range of stakeholders—not only students, faculty, and staff but also alumni, donors, and corporate and community partners who have a commitment to the college. The answers should help the planning committee understand what is happening in the college now and what people dream will happen in the future. Creative questioning opens up issues, opportunities, and concerns in unexpected ways. The committee may ask what new words, symbols, or myths have appeared on campus in the last few years and what value or meaning people assign them. A project to replace concrete and asphalt walkways with brick pavers, for example, could symbolize wasteful spending to students and faculty members who see teaching positions being eliminated and are inclined to relate the two events.

What aspects of the college would a given stakeholder address if there were a magic wand? What changes would he or she make? Responses will probably range from the mundane, such as speeding up responses from the dean's office, to the visionary, such as reconceiving undergraduate programs or developing state-of-the-art teaching laboratories. Collectively, these magic-wand suggestions will contribute to a serious view of where and how the college might enjoy important changes. For insights into the college culture, a dean should encourage colleagues to tell stories about what priorities and mechanisms really drive the organization's decisions. They may claim that the quality of students is a big factor, or working closely with the national accrediting body, or gaining technological support for faculty. A good listener can identify themes in these various responses and use them in defining a vision.

Assessing the Environment

Because a vision statement embodies the future, the planning committee (as well as the dean) should be thoroughly grounded in national higher education trends and issues. Journals such as the *Chronicle of Higher Education* and *Change* are indispensable sources of news, opinions, and ideas, as are books and monographs in various series devoted to higher education, and leading newspapers, such as *The New York Times* or *Washington Post,* that often report on relevant topics. The journals and agendas of national organizations for the specific disciplines in the college are another source of information about hot topics and new directions. Finally, work by futurists can stimulate thinking and draw attention to areas—such as continuing education and training in business and industry, current areas of intense interest—that offer both models and cautionary tales for the college.

Most useful are reports and analyses dealing with the trends in the institution's own state and region. Indeed, the campus economics or public administration program may well be the source of such reports. Environmental assessment—that is, a consideration of the economic, educational, social, and political factors affecting the institution—is important because the college vision must be realistic as well as forward-looking. What are the projected enrollment trends? What kinds of technological support will be needed for students and faculty, especially those in emerging fields? Where is job growth expected, and at what levels and fields of education? Are there ways to develop new ties with external entities that can strengthen research and contribute to economic development? Understanding these external forces allows a college to enhance opportunities associated with them. A state that is tackling the problems of pollution from wastewater, for example, may offer opportunities for joint research and numerous projects uniting students, faculty, local industry, and the larger community.

Defining the Key Stakeholders

Whom is this vision designed to motivate? Many groups of individuals from inside and outside the college have already invested, or are ready to invest, in the college: students, faculty members, department chairs, staff, donors, alumni, parents, central administrators, trustees, legislators, and local leaders in business and industry, to name just a few. The list is long, and individuals may well belong to more than one group at the same time (faculty member-parent, parent-alumnus, trustee-industry leader). The challenge is to identify those with a stake in the future toward which the vision tends. Again, questions set up the context. Who can help with the process of envisioning a future for the college? Who can actuate that vision? Who will benefit from the success of the college? Not all of the members of any one group are necessarily key stakeholders. The more activist and optimistic members who look ahead in confidence rather than alarm and work to get things done will have the greatest impact on formulating and achieving the college vision. A department chair with ideas about coordinating and expanding international activities in the college; a faculty member who arranges new, specialized internships for her or his students; a student who requests college-level activities to promote interaction with faculty, staff, and administrators in order to give students a better sense of a college, in addition to departmental, identity; and a business leader who negotiates for college courses to be taught at the worksite—each of these is a stakeholder.

Envisioning the Future

By definition a vision statement is forward-looking, and this must not simply amount to extrapolating the present into the future. The hardest but most important skill is to recognize those present realities that impede or damage the college, such as an inadequate infrastructure to support research and teaching in molecular biology, and must not be allowed to carry forward if the college is successfully to imagine a better version of itself and act on that image. Given resources that are at the top end of the realistic spectrum, a supportive and adaptable environment, and aspirations that are daunting but not reckless, where can the college go? What can and should the college be in five years? Why is achieving that vision important? The answers to these questions, generated by the planning committee and the dean, will define the vision.

Communicating the Vision

There comes now a delicate balancing act: the dean and committee naturally want to excite enthusiasm for the whole endeavor as it proceeds. Obviously the initial steps of seeking input, as described, should have that effect, but if the whole process then advances behind closed doors until the vision and plan are unveiled for an admiring populace, that enthusiasm will wane and eventually (perhaps sooner than anyone expects) turn into unformed suspicion that nobody's view is being incorporated into the document except the committee's or that the real purpose is to manage a crisis rather than step toward the future. Such souring expectations are fatal to the process, and yet it is risky to display one tentatively conceived snippet of a plan after another, because that merely confuses without encouraging. Therefore, candid but not detailed progress reports at predictable intervals help everyone. The committee accepts that it has a schedule to meet and is more likely to make progress; the college community hears of that progress—and also of difficulties not yet solved—and feels a growing ownership of the plan that is taking shape. But all that is tentative, gradual, fragmentary. The main work of expounding the vision comes after the plan is complete. This communication should be quick, emphatic, clear, and widely disseminated. It will stand at the head of the plan itself, but it can also be divulged with comment and analysis in newsletters to alumni and faculty, presentations at meetings of college faculty and governing bodies, discussions with department chairs and directors, case statements to potential funders, and updates to trustees and other advisory bodies. The goal is to reach all the constituencies who are necessary to achieving the vision, to sell them on its merits, and to help them see that their aspirations are actually embodied in this declaration of what the college can become.

Refining the Plan

Preparing and articulating mission and vision statements actually make up much of the planning process because doing so compels an assessment of realities and prospects and drives decisions about priorities. Nevertheless, the plan is a different creature from a vision statement. The vision statement is brief and global and talks about an endpoint in the future, whereas the plan is specific and systematic and addresses issues of staging and incremental accomplishment.

The dean may circulate the mission and vision statements for input and discussion before the final plan is drawn up. Some even ask their faculty and staff to vote on elements of the plan. The details of this stage depend on the college governance structure and any additional steps the dean deems prudent to ensure an endorsement of these vital parts of the plan. Assuming approval, the intermediate goals to fulfill the mission and vision still need to be specified and the necessary resources to achieve them must be stipulated. This is where the hard work of planning comes in. A vision statement may seem sufficiently detached from the fortunes of any one unit that all can agree it represents the institution as a whole. But as departmental oxen begin to get gored, the level of agreement and amity on the committee can drop quickly. A plan that calls for reductions in one part of the college in order to invest in another part will predictably be a stumbling block. Deans sometimes underestimate how difficult it is for faculty who earnestly and appropriately want the best for their own discipline to endorse actions that slow or even reverse their own department's progress. Moreover, they will certainly be questioned closely by their dismayed colleagues for sullying departmental prospects! In fact, what makes the role of dean so difficult is precisely the need to step back and take a comprehensive view of the college and then act in accordance with it. To see it the other way around, the dean can view all parts of the college with detachment, with the possible exception of his or her own, but each member of the committee will approach the question from inside a department, and that makes detachment very hard. Making tough decisions about the college—most amounting to reasoned guesses about the future—is part of the dean's job in a way that it is not for most individual faculty members. The dean cannot afford to have a permanently divided committee, or a report that is skewed by parochial intransigence. This may require longer deliberation, diplomatic skills, and compromise on specifics without a surrender of core goals. If the final product is a good plan, it will gain the support of the faculty, and those who had the wisdom and guts to formulate it selflessly will get the respect they deserve.

In formulating the plan, it is best to begin with a list (not more than ten items) of the most significant things to be accomplished in the window of time covered by the vision statement. The goals need not be all of the same type—that is, some can be programmatic (for example, a new core for the MBA curriculum), others outcome-oriented and measurable (such as an increase in the number of graduates placed with Fortune 500 companies). Consider the following imagined set of goals for a nursing school:

1. Achieve fiscal stability.
2. Enhance research support and productivity.
3. Develop research, teaching, and practice emphasis on nursing and aging.
4. Develop a research emphasis on oncology nursing.
5. Develop research, teaching, and practice emphasis on public and community health nursing.
6. Develop leadership emphasis across all academic programs.
7. Begin work on an international nursing center.
8. Improve the organizational structure of the college.

Each goal then needs to be articulated into major steps and resources required to achieve it. To achieve goal number 7, for instance, the steps might include forming a planning committee, identifying a location, identifying leadership, estimating required resources, and seeking formal approvals.

Implementing the Plan

Implementing the plan too encompasses several specific steps.

Resource Analysis

However good a plan may be, well-suited to the needs of the college and programmatically brilliant, it will amount to nothing if the college cannot gain the necessary resources to support it. Resource analysis is thus the looming concern for any goal, and is by no means expressed simply in dollars. Curriculum revision and innovation, for example, require faculty time, funds for research and consultation, new positions, and technological support. Once the full picture of goals and objectives emerges, the costs of each step must be estimated and totaled. In most college plans, some goals such as revamping the admissions process will require relatively few dollars, but curricular ambitions, such as adding a new concentration, or capital plans, such as committing to a new building, will require a significant investment. At this point, the planning committee may wish to revisit the goals and prioritize, adjust, or even eliminate some of them before settling on a final set and related costs.

The next big step is to identify sources for the funds to accomplish the various objectives. If the planning process has been realistic, this should be a reasonable chore, although it is here that the committee finally faces the hard decisions that will have to be defended to colleagues. The committee may wish to leave such recommendations and decisions to the dean, but they ought at least to sketch out alternative scenarios that would produce the needed resources. Again, widespread communication about the goals can help to prepare the college for the steps to come, in the sense that choosing to go in a certain direction implies choosing not to do some other things. If the mission and vision have gained acceptance, approval of actions in support of them will usually follow. Without this kind of scrutiny and testing of specific goals, the whole plan is no more than a wish list.

The dean and planning committee together should share the task of explaining to colleagues what resources will be needed to accomplish the goals of the plan. They can also identify potential external sources of funds and other support so that the burden does not fall fully on the college budget. For example, companies that hire graduates of specific programs or manufacturers who may be interested in a partnership can be approached for support of new technology. To the degree that the plan has demonstrable potential to generate new resources for the college, it will gain faster acceptance. Fundraising, then, is inevitably a part of the objectives in support of goals, but no plan depends entirely on the kindness of unidentified strangers. A shift of priorities finally requires some reallocation of existing funds.

Implementation

After a process that fluctuates between exciting and grueling, the committee shapes its plan. Now what? At this point, some committees choose to develop a separate implementation plan, others a planning grid or timetable. The selected method matters little; the crucial point is to specify for each major goal a series of steps, the dates by which each step is to be completed, and the individuals responsible for doing so, for at least the first year.

The final product, then, includes a mission statement, a vision statement, a list of goals, and an implementation plan.

Implementing a plan takes time, but this axiomatic point gets lost in the excitement of producing a bold new vision and the converse anxiety that any delay implies a lack of commitment to the project. The plan's timetable should make clear that implementation will be on an incremental basis, not an explosion of prosperity and improvement. After all, resources, energy, people, and attention are all finite in any given year. The dean who drives to accomplish more than the community can make use of may be seen as Napoleonic, but conversely, may also be seen as indifferent or even incompetent unless something significant gets done and gets noticed each year. The ongoing sense of momentum is at least as important as any single achievement. It is not self-aggrandizing to draw attention to these accomplishments; it is a perfectly appropriate act of communal self-understanding. Everyone needs to see what was planned, that the vision supported by that plan is coming into being, and that more progress can be expected as each year goes by.

Finally, it is important to revisit both the details and the framework annually, not with an eye to constant tinkering or wild digression but to be sure that the plan is truly on the right track as external circumstances change. After all, hula hoops and Nehru jackets once figured into plans that were made with a lot of effort and met with approval. So was alchemy.

Pitfalls

Anyone who has served on a planning committee knows that the way is fraught with peril. Some dangers arise from context, or from unforeseen circumstances. Others, the most frustrating kind, come from lapses of attention or judgment by the committee. Roger Cason (2000) offers a list of the most frequent pitfalls in developing plans:

1. Forgetting that the aim is to stimulate action (not just produce a plan on paper)
2. Failing to think seriously and in depth about the external environment
3. Taking so long to prepare the plan that its assumptions are no longer valid
4. Failing to review the plan at appropriate intervals (every year is ideal)
5. Having too many goals
6. Producing a list of goals without action plans, dates, and people responsible (that is, writing a wish list rather than building a strategic plan)

To these we could add a seventh: failing to follow up. Whereas an annual review offers the chance to revisit the goals, check off the ones that have been accomplished, and perhaps add new ones, throughout the year someone—probably the dean—needs to check with the people responsible for the various steps to see what progress is being made. Because plans are time-sensitive, a dean cannot wait months to discover that someone has failed to pursue an assigned role or that genuine effort has resulted in failure. A setback, in fundraising, for example, may call for redoubled efforts in other areas, or even reconsideration of some goals.

Another reason to keep the plan on the front burner is discipline. Deans are never short of good ideas suggested by colleagues and therefore they need to train themselves to stay true to the goals of the plan. If the dean does not stay on course, no one else will.

Suggestions for Further Reading

Bérubé, Michael, and Cary Nelson (eds.). *Higher Education under Fire: Politics, Economics, and the Crisis of the Humanities.* New York: Routledge, 1995.

Cason, Roger L. "Bird's Eye View: Typical Strategic Plan." Paper presented to the board of the Delaware Chamber Music Festival, Wilmington, Mar. 2000.

Feiss, P. Geoffrey. "Working with a Strategic Plan." Paper presented to the Council of Colleges of Arts and Sciences' Deans Seminars, Spring 2000, Charleston, S.C., and Albuquerque, N.M.

Hahs, Sharon. "Setting Goals and Achieving Them: The Art of Planning." Paper presented to the Council of Colleges of Arts and Sciences Seminar for New Deans, Williamsburg, Va., June 1997.

Higgerson, Mary Lou, and Susan S. Rehwaldt. *Complexities of Higher Education Administration. Case Studies and Issues.* Bolton, Mass.: Anker, 1993.

Kaplan, Matthew (ed.). *To Improve the Academy. Resources for Faculty, Instructional, and Organizational Development.* Vol. 18. Bolton, Mass.: Anker, 2000.

Keller, George. *Academic Strategy: The Management Revolution in Higher Education.* Baltimore: Johns Hopkins University Press, 1983.

Keller, George. "Examining What Works in Strategic Planning." In Marvin W. Peterson, David D. Dill, Lisa A. Mets, and Associates (eds.), *Planning and Management for a Changing Environment: A Handbook on Redesigning Post Secondary Institutions.* San Francisco: Jossey-Bass, 1997.

Leary, David E. "Strategic Planning." In George Allan (ed.), *Resource Handbook for Academic Deans* (pp. 125–131). Washington, D.C.: American Conference of Academic Deans, 1999.

Oblinger, Diana G., and Richard N. Katz (eds.). *Renewing Administration. Preparing Colleges and Universities for the 21st Century.* Bolton, Mass.: Anker, 1999.

Peterson, Marvin W. "Using Contextual Planning to Transform Institutions." In Marvin W. Peterson, David D. Dill, Lisa A. Mets, and Associates (eds.), *Planning and Management for a Changing Environment: A Handbook on Redesigning Post Secondary Institutions.* San Francisco: Jossey-Bass, 1997.

Peterson, Marvin W., David D. Dill, Lisa A. Mets, and Associates. *Planning and Management for a Changing Environment: A Handbook on Redesigning Post Secondary Institutions.* San Francisco: Jossey-Bass, 1997.

Rowley, Daniel James, Herman D. Lujan, and Michael G. Dolence. *Strategic Change in Colleges and Universities: Planning to Survive and Prosper.* San Francisco: Jossey-Bass, 1997.

Schuster, Jack H., Daryl G. Smith, Kathleen A. Corak, and Myrtle M. Yamada. *Strategic Governance: How to Make Big Decisions Better.* Phoenix: American Council on Education/ Oryx Press, 1994.

CHAPTER EIGHT

BUDGETS AND RESOURCES

In the realm of college finances and resources, several truisms prevail: there are never enough resources to cover all or even most needs, there is much less flexibility in college budgets than any outsider could imagine, the primary component of the recurring budget is salaries, it is very difficult to find the funds for large onetime projects, and the cost of technological support is already great and has more potential to devastate the financial stability of the college than any other cost. At the same time, the dean is perceived by faculty, staff, and even department chairs to be the holder of riches (millions!) for whom a small request, say $25,000, is trivial. And surely the dean has the funds to respond to an emergency—a flood in the chemistry department's research labs or a window of opportunity to hire a fabulous scholar who has just become available, for example. So what should a dean do to manage resources effectively to keep the college sound and moving ahead?

Budget Assistant

Although each college has its own budgetary idiosyncrasies, a number of basic principles are normally relevant. The most important pointer we can give is in some ways the most obvious: when possible, find a first-rate budget officer, whether an associate dean or a professional staff member. Ideally, the dean finds such a person in place and quickly builds a relationship of mutual support and confidence. In less happy situations, the dean discovers that the incumbent lacks the skills to perform at the necessary level and has to make a change.

What to look for in a budget officer? Reliability and a keen eye for detail, but also creativity in solving puzzles—and openness. Although the first two traits come immediately to mind when considering anyone to handle a budget, the third makes the difference between having a bookkeeper and a colleague in responsible administration. A budget officer who does not have the fourth quality—a disposition to share rather than hoard information and ideas—will imperil the dean's ability to manage fiscal responsibilities. Yet some assistants, correctly perceiving that much of the power lies in knowledge of the budget, are reluctant to share information even with the dean and quietly assume as much decision-making authority as they think they can get away with. Their decisions taken one by one may be shrewd and well thought out, and make good use of the money, but that is beside the point. A new dean's predecessor may even have allowed this to happen, preferring not to be bothered with the details of budget oversight. It is important to address the issue directly and specifically, without delay, to get a handle on the budget and to determine roles and responsibilities.

In addition to learning the shape and processes of the budget, it is important for the new dean to take the time to understand and assess the accuracy of the information the assistant provides. This can be done by reviewing statements, spreadsheets, and records of past budgets kept in the files. The dean must be confident that the budget officer keeps full and careful records of all transactions and does not assume anything based on memory or a hunch. Difficult as it is to imagine nowadays a budget officer who is not well-versed in the institution's financial systems and software, such persons are still not uncommon, especially in smaller colleges with fewer opportunities for specialized training and fewer staffing options. But such inadequacy cannot be allowed; if an assistant has difficulty with changing roles or technologies, and if further training does not help, the next step is to replace him or her. Here is an easy test: if the dean knows more about the software than does the assistant, then it is time to make a change. Deans at small colleges, however, often must be their own budget officers, and for them the challenge is to design or fine-tune a system to allow them to access budget information as needed.

The level of detail deans want to review on a regular basis varies widely, as does the frequency of those reviews. If there is a high level of confidence in the assistant's abilities and promptness in raising any concerns, then consultation can be less frequent and less detailed. This also depends to some extent on the size of the budget. In a small operation with relatively little room for innovation—or for error—it may be necessary to keep closer tabs on the ongoing situation. Some deans in small colleges begin each day with a status report. In contrast, in a larger enterprise where such frequent reviews are impractical, or if the categories of funds are relatively inflexible, a weekly or even monthly report may suffice.

Certain areas require special attention each year:

- Funds for temporary teaching, which depend principally on released salary dollars, require the college office both to gauge enrollment demands closely and to predict how much money will be available. The financial assistant should have a sufficient history of spending patterns in the college and departments to give sound guidance and to recognize a rising problem.
- The dean *must* learn, as soon as possible, what responsibilities the college has for physical furnishings and maintenance, and which funds can be carried over from one fiscal year to the next to address big-ticket needs.

As we will discuss later in this chapter, these are areas of great variable demand but also of potential resources in the college budget, and both need the dean's attention.

When There's Month Left at the End of the Money

All but the most stable and dull budgets seem like calamities waiting to happen. We cannot imagine all the potential problems for a college budget, but we can identify some of the more common ones.

Unexpected Cutbacks

Even assuming an able budget officer and regular oversight by the dean, an unexpected budget freeze or a rollback is a significant challenge. Such reversals of fortune have been far less frequent during the prosperity of the last decade, but they will surely recur—and be all the more alarming if we have been lulled into false confidence! Reductions may be onetime or permanent; the difference is extremely important. First we will consider the onetime version.

At the slightest whiff of either a freeze or a rescission, the college should begin unobtrusively scaling back its commitments and expenditures until the picture is clear. The temptation to spend without scaling back, based on the cavalier idea that what is gone cannot be returned, is not only defiant but foolish. The college may well be *taxed* a percentage of its annual budget, and if this happens even as early as midyear after aggressive spending, there will be no real way to stay solvent through the remainder of the year. In contrast, if the cut does actually come, the prudent dean may not have to force departments to make across-the-board reductions.

Shortfalls

Another distressing and regrettably not uncommon problem is a significant shortfall in anticipated income—not because of bad planning or rash spending but rather, perhaps, because of a shortfall in enrollments that reduces tuition revenues. How well the campus responds to this situation will depend on a range of factors, from the general fiscal health of the institution to the provost's existing view of the dean's management record. Worst of all is a shortfall resulting from the campus not following through on what appeared to be commitments. More than one dean, to put it gently, has fallen victim to central administration promises that are written in wind and water or policies that have more loopholes than the federal tax code and somehow always work to the detriment of the college budget.

If the dean has tried to proceed carefully and still ends with a significant shortfall that could not reasonably have been prevented, perhaps the campus will agree to spread recovery of the deficit over two years. In any case the dean will probably have to postpone plans for projects until the debt is covered. Raiding department budgets, however, can only be a last resort. Even if the dean has been blindsided, departments will feel the blow proportionately more keenly. Their budgets will have been cut to solve a problem they did not devise or foresee, and they will inevitably feel that such a move means they are paying for the dean's incompetence.

Excessive Spending

Conversely, department chairs may create budgetary problems for the whole college by making reckless commitments before they learn better, or as parting gestures before they leave office. These situations are usually not simple. It is often the high-power chair vigorously recruited as the department's new leader who decides that the only way to fulfill his or her mandate is to spend heavily. The impact on quality of faculty and programs may be wonderful, but the method may wreak havoc on the college's finances. That chair must be held accountable for the overrun to the degree feasible and then be either sternly instructed on achieving quality within available resources or asked to step aside. Occasionally, chairs who are stepping down but remaining in the department feel prompted to bestow resources on their friends, themselves, and their pet projects. The dean or college budget assistant needs to keep a close eye on purchases or requests emerging from a department in transition.

Permanent Cuts

The situation is far trickier if the cuts are to be permanent. Again, timing is a vital consideration. One can hope that the institution sees the emerging problem and has the time to make plans for an orderly retreat from some fraction of its current operations. A multiyear decline in tuition revenues, or a legislature that steadfastly refuses to increase the appropriation for several years (which in the face of any inflation has the practical effect of an annual budget cut), can leave a dean no choice but to scale back. Strategic planning ought to incorporate the prospect of such unpalatable situations, and in any case the budget must make some room for surprises, no matter how tight it may be overall.

But sometimes the blow is unforeseen. In the 1970s and 1980s, many public universities and colleges found themselves taxed in midyear by a legislature that in turn faced shortfalls and somehow always concluded that the education budget was flexible. It is not so many years since the stock market was cruel to endowments and private schools faced calamitous choices, especially as they competed for students in an already expensive market. Soaring fuel prices also took their toll. Some things never quite go away! Other costs have strained budgets in more recent years. Skyrocketing library costs, especially for scientific journals, and above all the meteoric rise of technology can sweep all before it. As they say, resistance is futile.

Although the cut will come expressed as a percentage of the budget, undoubtedly the worst action to take in response is mindless across-the-board percentage reductions that punish the efficient along with the large and complacent, the emerging along with the evanescent. Some parts of the cut can be distributed in this fashion—for example, a percentage of nonpersonnel operating budgets— but the largest portion of the budget is always personnel, and 2 percent of a small unit's budget translates into a fraction of a person's line. It is hard to fire 20 percent of a person, and devastatingly unfair to extract a full line that may represent a hugely disproportionate sacrifice. In contrast, an ongoing assessment of program quality, demand, centrality, and standing prepares the college to make decisions related not only to dollars but to academic worth. Such an assessment must be current, based on credible facts and objective criteria. The reductions can then be modulated according to the extent of the fiscal downturn, and also be sensitive to the health of the academic programs. It is a form of academic triage, hideous to perform but necessary under drastic conditions. It is never too early for a dean to devise a set of measures by which to judge departments and make decisions about resources. There is a glimmer of a silver lining here: if the dean has good reasons for reducing or eliminating a program but has been hampered by political considerations, this could be the time to take action on what is always a distasteful duty.

Then there are the emergencies: the flooded chemistry lab, the breakdown of the electron microscope, the damaged roof, the discovery of asbestos, the case of theft or vandalism. Needless to say, the dean needs a contingency fund for such losses that must be covered by the college budget but should also be prepared to ask hard questions about need, maintenance, and security rather than replacing or repairing items automatically. Much further down the scale of costs, temporary substitutes must be found for faculty or staff members who need to take emergency medical leave. Depending on the level of the position and length of time, these costs can mount up, especially if, as often happens, they occur in clusters. There is no exact rule of thumb for the size of a contingency fund, but the budget can provide an approximate record of the annual impact of emergencies. We would advise sequestering 150 percent of that estimate.

Getting Advice

Based on the options we have outlined—and there are others, none easy or appealing—how should a dean proceed when disaster strikes? A frequent strategy is that academic panacea, an ad hoc committee, possibly including some seasoned department chairs, to review the situation and consider alternatives. In the final analysis, permanent cuts to the college budget mean personnel cuts, and in most cases vacant faculty lines provide substantially more dollars than staff lines. Cutting entire programs also yields some operating funds, but that is a severe action and it is permanent. If the reduction is onetime, it is better to drain contingency funds along with the year's operating budget, suffer short-term hardship, and stay the course for future years. Permanent across-the-board cuts are usually unwise because they signal that the dean is unwilling to make hard choices. Having an advisory committee to work with the dean in these situations obviously is invaluable.

The members of such an advisory committee are very visible and exposed to resentful faculty colleagues. Committee members must have two qualities: broad confidence in their fairness and acumen, and a sure foundation of comparative data (as well as the college mission and vision statements) from which to develop recommendations. Clearly the questions will not be purely quantitative, but the numbers can highlight some forms of opportunity. Cost versus student credit hours produced, and more generally, all income generated against the separate categories of expenditures, will highlight programs that are expensive but perhaps marginal to the college mission. In other cases the anomaly is ratio of staff, or operating budget, to faculty numbers. Acting on such data is painful but relatively simple, although giving appropriate notice to personnel can easily negate the benefits if the funds must be retrieved rapidly. Depending on the deadline for identifying reductions, the dean and the committee may have to gather up all vacant positions without regard to program quality or college goals. This is one of the hardest parts of the dean's job and in the end there is no way to justify doing it other than expediency.

Budget Proposals

Turning in relief from budgetary problems, we should consider further the opportunities for improving the college that budgeting offers the dean, starting with the reminder that a budget is a planning document. It must not only be in accord with the college plan but also be pinned to the advancement of that plan. The impact of every budget proposal rests on its relevance to the college's plan. What goals will be reached with the requested resources? What can be moved from intended to actual, from temporary to permanent, from inadequate to excellent?

The requirements for budget proposals vary greatly in form and style from one place to the next, but in any culture they tend to be highly formulaic. The document will have to present justifications for requests, and the plan allows the dean to state and defend the priorities in the budget in a context that the campus has already heard and endorsed. The form that argument takes will differ considerably if the budgeting process is zero-based rather than incremental; the former requires justification for everything that the college does, whereas the latter focuses more on new initiatives or at least new resources. Both types, however, depend on their relation to goals as well as the support of data.

In the rhetorical combat of pleading for scarce resources, it is important not to neglect the college's edge over its competitors in the institution. Arts and science colleges teach a high proportion of general education courses and usually have a favorable ratio of income to expenditure per student, whereas others such as engineering and medical schools generate substantial income per faculty member from grants and contracts and can use this information to their advantage. Perhaps there is a strong record of attracting external gifts for capital projects, named professorships, scholarships, and the like. Such margins of achievement cannot fail to support the budget priorities and contribute to a strong budget presentation.

Grants and Contracts

In institutions that place a premium on externally funded research, getting grants, contracts, and external fellowships is automatically a priority in managing the college budget. Grants and contracts directly support faculty research, graduate student stipends, and research equipment; there are also many sources for grants in curricular, program, and teaching development, and especially interdisciplinary growth, available in institutions of all sizes. Fellowships (for example, Guggenheim or ACLS) provide salary support for current faculty members, whereas other programs, including exchanges, can bring temporary additions to the campus. The gains are obvious in every sphere, from research productivity to fiscal strength, prestige, student support, and academic program development.

The indirect cost recovery funds (ICR) associated with grants constitute one of the most important resources associated with research. These funds are intended to replace institutional costs, including utilities, impact on space, and administrative activity indirectly in support of research, and to provide for research-related expenses. Because they are not finely categorized, however, they are a precious and flexible resource that serve a variety of research-related needs (yachts, unless they are research vessels, are out of the question). The federal regulations governing use of ICR funds are complex and exacting, and woe to the institution that misappropriates such money! For these reasons, indirect cost recovery on a large scale is vitally important for the health of research but also entails complex issues of compliance and perilous political issues of allocation.

To manage this activity, large colleges may have an associate dean for research or for sponsored programs, usually a faculty member with a successful record of funding and a detailed knowledge of federal agencies' regulations as well as funding opportunities across the spectrum of disciplines. Faculty in technical and scientific disciplines all know the vital importance of the funding game (although not all are equally adept at playing it), but faculty in other disciplines often need help identifying and applying for grants.

The associate dean's office is a gathering point for records of funding opportunities, proposals submitted, and resources that can facilitate the process. More significant, the office can work with faculty to increase the number of proposals submitted from the college (and to increase the success rate). The associate dean's office strategizes with novice applicants, assists with their budgets, and basically shepherds them through the process until they become more experienced. There are probably campus review committees on human subjects and animal facilities clearance with which this office coordinates.

The associate also helps the dean with important resource decisions, such as determining when and how much to waive indirect cost recovery, matching fund agreements, locating and renovating space required for projects, and identifying personnel costs to be covered by the grant. These decisions require cost-benefit analysis with a keen eye to the bottom line if the grants process is to work for the benefit of the college.

Colleges with large indirect cost recovery funds are in a strong position to negotiate deals with other persons and units on campus. They also face a thorny allocation problem: Who should control the use of this ICR, which can run above 70 percent of the direct costs funded by the grant? Although the money arrives because of individual grants and thus because of specific faculty members or research teams, it goes toward the maintenance of institutional premises and pays for activities that neither originate in the principal investigator's department nor are paid out of departmental budgets. Thus both the researchers and the administrative offices can lay claim to the use of the funds.

Needless to say, everyone does. The dean has supported the pursuit of the grant and the researchers will work in college premises (for which the dean may need to find replacement or supplement), and these dollars are a precious opportunity to advance research in other parts of the college. The investigator can find a hundred reasonable uses for additional funding that he or she has brought into play. The department absorbs the impact of the activity undertaken on the grant by providing space, probably some reduction in teaching coverage, and an increased number of people for whom to provide administrative support. One might say that all three parties should share in the benefits. And we have not mentioned the campus itself, which has as good a claim as any other entity and the controlling hand in setting policy at all levels. As this summary suggests, the issues related to research support, particularly ICR policies, are not only important but highly contentious.

The associate dean often mediates among the department and faculty member, the college, and the campus research or accounting office on a host of related questions:

• *What priority attaches to improvements that could not have been accomplished without ICR funds—for example, the acquisition of an instructional computing facility?* Normally these receive high priority as an incentive for faculty to continue seeking external assistance. What is the policy on helping faculty members with potentially fundable projects and bridging proven researchers between grants? The dean should try to set aside a certain amount of venture capital each year, and either conduct a competition for it or consider requests on a case-by-case basis until the funds are exhausted. A savvy associate dean should be able to assess the best bets.

- *What happens when a funded faculty member accepts a position elsewhere and wants to take equipment and grant funds along?* And how do we facilitate the transition of a newly funded faculty member who wants to bring a truckload of equipment and a cadre of graduate assistants from the former institution? In both cases involving a move, the two institutions negotiate formal agreements indicating who keeps or pays for what. If the college was involved in the acquisition of the grant it will be part of the separation agreement, and the dean's office may be asked to represent the department and institution.

- *What happens when the college can send on only one proposal out of three for a competition?* An in-house review session of senior scholars with relevant expertise is both efficient and fair. All unsuccessful applicants, however, should receive a full explanation as to why their proposals were not selected.

- *Who has final responsibility for financial oversight of grant expenditures?* In addition to a departmental review process, the college must remain accurately informed. This function can normally devolve on the dean or the budget officer, but the associate dean (if such exists) is the logical endpoint of the reporting.

- *What is the college's responsibility in securing matching funds for a proposal?* Here the dean or a designate can help by staying alert to proposals as they take shape and assisting with negotiations before a proposal is submitted. If the figure is fairly modest, the college may cover it fully; for larger grants, and particularly those involving investigators from outside the college, some fraction must be secured from the campus and that diplomacy means more lead time in preparing the budget. The record of standing commitments by the office means prioritizing and capping the college's investment in grants, always an unpopular constraint.

- *What are appropriate levels of start-up funds?* This is a frequent topic of discussion as deans sort through departmental recruitment recommendations, financial limitations, and the national scene. Various deans organizations associated with the sciences study this issue regularly and can provide comparative data. But of course the institutional norms have to be considered as well. Research institutions have more to offer because they generate more ICR funds that can be used to support the research enterprise, but they also have far more—and more costly—cases to fund. Liberal arts colleges, in contrast, may have neither the resources nor the desire to invest heavily in a research infrastructure and so must consider programmatic needs, such as providing undergraduate research opportunities, in the mix.

- *What happens when a faculty member is awarded a prestigious fellowship, such as a Fulbright, that is insufficient to cover full salary and benefits for the year?* Although the professor's teaching will be forfeited for that period of time, it would be punitive to the scholar to prevent acceptance and punitive to the department to refuse any replacement. Moreover, even though the stipend of the fellowship is almost certainly well below the faculty member's annual salary, the freed-up funds can probably cover the salary-benefit gap and provide for some part-time teaching. Thus the faculty member gets the recognition and the time, and the department gets the teaching and the reflected glory. Some colleges with few replacement options (for example, those in remote locations with no local prospects for course-by-course teaching) require the faculty member to make up the teaching before and after the leave. This option is better than declining the award but should be considered a last resort, because it dampens both the spirit of the award and the faculty member's effectiveness by overloading the teaching.

Outcomes

Follow-up is critical to the success of the college. The dean not only needs to see that resources are distributed as agreed but also needs a good accounting of the outcomes. Was there a documented increase in student credit hours to reflect an increase in the instructional budget? What percentage of seed grants and start-up funds is paying off in funded research? Is an increase in graduate stipends resulting in a demonstrably higher quality of recipient? Even—at the lowest level of expectation—are grant recipients filing their reports on schedule? If the campus does not have a reliable system for tracking such data, the college needs to have its own. Good information like this is essential to effective budget management and to the college's credibility. We all know of departments and colleges that have resource constipation. It is important not to let this happen, but rather enhance data collection to evaluate current allocation of the budget and its results.

Personnel

People occupy lines (and space!) and cost money. One can track the positions, or the lines, or the dollars. Fringe benefits normally add 25 to 30 percent to salaries, and are sometimes reflected in the dean's budget, sometimes centrally. The positions-dollars must meet the demands of enrollment and program support for all the departments and other units reporting to the college. Every vacated line generates a battle between department and college over "ownership" of the line—and its accompanying dollars, whatever the rank of the last incumbent. In some universities, the provost retains control over vacated lines. When control over faculty lines remains at the decanal level, many deans sweep all vacant positions back into the college budget for reconsideration before distributing them to units even as minimal replacements—a form of zero-based budgeting. The review may be relatively simple, based on annual recruitment requests from chairs and directors, or the dean may require a more elaborate and quantitative justification with relevant data. Spreadsheets with categories for the most important data points, such as cost per FTE, can help the dean survey the college and determine where the need for positions is strongest. Such a method also helps the dean defend decisions about positions and other resources (see Chapter Nine for further discussion of faculty recruitment authorization).

A related issue for most academic deans is when and how to fill positions with part-time or temporary faculty members. Some colleges have developed a percentage limitation. No more than 25 percent of courses can be taught by persons who are not part of the permanent (that is, tenured and tenure-track) faculty, for example. Some institutions have adopted policies to stabilize the appointments of faculty not in the tenure stream. A new dean begins by learning such policies and assessing the makeup of the college—number of professional programs, size of continuing education components, need for specialized faculty such as teachers of Japanese, extent of graduate programs, emphasis on a traditional four-year curriculum—before determining the appropriate mix of faculty. Budgetary constraints are obviously another factor because part-time instructors generally are paid less and receive no benefits. Without repeating the well-known advantages of full-time over part-time and temporary faculty members, let us say that the dean ought to do everything possible to avoid exploitative situations and argue for the qualitative improvement to be gained by doing so. It may be preferable to offer fewer, larger classes in order to hire more full-time faculty.

All of this is not to say that the dean should try to eliminate part-time positions as a college resource. Uncertain budgets, unstable enrollments, or anticipated needs of a higher priority in the college are just a few of the situations that caution the dean to maintain a certain degree of flexibility in managing instructional funds. As we all know, it is much easier to release a person teaching on annual contracts than to eliminate a tenure-track, or tenured, position. In fact, unless the institution formally declares financial exigency, even the elimination of tenure-track positions can result in lawsuits. One dean, who was forced by the president and provost to reduce faculty members in one department, and so began with the last-hired, saw those appointments restored several years later when it became clear that the terminations would not hold up in court. Another consideration that comes up repeatedly is the moral claim that part-timers or temporary faculty believe they have when a full-time position is created. Many times these are women who are bound by location and have lacked opportunities for professional advancement. In any case, these individuals often will not have the credentials to succeed in a national search, and will appeal to the dean to intervene on their behalf. Normally, the dean will resist doing so, but it is easy to forget that relying on temporary faculty members can result in excruciating, even disruptive, personnel decisions and subsequent lawsuits that can take a toll on time and energy, even if they can't succeed. Our point is that, despite what the dean inherits, he or she should move to control the situation and to develop a balance between efficiency and quality.

What criteria should the dean consider before awarding a staff position? The complexity of the department as well as the number of people served are equally important. Foreign language departments, for example, soak up staff because of the number of students and the need for small sections, but mainly because of the diversity of the faculty and their needs. Departments using complex instructional equipment, whether technological or scientific in nature—such as freshman biology laboratories or computer science workstations—are also heavily dependent on staff assistance.

Distinguishing between *nice to have* and *necessary* is no trivial challenge. A number of research support positions in engineering and the sciences, such as the manager of the stock room, or the machinists, are a proper use for ICR funds from grants; the dean's contribution here is to look for ways to consolidate these operations across departments and save in more than one unit. The departments will resist, each claiming unique needs, but in fact there may be opportunities for significant savings to the college in coordinating support functions. As with other questions, faculty self-determination helps work through this question: a task force of concerned faculty members can make recommendations about the joint operation. Predictably, the hardest part is finding space to house it. It is necessary to use great caution in reducing positions from consolidated facilities until the transition is complete and it is clear what functions if any are redundant. Especially when times are tight, it makes good sense to move or even cut staff positions that basically serve only one person, even if that is the director of a program.

Physical Facilities

The physical facilities—buildings, offices, classrooms, studios, library, laboratories—of the college are an even more enduring part of the landscape than the faculty, but often in far worse repair. Like faculty and staff positions, these spaces will have many more demands made on them than they can accommodate. As programs grow or space use changes—classrooms become offices or computer rooms, or vice versa—both functions and people must move to new premises. Often the history of a building—for what purpose it was erected, the growth of the programs housed within it, even its aging and decline—is inseparable from its current use and occupants. Making a change, therefore, is fraught with problems.

A careful analysis of space and other resources can help justify or avert changes. How many hours per day are classrooms and instructional laboratories occupied? Are there better alternative uses, and what will it cost, both fiscally and politically, to make a move?

This is even more the case, if that is possible, with faculty offices. Range wars break out over office assignments with a difference of twenty square feet or a window that is a foot wider. For example, a department had one more faculty member than it had contiguous offices and someone had to move to the basement. An extremely cooperative and mild-mannered citizen of the department muttered darkly about the need for dynamite to dislodge him. Another (in another department) spoke of suing for compensation in the form of a 1 percent salary increase for every ten square feet his office was below the average for his rank. In fact, these squabbles correlate closely with rank. The lingering struggle is often lengthy—a decade or more—and easily spills over into unrelated issues from committee work to graduate student admissions. Which departments have coffee lounges and which do not? How much space, and of what quality, is allocated to staff members and departmental needs like the mail, copy machine, and fax machine? Inevitably there will be inequities and inefficiencies. The issues are less incendiary when departments occupy their own separate buildings, but when departments coexist under one roof and space is tight, pressures mount, transferred from weightier concerns—where the faculty despair of achieving change—to these relatively paltry issues. The college office ends up in the middle and had better have a very plausible reason for any decision. The dean may need to take an active role in the management of the situation.

Cold, hard data will only carry the argument so far. After reviewing the blueprints and numbers, the dean needs to inspect the premises personally to see what actually happens there. One dean was surprised to learn that a *vacant* office intended for a new faculty member actually housed a robotic arm for researchers to *play with* in their spare time! A storage closet, so marked on floor plans, may long ago have been converted to another use.

Among the most frequent challenges are the following: departments that have grown or diminished without any adjustment in their space, new demands for instructional computing laboratories in disciplines that had not needed such space until long after the available rooms were all taken up, the gift of a large display collection that needs to be housed (this function eats space with a special voracity), the arrival of a faculty member with a much more extensive program of funded research than his or her predecessor, the creation of a new department or program. In general the smaller the department, the more generous the space arrangements. This situation usually dates from the time when all departments were smaller, but some simply have not grown comparably with the others. Partly because of their size and perceived vulnerability, these departments tend to be the most sensitive of all to adjustments in their space. Yet a dean cannot overlook the fact that faculty members in larger departments may be sharing small offices while others in "neglected" units enjoy relatively palatial quarters. There is nothing for it but to pick on the little guy and effect a new arrangement, doing so with diplomacy, data, and firmness. The dean should bring the chairs of the affected departments together, lay out the problem clearly, and seek their help in finding a solution. The small department, feeling it is shrinking even further in status than in area, will probably accept the new dispensation better if it entails some renovations, furnishings, or equipment.

Each term when courses are matched up with classrooms, the space crunch issue arises again. Even with new space available, the traffic is gridlocked from 10:00 A.M. until 3:00. The reason is very simple: departments and faculty members are reluctant to schedule a course early in the morning or after midafternoon. Students find it terribly hard to get up and stay awake for a class starting before 9:00, and by midafternoon many are off to jobs or in labs. The faculty, for their part, are getting ready for class in the morning and are in the lab or library as soon as classes end. The result is that large numbers of classrooms stand idle for several class hours each day. This is a vexing problem, because neither student nor faculty habits are likely to change. A common but unpopular step is to schedule required courses early in the morning. Freshman calculus or rhetoric is never popular at the best of times, goes the argument, so there is nothing to be lost by setting them at an unpopular hour. Another alternative is to schedule classes that meet once a week after 3:30 P.M. The attraction of meeting weekly can overcome the undesirable time slot.

There is also continuing pressure on deans to take classrooms out of the inventory and convert them to other uses. Provided that classroom spaces continue to be used for instructional purposes, a workable solution is usually at hand. Some space devoted to computing labs, geology experiments, ear training for budding musicians, and so on, can also be put to other uses if properly outfitted with locked storage units and other security devices. The dean can make such multipurpose use a condition of the conversion. The root problem is the belief that departments and programs *own* instructional space and therefore have total control over it. It is fine to give them priority in scheduling their dedicated facilities, as long as the dean also emphasizes that the space is needed for the instructional mission of the college. Arguments based on data that show demand versus utilization, square footage per faculty member and department, and so forth will appear to fall on deaf ears, but in fact such arguments do carry weight and faculty recognize that the next time they may need to make the same case on the other side.

Departments with contiguous office, research, and instructional space are the lucky ones but in many cases, the smaller ones. Departments that have grown or merged with other programs may be scattered in several places, including ill-kept property in inconvenient locations (which may be why the department was able to expand!). With patience, diplomacy, funds, and occasionally a strong arm, the dean can address these situations systematically. Sometimes the first step is persuading the higher administration that there really is a problem that deserves a solution, especially if the department is contentious or undistinguished. It is precisely the scattered departments that are least likely to be healthy because the faculty, students, and staff cannot interact productively on a day-to-day basis. The dean's management of space, therefore, can directly affect the quality of the programs in the college.

In fact, to look at it the other way around, most quality improvements in the college require space. High-powered faculty members, whether scientists or not, usually have extraordinary space needs for files, computers, assistants, and visitors; a prestigious collection of rare specimens, instruments, or books requires dedicated space; new programs or especially new departments have special housing needs. The dean can work with department chairs to plan ahead for such developments. Surprisingly, at most colleges even now, institutional reviews of proposals do not ask about space in the way they routinely require budgetary details, even though space is more problematic than any other factor.

To help with this challenge, the dean should examine the institution's plan for renovation and new construction and look for ways to submit proposals for the college. At the same time, as suggested earlier, the dean should look thoroughly and creatively at current space and make changes to ensure optimal usage. For major projects, particularly new construction, external support from donors or foundations is often a practical necessity to get an idea off the drawing board. The argument is not that new space is needed, but rather what that space will do for the quality of the programs. Keep the horses before the carts, however: until there is a reasonable expectation of premises to house a new program, faculty expansion, or that remarkable collection of dinosaur fossils, it is extremely unwise to acquire any of them and expect them to function.

Technology

The last major category of resources within the dean's purview is technology, including computer support, instrumentation, and equipment for teaching, research, and office operations. As we indicated earlier, keeping pace with the explosive growth of technology both in uses and in equipment is as great a challenge to the college's resources as any other part of the enterprise, including faculty growth. Yet funds invested in improving the college's technological capabilities are giving the same access to people, knowledge, and processes that the building of libraries gave a century ago. Without that linkage and that capacity for keeping pace with the advance of knowledge, an institution's quality will decline swiftly and fatally. As a very high priority, the dean must learn the state of technology in the college, what sources are funding it, and which needs are the most urgent.

Not all technology is in the service of research, but the most sophisticated and rapidly evolving equipment is. Unless the dean is personally expert in these fields it is wise to ask the already-overworked associate dean for research, or a savvy faculty member, to act as technology adviser. The budget officer may also have the needed expertise, or connections, for administrative computing needs.

Precisely because technology is so important, deans are called on to make many decisions about it, and there are few prospects more daunting for someone from the other end of the intellectual world than making costly decisions about powerful but inscrutable devices. One nonscientist dean recalls that almost the first question he was asked after arriving on campus was what type of supercomputing would best serve his faculty. How can one gauge the individual and collective needs of hundreds of faculty and staff (and students) in a score of fields? A place to begin is with a modest commitment that faculty and staff will have the tools they need to perform their jobs effectively. In practice, of course, that is hardly modest, and yet no less necessary despite its alarming price tag. Going beyond the necessary requires a strong rationale and a cost-benefit analysis. Technology advisers can develop a college technology plan coordinated with larger goals and objectives, including projected start-up needs for new faculty members, upgrades for desktop computing, new or improved instructional laboratories, and basic research support. Some plans call for the cascading of equipment, that is, giving the newest and most advanced computers to the most sophisticated users with demonstrated need and passing the older machines along to those with simpler needs. But maintaining a floor of capability for all faculty and staff to have access to e-mail networks, or Internet connectivity, means periodic replacing, not just upgrading, as the technological horizon continually recedes.

We always test the limits of our current environment. Whatever level of support is provided sets up the need for the next, more expensive level. Faculty who make aggressive use of what they have and want to be competitive for the next grant discover that the proposal requires the institution to commit to assorted costly equipment, or another faculty member reports a remarkable bargain on a half-million-dollar item if the college can commit to it in the next twenty-four hours. This is when having both a plan and a knowledgeable adviser is invaluable.

If the proposal truly requires such an investment perhaps it is not feasible for this college now, but that is not a decision to reach off-the-cuff, foreclosing on an exciting opportunity. The advisers can also help by conferring with colleagues around the college. What problems are they experiencing, and what could they do if they had better equipment? There might be an angle to use in seeking external support for some initiatives. And, of course, funds for equipment should be built into research proposals to the full extent allowable. There was a time when it appeared that desktop computing could eliminate many support staff positions. We now know that prediction was absurdly optimistic: clerical staff have not been reduced because the scope of the enterprise continues to grow, and indeed they have been joined by an army of troubleshooters. Thus the college's technological advances often carry personnel costs that are not always anticipated. The support necessary to maintain a calculus teaching facility, for example, can amount to the equivalent of a new faculty position. The dean's role is to bring the issues to the department to help them make informed decisions about instructional priorities.

In the end, although we all hope that our chief contributions to the college will be based on our wisdom and intellectual leadership, those contributions will stand or fall by the availability and management of resources. This is one of the greatest changes for a faculty member who enters full-time administration. The experience may be likened to that of a regular theatergoer who is invited backstage to see the wonders of production and then asked to become stage manager. The play suddenly looks different from this new position!

Suggestions for Further Reading

Anderson, Richard E., and Joel W. Meyerson (eds.). *Financial Planning under Economic Uncertainty.* New Directions for Higher Education, no. 69. San Francisco: Jossey-Bass, 1990.

Bowen, William G., and Harold T. Shapiro (eds.). *Universities and Their Leadership.* Princeton, N.J.: Princeton University Press, 1998.

Chafee, Ellen Earle, and William G. Tierney. *Collegiate Culture and Leadership Strategies.* New York: ACE/Macmillan, 1988.

Higgerson, Mary Lou, and Susan S. Rehwaldt. *Complexities of Higher Education Administration: Case Studies and Issues.* Bolton, Mass.: Anker, 1993.

Katz, Richard N., & Associates. *Dancing with the Devil: Information Technology and the New Competition in Higher Education.* San Francisco: Jossey-Bass, 1999.

Rowley, Daniel James, Herman D. Lujan, and Michael G. Dolence. *Strategic Choices for the Academy: How Demand for Lifelong Learning Will Re-Create Higher Education.* San Francisco: Jossey-Bass, 1998.

Whalen, Edward L. *Responsibility Centered Budgeting.* Bloomington: Indiana University Press, 1991.

CHAPTER NINE

FACULTY DEVELOPMENT

"I will still be here when this dean is long gone!" What dean has not heard this comment, either from a faculty member in person or reported secondhand?

And it is true. The average tenure of a dean in a given post is now about four years—less than the probationary period of an assistant professor. It does not matter whether the dean rose out of the local faculty or came from outside, whether he or she returns to the faculty or moves elsewhere. At the end of service in the dean's office, that *dean* is gone. The same is true of any full-time administrator—dean, provost, president.

In contrast, a fresh assistant professor who stays through tenure and promotion to become associate and then full professor serves at least a dozen years at the same place, and for those who spend their whole career in the same community, perhaps thirty-five or forty years. Truly the faculty embody a college and make it what it is. They create the curriculum and teach the courses, publish research on every imaginable topic, shape the minds of countless thousands of students, and manage their own collective fortunes as a self-governing community. The dean's happy responsibility then is to recruit, foster, retain, and reward the faculty and provide the best possible conditions for the exercise of their intellectual talent and their capacity for collegial interaction. At least on the good days, the key to a dean's role in faculty development is optimism. Every college offers examples of what faculty can be, and the dean's emphasis must always be on appreciating and increasing the ranks of the exemplary, not on lamenting the prima donna or curmudgeon. From recruitment to retirement, faculty depend on the support and understanding of the dean, sometimes gratefully and sometimes in anger or frustration. Without the faculty, there would be no need for a dean. It would be wise to remember this, because certainly the faculty never forget it!

Recruiting Faculty

Each year, the dean may ask departments to submit requests for authorization to recruit faculty. The results are always interesting; every department wants to recruit at least one faculty member. Every year. At senior rank. But even the richest college cannot afford to approve every recruitment request, or even all the searches for which the DEO makes an excellent case. So how does one manage this abundance of academic good intentions?

Before Saying Yes

Recruiting faculty is one of the most unpredictable activities of the academy. It is complicated by countless unexpected twists, most of which make the process more expensive than anyone imagined. Unless the ground rules are very clear at the outset, the year will yield more exasperation than new colleagues. The best way to prevent this kind of frustration is by having the department describe its needs and capabilities in as much detail as possible beforehand, and then respond clearly to the request with approvals, provisos, or boundaries. The DEO should be asked to explain the purposes for the recruitment. What will this appointment add to the department, other than replacing a departing colleague or adding to the faculty ranks? The case made should include a compelling argument for the teaching field. This may be enrollment pressure from majors, contribution to general education programs, needed coverage in the graduate program, a new area that fits with current efforts either in the department or in other programs. The last item is especially important for the dean to consider. What are the potential benefits outside the confines of the department (lending coherence to an international studies program, for example, or launching a professional initiative that links law and public health)?

Clever departments come up with creative approaches to which the dean responds gratefully. They are willing to mortgage a line that is due to fall vacant in a year and meanwhile will forgo some TA support during a dry spell for the graduate program. Or they will share office space or phase a retirement that allows the line to open sooner. In one inventive proposal, the history department persuaded the school of public health to pick up a fraction of an appointment in the history of epidemic disease. Another ploy is to allow the department to keep all the proceeds of a senior retirement by splitting it into two junior lines, provided the second addresses a college as well as a departmental need.

Recruit at what rank? Ideally, faculty will stay and rise through the ranks so that the department grows its own senior colleagues. New hires can then normally be at junior rank unless other factors intervene (numerous retirements, losses from recruiting raids, or senior colleagues who lack the punch to lead the department's academic effort). However, departments always hear the siren song of a dazzling, distinguished appointment that will instantly put them on the map, replace retired colleagues, lead the department, and so on. Such arguments are not trivial but they should be compelling in a particular context, rather than follow the general argument that experience is better than inexperience. The cost of a senior appointment is not better than the cost of a junior appointment, and the novice may be a star in the making—or a far more useful colleague whose actual virtues outshine the public visibility of the star.

What are the prospects of actually finding someone for this position? The department may be looking in a well-established field with plenty of potential candidates. Is everyone else looking too? The department may want someone for a hot new field. What is the competition like, given what we can pay? They may want a rare bird, whose field of research is especially arcane and unlikely to be supported by the library or laboratory resources on hand. Are such people out there and potentially available? Is this actually a ploy to recruit a specific and very expensive person the department has already identified? A department of biology had such a quarry in mind but knew that the dean would not commit to the anticipated salary and other costs, so they made a case for an open search, probably at junior level but with the chance to go higher if a special opportunity arose. They then promptly brought in Distinguished Professor Jones—who could have imagined such good fortune? The dean had not put careful boundaries on the search, and was faced with turning down a golden opportunity or going broke.

If space is limited, which it usually is, the dean must ask for details about where the new person will be housed. If this is a replacement, will the vacated premises suffice? For an office, probably so, but for lab space almost never. This can be particularly problematic when replacing a scientist who has not been active in research and has not had much or any lab space. The new person will need a real lab. Even if there is a new building coming on-line, it is important to sort out these questions in advance, because claims on the space will rapidly account for every square foot!

Faced with requests that answer all the questions and make wonderful cases, the dean must maintain a collegewide perspective on faculty growth. The condition of an individual department is important, because the dean obviously wants to provide for the best possible program in that discipline and sustain the faculty in their task, but the place of that department in the overall needs of the college may help or hinder the argument for recruiting there this year. The size of the biology department depends not only on the number of majors or the large freshman courses but on the impact of the premed program, and that may outweigh the perfectly reasonable argument for adding a hot new subfield in anthropology this year or even for replacing a successful teacher who has retired but whose success was the result of her own special effectiveness rather than the centrality of her subject.

Authorization and Stipulations

The department should get a letter from the dean that lays out the authorization, including any special provisos. It should specify whether the search must be at the assistant professor level, presumably junior but possibly higher level (under what conditions?), or open rank. Once the position is advertised at a single rank it will be difficult if not illegal to alter that. Salary is harder to predict unless economy overrides all other considerations. With great discrepancies in salary from one place to another and a competitive marketplace, it is unwise to be inflexible unless, of course, local contract conditions require it. In any case, the dean should avoid pinpointing the salary in advance and certainly not look for the lowest figure the market might conceivably tolerate; you may or may not get what you pay for, but you will surely pay for what you get. The committee chair will need to know a reasonable range (such as $38,000 to $43,000) but also know that the figure is open to discussion under exceptional circumstances.

Likewise, it is important to lay out any special conditions, including the scope of start-up costs the college can support. This is one of the most widely varying items, from basic desktop computer support and some library development for a junior humanities appointment, to $700,000 or more for an established experimental physicist. The dean should contact a colleague at a comparable institution to check the going rate for various fields. As part of this determination, the dean should also explore what the department can put toward equipment, space remodeling, or technical and support staff from its current inventory. Chemistry departments have an eerie knack for looking in the back room and finding equipment that the new person can share, at least until grants can fund the rest.

Responsibility for a Clean and Diligent Search

We have already touched on the DEO's role in searching (Chapter Six). The college has a crucial responsibility to ensure that all necessary procedures are universally understood and followed. There is probably a campus office that oversees affirmative action, EOE, and other employment safeguards, and the college should have someone—an associate dean if the staffing permits—to screen the department's paperwork and clear its plan for the search, ensuring diligent regard for such matters as gender and ethnic diversity. Where will the department be advertising the position? What are the relevant deadlines? Are the criteria correctly and clearly laid out in all notices? No less important is to lay out a realistic budget for the search, reflecting reasonable expenses, including advertising, travel costs for committee members who may be interviewing at a professional convention, bringing finalists to campus, lavish dinners with everyone in sight. College and departmental budgets may not run to such complete support, but that makes it all the more important to agree on what resources are available—and from whom. Otherwise the search will inevitably cost much more than the college intended. One way to encourage thriftiness is to put the full amount (about $5,000 per search is sufficient for the purposes just listed) into the department's coffers with the agreement that if the search costs less, the department can keep the difference for its own appropriate uses.

Involvement in the Search Process

Before the department launches the search, the formal plan for recruitment should be checked—not merely to assure compliance with regulations but to ensure timely action. Once the search has begun, periodic progress reports will be necessary. The dean must be sure to review the interview list, and not just the short list before anyone is brought to campus. Even before that, committee members may go to a professional convention, where they may interview a dozen candidates. By gaining affirmative action clearance and the dean's approval for the entire dozen to be potential finalists, subject to the department's scrutiny, the committee can move swiftly to campus invitations and perhaps steal a march on the competition.

When funds are tight, a department or a college may try to save by conducting phone interviews, not just for the intermediate list but even for finalists. This is very risky. We recommend that all finalists be brought to campus, even if it means scaling back on other expenditures during the year. When they arrive, the dean or a designee should interview all of them. For consistency, the same person should meet with all candidates in a given search; if the position carries tenure, the dean is the one to meet them. As with the recruitment of chairs, this interview at the college level is a critical step in the process. The dean is probably the first person the candidate has met who can answer questions about the department's condition and prospects, and as ambassador for the college the dean can discuss the wider context with authority. As with interviews for DEO, this is the chance to look for hidden issues such as the spouse or partner, special leaves or unreasonable salary hopes, as well as virtues that perhaps have not emerged yet in conversations with the colleagues, such as unsuspected versatility, eagerness to develop a new program, and so forth.

The final choice, based on grounds of scholarly strength, rests with the department; the dean is obviously not chair of each and every department nor a scholar in every discipline. However, feedback from the college to the search committee concerning the candidates interviewed only makes sense. The college assessment should not be pro forma but add to the overall impression made by each interviewee. Furthermore, the dean has to endorse an appointment or it cannot proceed, so if he or she has serious concerns about the winning candidate, they must be sorted out with the department. To avoid needless confrontations, some deans ask for an annotated, ranked list before the department notifies its choice; in any case a conference with the DEO before agreeing to make an offer should help to resolve differences of opinion.

Occasionally the dean discovers that the department's winning candidate is not qualified for the announced position. Perhaps the department found an individual who was only marginally qualified in the area of the search but had other important strengths that fired the committee's imagination. In short, the candidate is not weak but inappropriate. Approving this candidate while passing over others who are genuinely qualified for the announced position is not merely unwise but illegal, particularly if doing so eliminates protected or underrepresented individuals. In these situations, the faculty is quick to object that the dean has no business making such judgments. It helps to keep handy the original position request to contrast with the unsuccessful candidate's record or interests. The college may be able to provide another position or make other arrangements, but it cannot make an appointment that turns the original position notice into false advertising.

No doubt the DEO or search committee chair will contact the winning candidate with the good news that an offer is imminent, and at that time may learn whether he or she is disposed to accept, but it is the dean who sends out the formal letter of offer. For senior appointments, the dean should also call. This sends the right signal to a senior colleague and often increases the chances of an acceptance.

Mentoring

So by dint of inventive pleading and skillful recruiting, the college faculty is grow-ing by leaps and bounds. But the traffic is by no means unidirectional or planned. In addition to retirements there are two main classes of departures: a fraction of junior faculty fail to receive tenure (the rate varies tremendously from one place to the next—less than one a year in some colleges, 40 percent or more in others) and a number of faculty at all ranks accept competitive offers elsewhere. In most cases, these are undesirable developments, and so we should consider how to reduce losses in each group. Let us begin with the probationary faculty.

Nurturing and Assessing Faculty

For generations, an ever-wider variety of colleges and universities assumed that earning a Ph.D.—a certification of the ability to do research—was sufficient preparation for a teaching career. Research universities led the way in emphasiz-ing the primacy of expertise in print over expertise in the classroom, but even col-leges whose historical mission has centered on teaching have been affected by that view of the intellectual life. Now it seems that colleges of every stripe across the country are recognizing the inadequacy of this approach, and in the past decade or so we have seen a rising tide of programs aimed at developing faculty teach-ing skills. Unfortunately, this still addresses only one of the three facets of profes-sional effort. The doctorate may certify a level of competence and achievement sufficient to enter an academic career, but what (or who) will guide continued growth? And what of academic citizenship, which is closely tied to the culture of each campus, and for which little in graduate school prepares anyone?

Here is no mystery. It is important for the dean to work with the faculty so that they will be able to stay, will want to stay, and will make the dean glad they did. Such programs do not need to be expensive or elaborate. They can be simple, old-fashioned mentoring by a skilled and caring senior colleague or include seminars on teaching and grant proposals, videotaped lectures, cross-departmental pairings of faculty for mutual development, centers for excellence in teaching—the possi-ble approaches are endless, but the possible results are not. They are but two: suc-cess and failure, and the institution shares in the failure of any colleague.

Departments are the natural setting for this development, but some are very small. They may care deeply but lack the experience or the resources for special training. In any case, the college leads the way both by getting the departments to establish agreed-upon expectations and by providing the more costly forms of support—the teaching center, the grant support office, and so on.

Active Mentoring

Thus the dean works with the faculty leadership, the DEOs, and the governance structure and clearly defines the level of performance expected in each aspect of the faculty role. More specifically, each newly recruited faculty member must know at the outset what this means for him or her, because each department lives these guidelines differently. The onus does not rest solely on the new person, but on the colleagues who know what is required and have already shown they can do it. The dean's office should take a continuing interest in how departments are mentoring their faculty and lead the way in providing resources, occasions, and examples. Mentoring does not mean distributing a handbook—as it were, winding up the tenure clock and letting it tick until it slowly runs down.

It is important to make sure that the chairs are reaching out to junior faculty—providing advice or encouragement without waiting until they are desperately needed—and to urge them to assign successful faculty colleagues as mentors to new members. The signals can take various forms. The most emphatic is through salary decisions, and the dean ought to pay special attention to the increases assigned to junior faculty.

Finally, we should note that although the emphasis in this section in on junior faculty—and what we have said applies most particularly to pretenure—guidance and encouragement are also essential for midcareer faculty, some of whom may otherwise become somnolent, ineffectual, disruptively selfish, or all of the above.

Centralized Faculty Development Programs

Most institutions have some form of centralized faculty development programs with which the dean coordinates. One of the most common is a center for teaching improvement that offers consultation, feedback, programs, and possibly evaluation mechanisms to faculty members. Information from the center may appear in annual evaluations, promotion and tenure dossiers, or aggregate data provided to deans and department chairs. Deans may have the opportunity to express their needs and to ask for specific help from the college. In addition, sabbatical requests, support for research or course development, and travel funds may be awarded centrally. In these instances, if proposals and requests are not already channeled through the dean's office, such a step should be taken. In smaller colleges, awards may be made by faculty committees. In larger institutions, deans may wish to establish college awards tailored to college needs (usually with overhead recoveries and gift funds) in addition to whatever is offered centrally.

Deans report some tension on the issue of faculty development funds where they believe that their college may not be treated fairly or where their recommendations are ignored. Centralized faculty development units certainly offer the potential for such problems, but the wise dean will try to learn the dynamics of these situations and fashion college procedures that complement the institution's goals, much the same as in promotion and tenure considerations.

Developing Teaching

We begin with the emphatic statement that the majority of faculty enjoy teaching, put a great deal of effort into it, and see it as a positive reason for a career as a scholar. There are two main difficulties. First, most faculty have not been trained to teach and therefore need training after they have already begun their careers. Second, the relative emphasis and interaction between teaching, research, and citizenship shifts from one college to the next, one person to the next, and one stage of an individual career to the next, making it very difficult to articulate, much less legislate, durable guidelines for how to support each aspect of professional activity. Nonetheless, with whatever blend of hope and resentment, faculty expect the dean's office to clarify these matters so that they can get on with doing what they were hired to do and be productive members of their community.

The Importance of Disciplinary Differences

"Teaching" means such different things to scholars from various parts of a campus—and various institutions—that any generalization is likely to be misleading. A typical teaching load in a small college with limited resources may be four courses a term. In a research university, much depends on the field; two per term is common in arts and sciences, except in the lab sciences (more commonly one course per term), whereas in medical schools a "six-hour teaching obligation" probably means giving six lectures in the term, not six hours per week.

The variations are as striking in class size (where the biologists often make up for it by having huge classes while their humanist counterparts have more but smaller classes), teaching style, technological sophistication, reliance on graduate assistants, fieldwork, and on and on. The dean of a complex college needs to become familiar with the pedagogical traditions and problems of many departments in order to understand the requests for help, the claims of achievement, and the sheer enthusiasm of the faculty.

In addition to recognizing the faculty's need for different kinds of resources, and for the freedom to teach by the best lights of each discipline, the dean needs to understand the picture because the nature and quality of faculty teaching will have to be documented appropriately for promotion and tenure, and as we discuss later that is a serious challenge.

Development, Not Just Monitoring

Our earlier admonitions about mentoring are particularly important here. Getting someone's teaching to mature is not detached anthropological fieldwork; nor is it like praying for rain in a drought. Colleagues from the candidate's department, elsewhere in the college, or even elsewhere on campus, are all involved in helping that person to grow. The advantage of cross-departmental partnering is that it moves the process from the realm of supervisory assessment into the realm of collegial support. There will be ample opportunities for evaluation in other settings, and if the two are blended the senior person will always be more of a supervisor than a colleague. Here again, although the activities ought to arise from faculty initiative and move independent of administrative intervention, the dean is best positioned to provide the necessary resources or coordination.

Encouraging Research

Research skills too must be developed and rewarded appropriately.

Allowing Enough Time for Faculty to Succeed

Conventional wisdom has it that faculty are hired to teach but are rewarded and promoted for research—even at many colleges where teaching is the declared priority. Whether in joy or in sorrow, faculty at all kinds of colleges say their research is the most "crucial" part of their job, not to be confused with "enjoyable" or even "time-consuming." Whatever the local research expectations may be, it must be possible for the faculty to meet them or frustration and disaffection will bring the teaching enterprise to a halt along with everything else. If there are no labs that accommodate high-powered research, the college cannot reasonably fault faculty for not engaging in such work. If the library is inadequate to anything more than undergraduate teaching, then a book should not be demanded for tenure (along with teaching seven courses a year!). The dean should talk with DEOs, and with the college P&T committee, about this issue in general. More specifically, each discipline should be encouraged to develop guidelines for what the faculty regard as appropriate levels of accomplishment. In the same way, teaching responsibilities in various disciplines should be discussed. How many different courses do junior faculty teach, and does that allow them to do the necessary research? If not, is the solution to reduce teaching loads or readjust research expectations? Few departments will appreciate this question, at least in this form, but it does focus the conversation on the hard alternatives! Unionized faculty will have departmental workload agreements developed in this way, though these will have to be reviewed and approved by the dean. Calibrating such agreements, whether or not the faculty are unionized, with requirements for promotion and tenure is essential.

Interrelation of Research and Teaching in Assignments and Evaluation

Few themes in campus debates generate as much heat and as little light as the "balance between teaching and research." Although a casual listener would never guess it from the endless wrangling over the relation between these two in tenure expectations and the reward system, they are not fundamentally different things at odds with each other but facets of the same pursuit. Faculty in political science, art history, advertising, plant pathology, and ophthalmology define that relationship very differently, and nothing is gained from striving for a one-size-fits-all approach. The dean has to learn how the symbiosis works in each department, and then work with the departmental leadership to optimize that arrangement. For instance, how much graduate supervision do faculty members undertake, especially junior faculty? This is the lifeblood of science faculty, whose graduate students make up much of the research team in the lab. For other disciplines the supervision of graduate student research is intimately linked to ongoing projects, although more one-on-one than in groups. And just because a department lacks a graduate program does not mean that the faculty forgo research—or that there is a weak tie between that research and the faculty's teaching, both in classrooms and in directed projects. For example, Miami University of Ohio has only a carefully selected array of graduate programs but one of the nation's most extensive programs of undergraduate research projects.

Auxiliary Support for Equipment, Grants, and Other Necessaries

Every dollar spent in support of the faculty's intellectual curiosity and exploration will pay off, and the primary meeting place for this effort is the dean's office. Some needs are isolated, individual, and relatively modest—a trip to Munich for a month to work with colleagues or to the Folger Library to use the archives. Others are individual but have a wider impact—the crucial matching funds on parts of a grant, or a couple of years' salary for the last member of a team project that can then sustain faculty and graduate students in a major undertaking. Still others affect the entire college, such as periodic upgrades or replacements of faculty and staff computers, or a central office to assist with grant proposal writing.

Cost sharing in equipment on grants will make the difference between success and failure. Funding a research assistant for a humanities scholar at a critical juncture in a book project can ensure completion, promotion, and career momentum. Even a modest fund to which faculty can apply for publication subventions, small equipment purchases, or international travel to conferences can mean the difference between a deferred project and a successful promotion case. If these awards are very visible and the results publicly recognized, both the dean and the faculty will feel that they work in a supportive environment.

All this is more easily said than done. Large colleges often have more discretionary funds, but of course they also have a larger population of scholars putting pressure on those resources. And not all large colleges enjoy any predictable source of discretionary funds for research support. Perhaps they are retained at the campus level, in which case the dean can make a request under the rubric of faculty development; a strong record of results can perhaps be parlayed into a recurring line in the college appropriation. Another important source of support for special research initiatives is annual fund appeals to alumni. Many graduates retain pride and interest in the accomplishments of the faculty and are glad to have a specific focus for their gifts. The dean then reports on the results of these gifts in the college's alumni newsletter or annual report; thanks to the generosity of our alumni (making particular mention of the lead donors), Professors MacLeod and Xiang were able to achieve such-and-such results. This personalizes both the contributions and their effect and can create an ongoing flow of private support for college research. The dean's office will almost certainly gain some share of indirect cost recovery funds (see also Chapter Eight for more on this), and these can likewise help to start, sustain, or finish projects that would otherwise run dry.

Academic Citizenship

Finally, citizenship issues must be addressed.

The Importance of Citizenship for the Life of the College

Two opposite things are true. First, the civic roles of self-governance on campus and service in professional organizations are valued little and have a measurable drag effect on a faculty member's progress in both teaching and research. Second, many faculty put in countless hours on committees, task forces, review panels, and so on. Not surprisingly, there is a high burnout rate for this unappreciated side of academic life, and often it is very hard to persuade faculty to take on another time-consuming assignment.

Who wants to be chair or director of graduate studies? How about planning the speaker series? Will you at least serve on the library committee? In a value system that in practice deemphasizes institutional engagement as against individual achievement, it is a minor miracle that faculty come forward to provide leadership in any of the forms needed in the academy. They do, but there are not always enough of them or the most appropriate volunteers. As a result, people get elected as directors of graduate study because they skipped the meeting and could not decline, and who among us does not know someone who wanted to be department chair in the worst way—which is exactly how they did the job? Small wonder, if we see committee roles as a burden to be carried like a hot potato or a malodorous sack, handled as briefly and as gingerly as possible and then passed along to someone we want to impede.

The worst disservice the academy has done itself is to use the term *service* for everything beyond teaching and publishable research. In this way, a noble term becomes condescending, dismissive, pejorative. A distant third after teaching and research in evaluation of faculty contributions, service can include an amazing range of activities on various campuses, from membership on a minor departmental committee to the presidency of the American Historical Association or editorship of a major journal. Perversely, some places even include under this heading the revision of course materials or the writing of textbooks published by respected academic presses. In short, it is the place to put other people's activities that in your view do not or should not count.

But colleges must have citizens who see service as a welcome obligation. We should recognize how different are the *kinds* of faculty activities other than teaching and research. On-campus involvement is different from holding office in a national organization, and working on a curriculum committee is different from participating in a review section for the NSF. Are we dealing with side effects of research activity or with teaching support? Is this village administration, state politics, or foreign affairs? Moreover, unless the very concept of citizenship moves closer to the center of faculty's view of their role on campus, and closer to the center of the institution's value structure in such matters as promotion and the reward system, it will remain a malodorous sack.

Of course, the last thing any dean or chair wants is to elevate this third realm to overshadow teaching and research. Rather, the college benefits from a shared understanding of how teaching and research relate not only to each other but to the civic duties that permit the existence of a community of free inquiry and mutual nurturing. It is certain that overtaxed faculty, however generous their contributions to the life of the college, will not be the ones to recommend an upgrading of service because it may also mean an increase in expectations. It rests then—no surprise here—with the dean to provide leadership in a delicate reinterpretation of faculty priorities. Faculty want to make things work but do not want to make unproductive efforts that go unappreciated.

What Counts?

The main task is to establish in fairly specific terms what counts as service, and how much it counts. We are not recommending a bean-counting mentality but rather, to the extent possible, the same clarity that is taken for granted in reporting and assessing teaching and research. Moreover, this effort will have meaning only if it is reflected in the reward structure. Ironically, the best way to ensure that the leading citizens of the college have a say in this is to form a committee on the reward system and take its advice. It is important to get clear statements on what counts under service and what weight this category has in annual evaluations of faculty and in promotion evaluations.

Evaluation

In a profession that relies constantly on examinations, grades, vetting proposals, and reviewing research, it is amazing how haphazard the annual performance review process is at many places! We believe that no student can do without the wisdom of our judgment, no external scholar should be deprived of our knowledge about his or her subject, and yet we are strangely reticent about the work of our own colleagues to whom we have an equally important responsibility. Written reviews, followed by a meeting if either party wishes, ought to be the normal practice for all faculty, but most assuredly for untenured members. This is not simply to fend off charges of capriciousness but to reestablish the bond between the faculty member and the department. Again, the dean sets the policy and the tone for faculty reviews, which should be available for reference by the dean as needed (in many colleges, the chairs file all annual reports with the dean along with salary increase requests).

Probationary Reviews

Without imposing conformity of style or content, the dean's office ensures that all probationary faculty receive annual comment and guidance from the department.

The trick here is to find a balance between intrusion on disciplinary habits and neglect that leads to indifferent or even misleading reviews. As a general guideline, pretenure reviews should involve someone in addition to the DEO so that they do not seem to be mere policing actions by the boss, and they should be positive in their approach. The topic should be taken up with the chairs, who can tell about approaches they find effective. At the same time the dean should underscore the importance the campus attaches to candid, supportive reviews.

Halfway through the probationary period, the junior faculty member gets a more thorough review, a dry run for the tenure process of the sixth year. Sometimes these are managed the same way as other annual reviews—internally by the department—with results going to the dean as well as to the "victim." At other places, the college office takes a more directive role, as it does for the final tenure process. The sweep of this midcourse review is broader, and the potential consequences more serious. If the initial appointment was for three years, it determines whether the candidate gets a second appointment, taking him or her through to tenure consideration, or is stopped with a terminal year.

Whether the department or the college office runs the review, it falls to the dean to ensure that it conforms to the procedures and expectations of the tenure assessment for which it is a preview and probable predictor. This is especially important because often faculty are mesmerized by the two Great Reckonings, for tenure and for senior promotion. And yet the preliminary pretenure evaluation is crucial for avoiding surprises or missteps, and the assessment of faculty continues each year from hiring to departure. Associate professors frequently need to make more than one attempt before being promoted to senior rank, and they deserve more than the annual raise letter to tell them how they are doing. They should have fuller periodic reviews to measure their progress and to help it along. Usually, associate professors get a full-dress evaluation at least every fifth year in rank, and more frequently if they request it. That process should have the same features and procedures as reviews at other stages of their career. In short, the entire ongoing process of evaluation, whatever the rank of the person under review, should be marked by consistency as well as fairness.

A rapidly growing form of personnel review for faculty falls under the general heading of posttenure review applicable to all faculty at all ranks. The practice has been prompted to some significant extent by public concern for accountability as well as closer scrutiny inside the academy on quality, use of resources, and such familiar phenomena as the long-term associate professor and the unproductive senior colleague. About one-half of the institutions in the country now engage in formalized posttenure reviews. These may be either generally applied on a predictable timetable (for example, every fifth year) with the goal of assessing what a faculty member has been involved in and what he or she has achieved since the last review, or they may consist in accepted standards and procedures that are initiated when a faculty member is apparently not performing at an acceptable level.

The individual department or program must be intimately involved in laying out the practices and traditions of its discipline so that the institution can be confident that it is adjudicating work on an appropriate basis. Once that account of expectations is agreed to, both faculty and institution can approach evaluation with clarity and confidence. Posttenure review concentrates not on extending the policing function of the college but on encouraging faculty to contribute in the most effective and helpful way—for both the individual and the college. The evolving interests and emphases of an individual's work over the span of a whole career are often at odds with the expectations of the department or the college not because the faculty member is doing irrelevant or incompetent work but because there is no mechanism for planning changes in emphasis (more time on teaching for the next few years, or a special opportunity to work up a new area of concentration, for example). To the department, using the same yardstick it used a decade ago, the faculty member seems off-target or detached. That may be the case and the department is right to be concerned, or the college may be passing up the opportunity to derive special benefit from a new phase of a colleague's intellectual life.

Tenure and Promotion

The college takes the lead in setting the level of achievement expected. The dean must never take on this process singlehandedly but should tap the wisdom of the strongest faculty, continually refining and advancing that definition of excellence. Each discipline has to translate that standard into its own terms. This is not to say that each department, however weak, can use its own record as the benchmark of excellence. Standards at other comparable institutions—preferably somewhat stronger overall—can clarify what it is reasonable to ask and provide a slightly tougher target to aim at. Here the dean plays a delicate but invaluable role in working with the departments to define their expectations more clearly and to accept a process of moving those expectations up a notch.

However, there is a grave peril of inequity in this matter. An assistant professor has six years to meet the standards of the department and the college for promotion. Meanwhile, in those six years, the department and college continue to improve and the level of faculty achievement rises. By the sixth year, the assistant professor who had what it took to get the job and has done what was expected of him or her is deficient by current standards. Success is a moving target, and the college moved the target.

The problem is not unlike salary compression, by which the salaries needed to recruit the best new faculty rise faster than established salary lines through annual increases until those who have been on the faculty for six years are proportionately less well paid than the newcomers, and associate professors may actually earn less than midlevel assistant professors. The college needs to keep track of the *progress* of probationary faculty and keep the pace as strong as possible, without assuming that six years later they can arbitrarily match whatever new standards have emerged in the marketplace. In most cases, faculty can achieve more than they originally imagined, and they should be both monitored and encouraged at every step without fear of being fired if they do not meet standards not yet articulated for the future.

From the start of the appointment, the candidate must know the requirements for promotion and have a reasonable idea of what will be needed to meet them. The annual review should not only comment on how this year went but how it contributed to achieving the goal: How am I doing for this stage of the process? The third year review is crucial in laying out the big picture, using the same template as the tenure review itself.

The sixth year, when that decisive tenure review takes place, is like a three-ring circus with candidate, department, and campus each performing in turn. The dean's office plays a vital role in describing expectations and procedures for all departments to follow.

Candidates present their dossier as the basis of the scrutiny. What goes into that dossier? All the evidence that two different juries will need go into it: the expert jury of disciplinary colleagues in the department and the nonexpert jury at the college-campus level. If not planned carefully, the response can yield such prodigious mounds of material that few if any reviewers actually wade through it, which defeats the purpose.

On university campuses (as distinct from freestanding colleges), the campus usually has a template for promotion dossiers, stipulating the kind of information required and in some cases even the maximum overall bulk. In that case, the dean needs to work with the DEOs and the college P&T committee to ensure conformity with campus regulations. If there is no fixed form or method, the dean should develop a system of reporting and reviewing information that gives the fullest possible play to the individual discipline for articulating its expectations and its findings in a way that is accessible to nonspecialists. It is a teaching opportunity for the author of the dossier to explain a complex set of findings to intelligent lay jurors. Moreover, a college P&T committee with representatives from across the college may include members who know little about the disciplines under review. If the committee begins with a discussion of academic values, and of what has succeeded or failed in previous years, it can build a shared basis for judgment and avoid aberrations that are not only unfair but may lead to appeal, or even litigation.

The candidate is responsible for supplying information, which the department turns into a dossier for formal review. A good practical rule in assembling the information is that more is better. Excess information can always be winnowed out, but gaps in either information or explanation can sink a case if nobody in the room can fill in those gaps. If the candidate has team-taught courses, what was his or her share of the actual course development, instruction, evaluation, and so forth? In jointly authored papers or especially books, what was the candidate's role (either in the research or in the preparation of the paper)? Are the journals in which the candidate published well-respected, even prestigious? What sort of acceptance rates do they have? A book may be appearing from a press that is not generally seen as distinguished but happens to specialize in this field, or it may be little more than a vanity press reflecting a poor reception in the usual channels. If the teaching evaluations have any peculiarities (one or two with really bad evaluations but the rest are strong), the anomalies should be explained.

In short, if the record is strong, the department needs to be sure that all those strengths are in the dossier in such a form that committees at all levels can appreciate them. The departments must also realize they should never try to oversell or excuse a weak case. Any endorsement for tenure or promotion is a statement that this person embodies the department's standards for high achievement; it is not only the candidate's credibility on the line in these dossiers but also that of the whole department.

Letters from external referees are especially crucial to the case for research and sometimes also for teaching and service. The department must gather the most authoritative opinions it possibly can, not merely to persuade the committees outside the department but to have the best objective commentary at its own disposal before deciding whether the case deserves to be supported. Who are the referees, what are their credentials for commenting on this case, and do any of them have a relationship—personal or professional—with the candidate? The candidate's dissertation director, for example, should not generally serve as an evaluator, and coauthors are naturally suspect because the work is as much their own as the candidate's. How should referees be selected? Practice varies greatly. In some places, the department or committee simply chooses and contacts scholars until it has the necessary number of commitments; elsewhere, the candidate makes suggestions that may or may not be reflected in the department's final list. Yet another approach is to negotiate the list between candidate and chair, with the department reserving the right to add names of its own choosing. There are colleges where the dean's office must approve the list of referees and even carries out all contact with them to avoid any signals from the department on the preferred tone of the letter. ("We are trying to get Liu promoted this year and hope you can help us," or "Although Anderson's file is a bit less than we normally expect, we must decide this year whether to tenure him. How does his record strike you, as a world-renowned expert in this specialty?")

If a case passes the department, it will come to the college committee and then to the dean; if it fails, it will surely follow the same route as an appeal. Either way, the dean gets to make a decision about every case every year. We make three recommendations.

First, despite the stacks of material, the dean should read every dossier with care, even those that are clearly winners—they help to define the desired level of excellence.

Second, the dean should think very hard before overruling the college P&T committee. Their conclusions are only recommendations, but after all, so are the dean's. Whether the committee members are elected by the faculty or appointed by the dean, they are probably among the college's best faculty and they are exposed to intense scrutiny for each judgment. If there are doubts about a recommendation, the dean should meet with the committee, explain those doubts, and hear their reasoning more fully. This courteous precaution has rescued many a dean from taking a step he or she would have regretted, whether it was to turn down someone approved by the committee or—less often—to reinstate a case denied by the committee.

And third, even though it is the department's responsibility to assemble the dossier, the dean should take care that each file is in the best possible shape before sending it on to the provost or president for final action. As a dossier climbs the administrative ladder, it goes to people who know less and less about the individual disciplines (a campus committee with members from agronomy, law, and dance do not want to try to figure out what is amiss in a file from civil engineering). The dean should not imperil a case by making the next committee uncomfortable with a lack of information and puzzled by the document they must rule on. In any case, the college wants a reputation for delivering strong cases that are clearly presented and easy to support.

Reward and Support System

Each year every faculty member receives a miniature version of a promotion in the form of the decision about salary for the coming year. Assuming the new number is not completely capricious, it conveys a judgment about how things are going, and even if it does not include advancement in rank or title, it should feel like advancement in tangible rewards. Salaries are the one issue affecting all faculty at the same time and in the same terms every single year. Quite apart from the benefits they offer for one's personal finances, salaries are a powerful symbolic system. Deans must learn to use that symbolism carefully and to good effect.

For the sake of simplicity in this section, we will use 4 percent as the basis for all illustrations.

Criteria for Raises

On what will increases depend? If the system assigns virtually all raises across the board, with perhaps a very small amount (say 0.5 percent) for merit, as happens in many state systems and most particularly on unionized campuses, then the criteria are not hard to define, although even the small bit for merit will require explanation of the rules. If at the other end of the spectrum the entire raise system is "merit-based," then every dollar is a deliberate comment that can be interpreted, resented, challenged, and generally used as a lethal weapon against chair and dean alike. In practice, even those places that claim to give only merit raises usually have a minimum (for example, 1.5 percent) across the board except for serious problem cases.

Within merit, what carries more weight? We are back to the research-teaching issue, but unlike tenure and promotion decisions, teaching tends to carry relatively more weight in annual raises than in P&T decisions, even in research-intensive institutions. (If nothing else, most research universities are large, and must account for a lot of teaching. Whether or not departments appreciate this, deans quickly learn to do so!) In a given year, some activity such as course development for a new curriculum or use of technology or extension work may be the object of special rewards, but overall the weighting of activities probably will not change much from year to year because it reflects deeply held convictions. Thus, raises are confidently based on annual activity reports.

Process

In Lake Wobegon, where all the children are above average, it is a safe bet that more people will be vaguely disappointed by their raises than will be vaguely pleased. It is important to be clear about the details of the process. For example, how much is there to work with? Answer: 4 percent. Does that mean a total of 4 percent including promotion bumps, counteroffers, equity adjustments—everything—or are some of those covered by other funds (such as turnover funds held in the dean's office) and the full 4 percent goes to "regular" increases? If the former is true, then even though the total salary budget will indeed increase by

4 percent most faculty will be sharing in a raise pool of perhaps 3.75 percent and that means even more will discover they have received less than they deserved. Describing the rules of the game clearly makes life easier for everyone.

Moreover, the dean has to keep back some funds to respond to special appeals from chairs on behalf of extraordinary cases. This further diminishes the amount sent out to DEOs, although of course it will all go into raises in the end.

Now we are down to about 3.5 percent going to departments. In the great majority of cases, all departments get the same percentage on their continuing base. But a troubling thought occurs: just as individuals vary in the quality of their accomplishments, so too departments, taken as units, vary considerably in merit. So is it fair to give all departments the same percentage pool to work with? Is it any fairer than giving across-the-board individual raises? A few deans take up this challenge and give differential rates to departments at the outset—perhaps 3 percent to some and 5 percent or more to others (depending, of course, on the relative size of the strong and weak units). At this point, however, they usually indicate that they have almost nothing held in reserve. In other words, they acknowledge where the strong cases are and put the funds into the hands of the DEO to reward them. A more common approach is to hold some back, give out the same percentage to all departments, and require the weaker units to handle all raises within that basic rate, including special merit.

And finally, who gets credit or blame for the resulting numbers? If the dean relies heavily on the DEO recommendations (and it would be a rashly self-confident dean who felt prepared to do a better job person by person, department by department, than the DEOs armed with annual reports and justifications), then that should be acknowledged. "The college laid out the criteria and procedures, and placed 3.5 percent in the department, with the opportunity to request special raises beyond that level. I have reviewed all the recommendations, but relied very heavily on the careful work of the DEOs." The DEOs do hard and thankless work, they deserve to be supported and acknowledged.

Sabbaticals and Other Leaves

Relatively few faculty would go so far in their appreciation of the academic life as to say that it is paradise, but we still re-create an important biblical moment: just as the Creator rested on the seventh day, so faculty in most institutions can request a pause every seventh year and refresh their intellectual energies with a paid leave of absence from teaching. (It is interesting that so far as we can tell, nobody has ever proposed a sabbatical term away from research by doubling the teaching load!) Apart from tenure itself, this is the most prized faculty perquisite as well as the most efficient engine for carrying major research projects to completion. The specific terms and frequency of sabbaticals varies from campus to campus; the most common is a semester at full pay after every six years, frequently with the option of a full year at half-pay. The dean has relatively little discretion in altering that calendar, but in most places must approve each leave and ensure the teaching operations will not be encumbered by too many faculty leaves. Not surprisingly, faculty with sabbaticals in the offing are very reluctant to have even a chair, much less a dean, tell them that their plans are subject to scrutiny, and deans report amazing reactions to requests for further information that would let them write a better endorsement of the application! Yet the dean's responsibilities—both fiscal and programmatic—make this review an absolute necessity.

Deans can also help in two very important ways. First, although the faculty member is on full salary and thus releases no temporary funds, the department still needs to hire a replacement or absorb that person's teaching somehow. Assuming one-seventh of the tenured faculty will wish to be on sabbatical in a given year, this can mean a significant problem in a large department, especially if nobody else can teach the absent colleague's courses, and all the more if he or she finds external funds to flesh out a full year of research leave. The dean's purse can usually provide at least some help for a visiting instructor, which can make the difference between approving or delaying a leave. It's also a good idea to have some contingency funds to be used on a case-by-case basis. Faculty should be encouraged to apply for faculty development funds from national foundations and scholarly organizations such as ACLS, but could also seek faculty development funds from the college.

Second, the value of a sabbatical leave often depends on relocating for at least part of the time, getting to an archive, or traveling to work with a colleague. Any help from the dean with such expenses will be a good investment in a productive leave, especially for younger colleagues who are less able to absorb these costs personally. If at all possible, deans and chairs should look for ways to give probationary faculty some released time from teaching in order to complete the research that they must present for tenure. Awarding course releases competitively offers both time and recognition; although it is costly to do for everyone, a semester of assigned research time is a precious gift that nearly all junior faculty will use to good advantage.

Dealing with External Offers

For years, the academy has implicitly encouraged faculty to generate an external offer as the best or only way to get a substantial salary boost—and then complained bitterly that the faculty are fickle because they cynically generate external offers without intending to accept them. In this game, the faculty premise is that, by definition, any university that makes me an offer I can take to my chair or dean is a Better University and will bring me a Better Situation here even if I have no intention of leaving. Yet the dean might quote from President Kennedy's inaugural address: "Let us never negotiate out of fear, but let us never fear to negotiate."

Each year, at least one faculty member comes in with a tempting offer from elsewhere, and wonders what to do about it, as if it had arrived uninvited and was strangely unsettling. "I love it here, but this offer! I just had no idea it was coming, and I told them I was happy here, but they keep pressing me and offering more salary, and they will give me a center to direct." This is a very slippery area, in which mistakes in either direction can have bad and lasting consequences. Failing (or declining) to respond strongly to an external offer can cost the college a valued colleague; responding with undue enthusiasm can persuade a mediocre faculty member to stay, squandering the best chance to create an opening for a stronger appointment.

Because most offers involve salary or other fiscal considerations, the DEO quickly takes the negotiations to the dean. Here are some guidelines for handling the process.

Is There Really an Offer?

Every dean, it seems, has a tale to tell of the faculty member who said he or she "had received an offer," which turned out to mean there was some prospect of an offer in the air. A faculty member may keep the DEO informed about a candidacy that is making real progress, both to test the waters at home and to allow the DEO to start formulating a response if the offer really comes through, but nobody should make any counteroffer in response to finalist status, second interviews, reported phone calls from the other place's dean, or certified letters that will be mailed to the faculty member next week. "The check is in the mail" is worth no more here than elsewhere. The chair can certainly alert the dean to the emerging situation, and can talk about the issues, but only on receipt of a copy of the offer letter does anyone make a formal counteroffer.

Is the Candidate a Valued Colleague?

The dean should consult with the chair before engaging the issue at all with the faculty member. Among the questions to discuss are these: If this person leaves, is the department likely to recruit someone better? How does this colleague fit the needs of the department? What about collegiality? And is he or she genuinely interested in the other job or is this basically a ploy to get a big raise or an extra year of research leave?

Who Made the Offer?

Even assuming this is a colleague that the dean and department want to retain, it may not be necessary or appropriate to match the offer in full. Such factors as the relative prestige of the other place, the difference in cost of living, climate, library, and department size should be considered. The list of factors is long and will be very different in each case. An associate professor at the University of Michigan who is offered a full professorship at an undistinguished four-year college is not negotiating from strength. There may be other personal factors (see the following sections) that make the opportunity more appealing and radically alter the counteroffer question.

What Should Be Included in Negotiations?

The list of possible bargaining chips is fairly limited, but the dean may be quite willing to negotiate on some items with this candidate but not others. Which is which? Early or extra sabbaticals, salary raises, released time for specified projects, administrative roles (or release from same!), funds for the center the individual has always wanted, added lines in the department to shore up his or her part of the field, summer appointments, study abroad leadership . . . the dean should understand which topics are on the table and which are not *before* talking to the faculty member. The chair can be very helpful in putting these issues into perspective for the dean. A second role for the dean comes into play because, when appropriate and feasible, the college can provide support that the department cannot.

Showing Appreciation

It is fatal to assume that a faculty member knows that he or she is properly appreciated. The promptness with which the dean meets the colleague, the issues raised and terms used in discussing the faculty member's role and department, the kinds of incentives that turn up in one's remarks, will all be signals. But above all, the dean should avoid the risk of losing one of the best faculty for the sake of a few— or even a few thousand—dollars. The margin of difference is paltry compared with losing an experienced and loyal colleague. Sometimes deans or chairs fall victim to a pernicious lure: if Smith leaves, we can split her salary into two junior positions and get twice the coverage! However, changing a ten for two fives may give equivalency at the bank but not in the department.

Making Deals

Negotiating counteroffers carries a high risk of distorting the status and reward systems of the department and the college. What is this person's value to the college? Is the dean willing to skew the salary distribution or other features of the departmental landscape? Who are the faculty most comparable to this one, and what will it mean to them when they hear (even inaccurately) what this person has gained by producing an external offer? It is important to be very sure who those comparable faculty are, because the issue will come up before the conversation is over, and if the dean does not have a clear sense of who is comparable, the colleague sitting in the dean's office will be glad to supply a list. Somehow, the comparable faculty always turn out to be members of the National Academy. And once a deal is struck and accepted, all who believe they deserved as much or more (a numerous band) will press for the same deal. No college has a perfect reward system, but every college operates on premises and precedents that are well known and generally understood. Once the dean does violence to that frame of reference as understood by the faculty, it creates not only a single injustice but a lack of confidence in the dean's fairness and judgment. The consequences of that can be long and damaging.

Why Is the Offer Attractive?

The individual's reasons for liking an offer may well be different from why an offer seems good or bad to the dean. The appeal may be a negative: it is not here, and there are personal reasons for wanting to relocate. Perhaps the offer appeals to a special interest or vanity—that is, the person feels underappreciated here and is responding to greater blandishment. Or the offer is in a city with opportunities for the spouse. And so on. In other words, the offer may hinge on factors the dean did not expect or cannot counter.

Talking Candidly to the Faculty Member

Before talking, it is important to listen. The colleague should be allowed to lay out the issues, including what makes the other place attractive, and why she would be glad or reluctant to leave here. Then the dean can talk about how he sees the college, the department's near and medium prospects, and what role they can play in that situation. It will do little good in the short run and much harm in the long run to be other than candid. Vague suggestions of good things to come for the department or the individual will only increase expectations in the counteroffer and resentment when these benefits prove illusory. Moreover, persuading an individual to stay in a situation that will clearly not satisfy for long is a recipe for lasting bitterness and reduced value in the years ahead.

Importance of Negotiating

If the dean already has a counteroffer ready to lay out, the inevitable inference is that the issue was settled before even hearing the question. That will make the faculty member resent wasting time on pointless inquiries. Much better to set a time for a firm reply, also to be delivered in person, and to be followed the same day by a letter affirming the terms and asking for a response in no more than a week.

Avoiding Promotion or Tenure Packages

Quite possibly the external offer includes promotion in rank (or for assistant professors, the prospect of tenure). The pressure to respond in kind can be almost intolerable. But the dean should not discuss that issue, for a simple, practical reason: these decisions have to go through department and perhaps college faculty recommendation, not to mention the provost and the president. The dean could promise to push the promotion through, but cannot really deliver if others are averse, and even if such a private exception works, waiving or forcing the formal review process in any instance undermines its legitimacy. It is better to promise a prompt review through the usual channels, but explain that it is not possible to offer a full professorship simply because the other place is doing so. If the faculty member really is good, he or she will have confidence in that review and trust the dean to follow through. If that trust is not there, the dean has a problem anyway.

Retooling and Retirement

Nature abhors a vacuum. Faculty dread one. After tenure comes the free fall of a career with relatively few compulsions or restraints. For most faculty, advancement to tenure means the freedom to imagine projects and courses and roles that were too risky to contemplate as a probationary faculty member. For a few—and it is very important to emphasize that we are talking about a small minority—the shock of possessing a lifetime appointment that only the most remarkable offense can interrupt leads to a kind of paralysis. Because everything is possible, nothing is required.

Every dean has such faculty members. With any luck, they are spread sparsely across the college rather than concentrated in a few weak units. For the department, a few faculty stalled at midcareer are often less of a concern than the dean thinks they should be. In the department's eyes, they are long-term colleagues and friends, perhaps very good at advising students and teaching lower-level courses, and close friends.

What can the dean do with this underachieving group? They are tenured, and removal from tenure is—as it must be—difficult in the extreme. The most common response is to ignore the problem. The perpetual associate professor gets lower raises, in some cases no raise at all for years on end, and thus costs less, and possibly teaches an extra course and thus avoids the need for costlier achievers who will want to teach less for more money. Best just to let sleeping colleagues lie. In extreme cases, deans who can afford it have been known simply to work around them, in effect treat them as invisible and hire their replacements while waiting for them to retire. The costs include office space, salary, and benefits, and drooping morale among the colleagues who see incompetence being rewarded.

The problem is almost impossible to address with the resources of the department. Moreover, the dean has more to gain from a just resolution. The first step is to get a good census of cases, ranging from the moderate and recent to the long-term and severe. The second is to tailor short-range (two-year) opportunities that will encourage faculty to become more productive in teaching or research.

Here are two illustrations. One dean at a large research university took stock of the English department and noted that fully a third of the faculty were producing little or no scholarship, but that most of this group were still effective undergraduate teachers who claimed to have a project in the works—a book deriving from a twenty-year-old dissertation, in most cases. In consultation with the DEO, he offered as many as three faculty per year a semester's release from all teaching if they had a project that could reasonably be finished in that time. The release time would not count against the sabbatical clock, and so there was still the incentive of another leave if this one bore fruit. At the end of the leave, the DEO conferred with the faculty member. What got done? How did the colleague regard the prospects for reinvigorated scholarship? Might promotion be on the horizon with completion of the book after all? Remarkably, at least one person each year was reanimated for research and eventually ended twenty years of languishing in rank.

Another dean at a small college that is centered on teaching saw the problem differently. The problem faculty here were those who had lost their intensity in the classroom, in developing courses, and in advising students. This time, the dean went directly to the faculty in question and asked for their help. You are senior colleagues who once set the pace as teachers, she said, but clearly the past few years have brought changes both in how we do things and in how engaged you feel with your craft. I know you are good teachers, so how can your younger colleagues benefit from that talent? And how can I help? In most cases the faculty were grateful that the dean cared enough to make a personal effort. Each faculty member adopted a junior faculty as an apprentice, and in most cases revived their own love of teaching by mentoring another teacher. As a reward, each was given the opportunity to devise and teach a special course together with the apprentice. Everybody benefited from this solution, not least the younger faculty who saw what a caring administrator could achieve and what they could learn from a colleague they had probably dismissed as over the hill.

Sometimes we should simply accept the evidence of the past decade and work out a plan for early retirement. For every faculty member who vows to die at his desk, there is another who fears that that is indeed what lies ahead of him. Given the chance to gain control over his or her time rather than slog away at a job that long ago ceased to hold any interest, who would not at least talk about the options? Here again, although the chair is most likely to know who could or should consider a deal, the department does not have the resources but the dean does, and the retirement can be a chance also to draw the department into a discussion of new directions.

Among the possibilities that have worked (private schools have far more flexibility than public, but the latter have some special advantages in being backed by the state coffers and a huge retirement system) is to offer a very substantial increase to the full-time salary base that will also involve ramping down the appointment from full-time to half-time over a three-year period. This keeps the contributions to retirement flowing, lets the faculty member adjust to the lower income, and increases the amount of free time each year. After three years, most are delighted to have their freedom; they have done the necessary financial planning and are grateful to an institution they long thought exploitative. Another successful approach is for the faculty member to retire and begin to draw benefits while the college agrees to engage him or her back for at least one course per year for a fixed period (this is not to be done if the chief reason for inducing retirement is bad teaching!). In return, the college tops off the retirement benefits to the present salary figure for three years.

In systems where the retirement benefit is calculated on the average of the highest annual salary for three or four years, one can give imposing salary raises for three years to raise the average on which retirement is calculated in return for a written commitment to retire after the three years. The advantage of this tactic is that it is an investment in retirement, not a reward for being mediocre.

Every place has the impossibly hard case: a terrible teacher who does no research and is not interested in retiring. (One thinks of Dorothy Parker's comment on hearing of Calvin Coolidge's death: "How could they tell?") This is the faculty member who is not physically unhealthy so as to justify disability retirement and is likely to stay until death do you part. Our best advice in such a case is not to inflict damage on students or colleagues just to punish this one for refusing to leave. If absolutely necessary, the salary can be absorbed as a dead loss (if increases have been fair—near zero—over the length of the dormancy, it probably is not much more than an entry-level line anyway) and the individual's presence and fiscal impact reduced as much as possible. There will be resentment and low-level scuffling on such a situation in any case. At some point the need to move on with the growth of the department takes precedence over the relative discomfort this individual engenders.

Of course, if possible, it is far better to find a positive approach that preserves collegiality and dignity, reignites the spark that brought the faculty members into the profession, and yet acknowledges that the landscape has changed and they cannot claim to be full participants in the new version of the department. If the dean has any power of moral suasion, now is the time to exercise it. Coming full circle from the beneficial impact the dean can make with recruitment, the dean can ease the separation process that marks the end point of a faculty career.

Suggestions for Further Reading

Arreola, Raoul A. *Developing a Comprehensive Faculty Evaluation System* (2nd ed.). Bolton, Mass.: Anker, 2000.

Bérubé, Michael, and Cary Nelson (eds.). *Higher Education under Fire: Politics, Economics, and the Crisis of the Humanities.* New York: Routledge, 1995.

Boice, Robert. *The New Faculty Member: Supporting and Fostering Faculty Development.* San Francisco: Jossey-Bass, 1992.

Boyer, Ernest. *Scholarship Reconsidered: Priorities of the Professoriate.* Princeton, N.J.: Carnegie Foundation for the Advancement of Teaching, 1990.

Chafee, Ellen Earle, and William G. Tierney. *Collegiate Culture and Leadership Strategies.* New York: ACE/Macmillan, 1988.

Graham, Hugh Davis, and Nancy Diamond. *The Rise of American Research Universities: Elites and Challengers in the Postwar Era.* Baltimore: Johns Hopkins University Press, 1997.

Kaplan, Matthew (ed.). *To Improve the Academy. Resources for Faculty, Instructional, and Organizational Development.* Vol. 18. Bolton, Mass.: Anker, 2000.

Katz, Richard N., & Associates. *Dancing with the Devil: Information Technology and the New Competition in Higher Education.* San Francisco: Jossey-Bass, 1999.

Keller, George. *Academic Strategy: The Management Revolution in Higher Education.* Baltimore: Johns Hopkins University Press, 1983.

Krahenbuhl, Gary S., and Patrick M. McConeghy. "The Integration of Faculty Responsibilities and Institutional Needs." Paper presented to the annual meeting of the Council of Colleges of Arts and Sciences, Seattle, Nov. 1999.

Oblinger, Diana G., and Richard N. Katz (eds.). *Renewing Administration. Preparing Colleges and Universities for the 21st Century.* Bolton, Mass.: Anker, 1999.

Project on Faculty Appointments, Harvard Graduate School of Education. *Faculty Appointment Policy Archive* (CD). Bolton, Mass.: Anker, 1999.

Rosovsky, Henry, and Inge-Lise Ameer. "A Neglected Topic: Professional Conduct of College and University Teachers" (pp. 119–156). In William G. Bowen and Harold T. Shapiro (eds.), *Universities and Their Leadership.* Princeton, N.J.: Princeton University Press, 1998.

Scarborough, Elizabeth. "Retirement Arrangements for Faculty." In George Allan (ed.), *Resource Handbook for Academic Deans* (pp. 125–131). Washington, D.C.: American Conference of Academic Deans, 1999.

Smith, Holly M. "Getting and Keeping Good Department Chairs." Paper presented at the annual meeting of the Council of Colleges of Arts and Sciences, Seattle, Nov. 1999.

Trower, Cathy A. (ed.). *Policies on Faculty Appointment. Standard Practices and Unusual Arrangements.* Bolton, Mass.: Anker, 2000.

Watt, Stephen. "Faculty." In Cary Nelson and Stephen Watt (eds.), *Academic Keywords: A Devil's Dictionary for Higher Education* (pp. 132–152). New York: Routledge, 1999.

CHAPTER TEN

THE DEAN'S ROLE IN ACADEMIC PROGRAMS

The academic program stands at the heart of the college, the point where all the forces that create the modern academy converge—the recruiting of faculty, the admission of students, the construction and maintenance of a vast physical plant, the patient nurturing of library and other resources. Without it neither faculty nor students would have reason to gather, and the campus itself would have no reason to exist. In that sense at least, the academic program is the central concern of the dean; however, it is also the property of the faculty who design and teach it, and the dean who acts unilaterally on the academic program without the faculty's approval is playing with fire. What then does the dean have to do with the programs of the college?

Types of Programs

We should begin by noting the kinds of programs that a college provides. Although all individual courses are offered by some unit, whether a department or program, they may be pertinent to several units as components of various curricular structures.

Collegewide Requirements

The great majority of liberal arts colleges, and usually all undergraduate colleges that form part of a university campus, have some form of general education requirements (GER). Their purpose is to ensure that all students have some breadth in their preparation, regardless of their field of specialization. This approach really began as a way to preserve some of the generalist character of a nineteenth-century college education while accommodating the specialist approach that became the hallmark of twentieth-century American curricula.

The variety of designs for GER is staggering; a comparison of options across the country may well lead the casual observer—and does lead many frustrated students—to conclude that what these requirements have in common is a determination to make students jump through hoops and to sustain enrollments in certain departments. To be sure, the purposes are far more sensible than that, but both charges are understandable. Some plans have a broadly stated requirement, such as three courses each from the humanities, social sciences, and natural sciences; others are more controlled, requiring choice from a specified menu in each group or from more closely defined categories (Western civilization, international studies, quantitative reasoning). Other colleges, such as St. John's, offer a specially designed group of interdisciplinary courses, perhaps packaged as a freshman year experience. Usually, the general education segment of an arts and sciences curriculum accounts for the equivalent of three semesters of work, or about three-eighths of the total coursework. In colleges of business or engineering or agriculture, the proportion is usually less, often no more than one semester's equivalent.

Majors

The academic major, a staple of American college programs for more than a century, is the inverse of collegewide requirements: it is a formulation by a single academic unit of what a student must learn in order to claim some level of proficiency in a given field. This may well require courses offered by other departments (for instance, ancient history for a classics major), but such decisions are made in the major unit.

Furthermore, although most majors still have their home in departments that profess to teach a single discipline—psychology or mechanical engineering or art history—with some addition from elsewhere, each year brings more programs that do not represent the mission of any one unit but are an amalgam of faculty and courses from several units. Some of these have become disciplines on their own right (women's studies, for example) and have attained departmental status on many campuses.

But whatever unit hosts a major, it is a distinctive form of academic requirement, which instead of proceeding from shared assumptions about what all students should know or be equipped to learn, lays out what it takes to have a distinctive preparation. Not surprisingly, departments and programs zealously guard the right to formulate and modify any requirements for their major, but no department of the college lives in such total autonomy that its academic requirements are free of approval by a broader faculty group, usually the curriculum committee.

Minors

Although the major is a nearly universal feature of the undergraduate landscape, the minor is far less common. What would it take to know enough about French or economics to mention it as a particular feature of your studies, but not enough to lay claim to any expertise? To be, as it were, a friend, as distinct from a casual acquaintance or a close friend? The minor occupies a middle ground between the GER, which provides a brief encounter with many subjects, and the major, with its relatively massive commitment to a single field (often about the same amount of course work as all the GE requirements together). A typical minor involves about five or six semester courses, or about half as much as the major. The other distinctive feature of the minor is that it is usually an optional pursuit. Students *must* fulfill the GER, and have a major, and they *may* also have a minor. Like the major, it is a departmental responsibility, but the students are less integrated into the department and really "belong" elsewhere, in their major. In this way, the minor can feel like an extension of the GER rather than a trimmed-down major, and it is not uncommon to hear students lament that they seem to care more about their minor status than the department does.

Interdisciplinary Programs

Finally, as programs continue to proliferate and to reflect the explosive growth of interdisciplinary work, more and more programs cross college or school lines to incorporate elements from other parts of the campus. Environmental studies, for example, often involves work from agriculture, engineering, public health, or law as well as several units in arts and sciences. As with general education requirements, such programs can be difficult for faculty in any one college to establish or monitor, yet such cross-campus collaborations are vital to the health of the academic programs as a whole.

The Dean's Role

Accordingly, despite faculty "ownership" of the curriculum at both college and unit levels, the dean has an indispensable role to play in its development, welfare, and renewal, in at least four areas.

Matching the College Mission

In addition to the faculty's broad concern about what kinds of knowledge and skill each student needs (GER) and the individual departments' concern about what their own majors need to know, there is a third question: What is the range of programs that the college needs to offer in order to satisfy its mission? Can a college of arts and sciences do without serious offerings, including a major, in a central field like philosophy or physics? Must (or should) it add a program in environmental studies, if it currently does not have one, in order to be respectable? Does computer science belong in the college of engineering or in arts and sciences? Is the proposal for a new program in antarctic studies consistent with the mission of this school?

The dean, with the best advice of the curriculum committee and other faculty leadership, needs to consider what parts of the current array of programs are not suitable for continued support by the college—from the standpoint of fit with the college's mission and goals. Other obvious considerations, such as resources, also arise, but there is no point in fretting about finding money for something extraneous to the college's real purposes. And conversely, what fields now unrepresented are necessary for the college to have an appropriate span? The temptation here is always to add the latest hot subfield, usually at great expense, in hopes of being seen as a leader and attracting more strong students, but if this hot subfield does not fit with the college's core mission and is competing with central, established programs for resources, it will soon become an expensive distraction.

Quality Control

Faculty are proud of their chosen disciplines, departments take equal pride in their programs, and the institution has much to gain from a reputation for quality in all its operations. Strong, mature programs take the necessary steps to protect the excellence they worked so hard to establish, and the dean is wise to direct both fiscal and political support to those programs: vigorous public acknowledgment of their achievements, merit raises that reflect their work, some margin of added resources to protect high-quality honors classes, and so forth.

Yet quality often seems to be the victim of other considerations, not the least of which are fiscal. The dean juggles numerous considerations, and with all the goodwill in the world, maintaining the quality of academic programs across the board is extremely difficult. Departments are always under pressure to make the most of what they have—handling the largest feasible enrollments with their faculty and TAs and making the most efficient use of classroom space, labs, and of course their operating budgets, for example. Simultaneously and without any apparent sense of contradiction, the college is boasting about its commitment to small classes, accessible faculty, and all the other benefits that are starkly at odds with such a press for efficiency.

Understandably, the response from a beleaguered department may well be to increase class size, cut back on courses that do not draw enough students (even though the courses may be among the most creative and best taught), and assign as many sections as possible to adjuncts or teaching assistants. In language and literature departments with graduate programs, for example, it is rare for a regular faculty member to teach the introductory year of the languages; the same pattern appears in mathematics and elsewhere. In this setting, the graduate students cut their teeth as teachers, and if the department is responsible for a collegewide requirement, a captive audience of undergraduates takes the courses no matter how indifferently they are taught. There is an important gain in this arrangement, in the training of graduate students to be teachers as well as scholars, and many graduate students are very good teachers indeed. But a cold-blooded analysis of this practice across the country suggests the motivation is more to increase enrollments and handle courses economically than to work on neophyte teachers' skills.

The graduate program also faces the opposite risk: that it will fall disproportionately into the hands of a few of the most senior faculty as a prized entitlement that comes with advancing years. This can isolate the graduate students from the rest of the faculty, and some graduate seminars plod on year after year with yellowing notes from readings a decade old. To all appearances, the department is giving an impressive program with well-known scholars leading seminars in their specialty and with the advantages of small groups, whereas in fact the classes are small because they are out of date and dull, a refuge for faculty ill-suited to undergraduate teaching or large classes.

Conditions like these put the quality of an entire department's program at risk. The dean should work with the department chairs as a group to be sure that any serious threats to program quality are known and tackled by all concerned. Perhaps the problem comes from a lack of vigilance in faculty committees such as curriculum or academic standards. The dean must sit with that committee, and then have a series of discussions of standards in faculty meetings, to be sure that departments understand what is expected in course or program proposals. The review committees will be glad to do their task with rigor and care if they know they have the backing of the college in pursuit of quality at every level.

Perhaps courses are being assigned inappropriately in some departments, as described earlier. The dean can talk with the chair, and with the entire department if necessary, about the distribution of teaching and other roles over the whole department. The question can be cast as one of sharing the load rather than as an attack on the privilege of senior colleagues; a positive approach seeking improvement is far more likely to produce results than punitive measures such as withholding raises or replacement lines or graduate stipends.

Consistency of Practice

Departments and programs design their curricula more by reference to prevailing practice in the discipline elsewhere than by looking at what other disciplines do locally. The strictly sequential design of a chemistry major is rather different from the more loosely designed history curriculum, for example, where there is more choice and freer movement among options. Fields such as sociology are more likely than English to include an internship as a normal component of their students' training. This is perfectly sensible, because each department wants to reflect best practices in its own field. And when introducing a new field, the planners inevitably use models in that field from elsewhere.

The result of this externally oriented gaze is the constant risk that the programs across the college will be individually appropriate but too inconsistent from one to the next in their demands. A biochemistry major can add up to three-quarters of the total course work a student takes, and that in turn may make it almost impossible to complete all college requirements within the obligatory total credit hours. If internships carry very little academic credit but require huge amounts of time, they can put students at a disadvantage for keeping up the rest of their studies without sufficient compensatory credit on their transcripts. The college needs to ensure that the legitimate variations in how programs define their expectations do not skew the overall shape of the college program or put unreasonable demands on students as they juggle the GER, their major, and other academic activities.

Coordination with Other Schools

Finally, most universities are interested in programs that reach across college or school boundaries to create fresh combinations of faculty, students, or courses or lend distinctive strength to existing curricula. In nearly all universities, colleges depend on one another for courses to fulfill teacher education, mathematics, technical writing, and other requirements. Similarly, freestanding liberal arts colleges may be part of a consortium sharing courses and faculty. It falls to the dean to resolve problems when the business school, for instance, adopts new requirements for its students that the arts and sciences college must provide, or when the courses currently offered are not what the students from another college actually need.

One approach is to set up special sections reserved for students from other colleges or even aimed at them (Spanish for engineers or statistics for public health, for example) or to offer more frequently an existing course that is adopted as a requirement elsewhere. The dean of the college that benefits from this effort may be asked to contribute resources for the added staff, or the two colleges may strike an arrangement of putting up required courses for one another.

Individual colleges in a university usually enjoy considerable independence in defining their academic programs, and so establishing a program that involves the participation of faculty and students from more than one school will require careful (that is, lengthy!) planning and some concession of autonomy on both sides. The deans or their representatives need to be involved with the appropriate faculty committees or departmental agents in laying out ground rules for the establishment of programs and for making the necessary commitments of budgetary and other resources. Among the questions that must be addressed are these: Will there be special committees to propose and review program initiatives? In which school will the program be based, and how will each college monitor its progress and quality? What are the budgetary arrangements for funding both teaching and research in the program? Who is responsible for staffing the course, how will the admissions process work, and how many spaces will be reserved for students from each school? Will the regular curriculum committees of each college serve as the reviewing agency, or does this distinctive new program require a special review board? Extra effort and care in setting up the first few intercollege programs will pay good dividends in faculty confidence, student interest, and funding stability for similar efforts thereafter.

Reviewing Programs

Departments change constantly, not only in the composition of the faculty and the number and kind of students who populate their courses but in the currency and general health of their programs. One year a department has the right number of faculty, with suitable specialties for its program, good facilities, strong undergraduate enrollments, and excellent graduate students. Five years later, faculty turnover has meant the loss of a key expert for the graduate program and the firebrand instructor of the big undergraduate course that attracted so many majors, or even a cluster of retirements that has downgraded the department. Growing use of computers has taken over two faculty offices; students have migrated to other fields whose experts and firebrands are still here. The result is that though there have been no bad decisions, and everyone is still working hard, the department is far less healthy than it used to be. What can the dean do to anticipate and forestall such problems?

Regular periodic reviews of all departments and their curricula is a crucial tool for planning and maintenance or enhancement of the academic programs. Generally speaking, conditions in a department change persistently enough that the college should conduct a careful review of each unit every five years. More frequent scrutiny feels like harassment and does not give the department enough time to implement programs and recruit students to see whether the changes have paid off, whereas waiting longer than five years for reviews may cause problems to multiply.

The goals of the review are to identify strengths and weaknesses in the unit's operations, personnel, and programs. What has the department done to capitalize on opportunities that the last review identified, or to remedy deficiencies? What ambitions does it entertain, and are these consistent with its mission and with the college's plans? Is the faculty the right size for its offerings and student demand? Are its resources used wisely? Underlying all these questions is the health of the academic program.

The department wants to impress the college with its accomplishments, quality, and ambitions. The college wants to find out what the department really needs, how good it actually is, and how well it fits into the college's overall purposes. In short, the department wants to use the review as a club with which to pound on the dean until it gets what it sincerely believes it should have, whereas the dean hopes the process will be more like holding up a mirror to the department so it can see itself more clearly as others see it.

Reviews often have three phases, all equally crucial. First comes the department's self-study, in which it lays out its mission and goals, assesses its current situation, and raises issues that it believes require attention. Some deans prefer a very structured approach to this phase, providing a list of questions used for all departments so as to give a consistent frame of reference in assessing the reports. Others take a more flexible tack, simply giving general headings such as those listed here and asking the department to give its own shape to the issues that concern it.

The first approach does mean more consistency in the resulting report, and a better basis for comparison among units, but it may undercut the opportunity to hear about distinctive issues or genuinely creative ideas that do not fit the template. Conversely, the second allows the department's voice to come through clearly, and that opportunity for candor may tell the dean things that would never have come up otherwise. These things are often not very encouraging, but they can be important to know. One dean was startled to find in a self-study from his art department a blithe admission that the department had been using funds in an improper way for several years and the equally surprising statement that the group realized they did not have enough students to justify even their current size—but wanted three new lines anyway.

Phase two is the visit of the review team. Much anxiety attends the creation of a visiting committee. The faculty are obviously more familiar with persons elsewhere who can comment knowledgeably on their programs, but they have a vested interest in having those comments support their own concerns. For this reason, letting the department simply choose its own team is unwise. The faculty should recommend potential visitors, and as with proposed referees for promotion, note any connections each has had with the department (was once visiting professor here, was the dissertation director of Professor Rodriguez, is currently a collaborator with Professor Huang on funded research, hired two of our Ph.D.s in the past five years, and so on). The dean should not only review this list carefully but also make inquiry elsewhere—perhaps talk to fellow deans who are in the discipline under review or have distinguished departments in the field. The goal is not to set up an adversarial situation in which either the dean or the department "wins" but rather to encourage a candid conversation that will allow department and dean together to assess the department's capabilities.

Before the visit, the dean should not only send the visitors the self-study with any relevant data but also send both committee and department a set of specific questions based on that report, in order to take fullest advantage of the team's precious time on campus. This step reaffirms the self-study as the central statement in the process but lets the dean focus the conversation on the key issues.

The schedule of interviews is all-important. Again, the dean's office should manage this process in order to ensure that the visitors have a chance to see relevant people outside the department as well as the various groups in the unit (faculty, staff, graduate students, undergraduate majors). For example, if the department is in some kind of trouble, DEOs in neighboring units may be able to offer perceptive comments on the situation. Or, if the department or the dean hopes to open up new ventures with other units, the committee will need to assess those hopes from the perspective of the other party.

The visit begins and ends with interviews with the dean, who can lay out the issues and concerns at the start and hear individually from the committee members before they merge their ideas into a report. The sooner that report can be completed the better, not only to keep the details fresh in the committee's mind once they scatter to their own regular business but also to keep the conversation with the department alive and productive. If at all possible, the report should be completed within four weeks of the visit. Most institutions withhold payment of expenses and honoraria until the report is in hand. The report goes to the dean, who distributes it to the department—not to the department with a copy to the dean. Many deans tell committees that if they have observations on discreet issues unsuitable for a public document, such as advice directly to the dean on coping with a difficult faculty member, they should address them separately in a letter.

Phase three is the follow-up once the visitors' report has been distributed. The only error worse than not reviewing departments is reviewing them and then doing nothing with the results. Every department puts significant time and effort into this activity, and sees it as the best chance to tell the dean about its virtues and its problems. The faculty, staff, and students—especially the faculty—have also invested much pride and worry, and deserve to see something come of it. More importantly, questions have been asked and answers provided. If either the dean or the department hopes to effect any beneficial changes, there will be no better opportunity than this.

The dean should ask the department to respond in writing to the report in order to complete the conversation that began during the committee's visit. Then a meeting with the department allows all parties to pursue the implications of the recommendations. The dean is certainly not bound by those recommendations but in all fairness should take them into account in his or her decisions, and if they are eventually ignored at least indicate why.

Finally, the department and the dean settle on an agenda for dealing with the issues that emerged from the review, with responsibility assigned for the various tasks. The dean may agree, for instance, to begin a search for a new senior faculty member in anticipation of a key retirement. The department may agree to eliminate a weak area in the curriculum and use those resources to enhance its strengths. By an agreed date, the department reports on progress. The most important part of this activity again centers on the health of the academic program, and the dean does well to keep that in mind. This is not in the final analysis a competition for control of the department but a search for ways to improve what the department does.

Special Problems

Cross-departmental programs and study abroad programs present special problems.

Cross-Departmental Programs

Cross-departmental programs are increasingly a problem for colleges of all sorts and sizes. The college is still structured around disciplinary departments, because faculty lines, tenure homes, and most courses reside in them. So do most of the resources, from operating budgets to dedicated teaching space. As long as the academic programs—majors, minors, and GER—were also housed there, the challenge was to make appropriate allocations among these units. But nowadays, interdepartmental and interdisciplinary programs are steadily proliferating, reflecting the current realities of intellectual life. More and more, faculty live in departments but do their research and much of their teaching outside the boundaries of those units, building links to other fields and methodologies.

Of course, the academy has always pressed for new ways to organize itself and new fields to pursue. The most striking difference today is the extent to which individual scholars and emerging programs have challenged the constraints of the traditional disciplines and competed for the resources that drive the enterprise rather than find ways to work within the received framework. The very fact of these efforts underlines the need to maintain flexible arrangements in the college to allow the worthy to thrive. And indeed, interdisciplinary programs have succeeded remarkably in capturing faculty and student support, even as most institutions still vest faculty lines, tenure, and assignment of time with the departments. This means that programs must find accommodation with the departments to borrow faculty for all functions. Despite all the difficulties involved in prying faculty loose from departments, teaching may often be the least of the problems because a good fraction of a program's courses are cross-listed with a department, and with careful planning, it is usually possible to borrow a faculty member for one course here and there that originates in the program. A harder challenge is to capture faculty time and effort to do the rest of the program's business: advising, exams, supervision of dissertations, committee work, and governance. Work done for another unit carries little weight back home in the department, and so the choice often comes down to accepting an overload of these roles or declining to serve, which frustrates both faculty members and program directors. There can also be the issue of research funds to resolve. A neuroscience program, for example, may depend on faculty grants to support interdisciplinary research, yet the home department naturally feels a claim on the overhead recoveries, at least.

It is very hard for either the department or the program to solve such dilemmas. Only the college office can provide the resources, and negotiate the terms, for supporting both parties. For that reason, the dean needs to take careful stock of the number and character of nondepartmental programs in the college. Because interdisciplinary programs can shift their focus as they evolve, it is not always prudent to move part of a faculty member's appointment permanently to a program, although for some that will be appropriate. But a commitment of one-quarter or one-third time for as long as all parties agree to the arrangement gives stability and flexibility. This commitment must include teaching, related duties, and research expectations. Some deans have experimented with a chit system, in which the program is recognized as having a certain total claim on faculty effort, and departments can enter into agreements with the program confident of regaining lost resources from the college. This allows both short-term and longer-term arrangements and is not tied to a single person (for instance, the psychology department will provide one course for the neurobiology program, but in a given term it may be offered by any of several interested faculty). Some deans have approved faculty hires for the purpose of providing a specified amount of instruction, service, and research to an interdisciplinary program outside the hiring department.

It also rests with the dean to ensure that a faculty member's contributions outside the department are duly recognized in both salary increases and consideration for promotion. The home department cannot really assess (and may not really appreciate) work done elsewhere, but regular reports to the dean and department chair from program directors on all faculty who have contributed to those units allow the dean to form a more complete picture.

Study Abroad

Students compete fiercely to get into the college of their choice, and then two years later compete just as fiercely to get away from campus and go study elsewhere! Student demand for opportunities to study in another country grows every year, as study abroad has become a key feature in the undergraduate program of all kinds of colleges. Some smaller colleges have the ambitious goal of providing an international experience for most of their students. A study abroad program that is accessible to all who want it is among the most exciting and valuable assets of a college program, and one of the hardest to manage effectively. We will merely touch on three areas where close attention and hard decisions are necessary.

Costs. For the student, the cost of going abroad can be significantly higher than staying at home. The travel costs are a large addition to the budget, as are most aspects of the cost of living in a temporary arrangement abroad. Assuming tuition is at the same rate (which is not always true), the difference in cost to spend a semester in London instead of back home can easily be $5,000 or more. For students at a state university, that is a huge percentage increase; for those who are already going into even greater debt paying tuition at a private college or university, such a surcharge can put the whole opportunity out of reach. In short, study abroad risks being an opportunity only for the wealthy, and very few would favor that.

To be sure, students can take most forms of financial aid with them to study at an approved program abroad, but not all, and in any case their aid is not likely to increase nearly enough to cover the new figure. If financial aid comes out of the college budget, the college faces a potential problem. Suppose the student is enrolling in a program offered by another institution. Then the financial aid the college has provided is going to pay tuition elsewhere. Yet the costs of operating the college will be just as great, even though it has lost the tuition of the students abroad. If the overseas program belongs to the college, it encounters major costs to run it and the tuition students pay will be needed there. For instance, ten students who would have taken American history are away this term, but that merely means the class will be smaller, not canceled. The college pays the instructor just as much to teach forty students as fifty. Multiply that effect by the number of students abroad, and the problem becomes clear. The dean's office then faces two opposite tasks. It needs to compensate for a reduction in available tuition revenue, whether students are paying to attend another institution's programs or they are still paying tuition to their own college but the money is needed to operate an overseas enterprise. One approach is to admit more students than previously, factoring in the probable number who will be away in their junior year. Another is to be slightly more cautious in running on-campus courses that attract only minimal enrollments. The other side of the equation is to find the requisite dollars to support the activities abroad. It is very unlikely that tuition revenues alone will cover all aspects of the program, and some state legislatures have shown an odd aversion to state appropriations for programs whose purpose is to send students to study outside of the state. As to the financial impact on students, there is a great diversity of mechanisms employed by financial aid offices, and so much depends on the nature of the college and its programs (public or private, large or small, targeted on a few places or spread over many countries) that it would be fruitless to generalize on strategies. But the academic office and the financial aid program must work together to protect the interests of all concerned—faculty, students, and the institution.

Programs. How many study abroad programs can or should a college sustain? The answer depends on whether a program involves renting instructional premises or relies mainly on attending the university in the distant city. Is there a residential facility or are students billeted or renting flats of their own arranging? In any case, every program that places students and college personnel on-site is expensive, which puts a limit on the number any college can set up.

Yet it is impractical to have only one or two. This skews the students' choices, privileging a couple of cities and cultures over all the rest, and also, assuming anything like current levels of demand, means a very large and very expensive enterprise, with rentals, housing, instructional, and administrative costs. A college is more likely to have a few sites with its own personnel and premises, and otherwise enter into arrangements with other comparable institutions to share functions and costs.

Impact on Campus Activities. Sending large numbers of students abroad, especially if most are at the same stage (traditionally juniors), inevitably has an impact on the college's normal activities. We have already noted one effect—the loss of tuition revenue unless registration is run through the college's own in-house course structure. But if a third of the junior class is away, this takes its toll on enrollments in the middle range of courses, including many requirements for majors. In some cases, students will come back and pick up courses they missed, but not everything will be available whenever they want it, and if the courses are strictly sequential, this can result in a longer time to graduation. If not usual and predictable, it will distort the usual pattern of course demand, which in turn affects the assignment of onetime teaching resources from the dean.

In addition to students and dollars, one other precious resource goes away to these programs: faculty. Who will teach abroad? Because the faculty members who go will not only be teaching a different kind of course but probably also have some supervisory responsibility for students' personal welfare, both department and college want to send experienced faculty. This feels like an added strain on the department, almost like having another person go on sabbatical (and these individuals do not leave behind any salary for replacement). In some instances, participation in study abroad can be a form of reward for a faculty member's strong contributions and leadership. Conversely, it can sometimes mean encouraging the selection of faculty whose role is less central—or who contribute less—in order to give them an opportunity to contribute.

Alternatively, if we rely on faculty sent from another participating institution, how confident are we in their quality? Will they teach courses that correspond to our own and can count in our students' progress? What if the institution engages temporary or marginally qualified faculty? What if the instructors are hired locally, and however impressive their academic qualifications, they have problems communicating with the students? One alternative is to have an on-site director for the program who can exercise quality control over the academic functions that must be contracted out. In fact, there are many fine instructors in Paris, London, and elsewhere who make their living by teaching in American study-abroad programs. Working through other established programs, the director should have no problem locating such individuals and assessing their competence.

Finally, we should remember that, for example, a program in Spain will probably originate in the Spanish department and be largely shaped by that unit, including an emphasis on work suited to Spanish majors or minors (particularly language courses). Yet for such a program to succeed, it needs to draw students from all academic areas: art history, political science, not to mention students in utterly unrelated majors such as chemistry or accounting, who can profit equally well from exposure to international cultures. Some colleges have solved this dilemma by separating the language students into a special group taught in the language of the country.

All these questions underscore how difficult a puzzle the dean has to solve in study abroad. Nonetheless, we emphasize again its importance for the quality of education the students receive and for the impact a well-designed array of international study opportunities can have on student recruitment.

Maintaining the Curriculum

The two most significant issues here are working with the curriculum committee and revising the curriculum.

Working with the Curriculum Committee

Although the faculty design the curriculum, the dean is ultimately responsible for the majors, minors, graduate programs, certificate programs, and college requirements that are included in it. As suggested earlier, one key element of this responsibility is working with the curriculum committee to make sure that body is taking the concerns of the entire college into account and not simply reviewing individual proposals in isolation.

Often curriculum committees focus on proposals for new courses and programs but neglect to take a broader view of the college offerings or to revisit programs already on the books. Thus they may not know that a crucial course has not been offered for several years because its only teacher retired or that there is needless duplication in offerings—statistics courses are a common culprit from one department to the next.

Depending on the wisdom of its leadership, this committee may need the dean's guidance on questions to ask about proposals for new courses or even whole programs. What new resources will be required, or what will the department stop doing to make room for the new activity? What are current enrollments in majors and minors throughout the college, and how do these affect existing and proposed programs? How often are courses offered? Is it wise to approve a new minor if none of the instructors are tenure-track and may all be gone in three years?

The dean may have concerns not only about the soundness of the curriculum as a whole but also its currency. Many professional deans' organizations and publications are devoted to the state of the disciplines and can help the dean stay informed, as can materials from the disciplinary associations. One measure of a good DEO is her or his ability to brief the dean about such matters and to show whether the department is keeping up with the latest developments in the field.

A related issue is the adequacy of teaching staff for the curriculum. Where requirements are routinely waived because of insufficient course offerings, or students have virtually no choice of courses in a program because the offerings are so slim, the dean can recognize misalignment that requires either additional faculty or fewer programs. Faced with evidence of such problems, the dean should consult with the curriculum committee as well as the department in order to find the least disruptive and most broadly tolerable solutions.

Although enrollments may not be a traditional concern of the curriculum committee, deans also need to monitor student numbers and be sensitive to the demand for certain fields of study, and the committee can be helpful in assessing the situation as well as recommending remedies. For example, in recent years communication departments have been almost overwhelmed with students, to the point that they could be saddled with nearly half the majors in the college if there were no controls to prevent it. Psychology is likewise an extraordinarily popular choice, often well beyond the capacity of the faculty to teach and advise.

To handle the situation, many departments, with the concurrence of the dean, have put caps on the number of students admitted to their programs. Business schools have often needed to do the same, usually through a minimum GPA. Although this solution risks fostering resentment among the departments to which excluded students reluctantly migrate, it makes sense to protect a department from having to do its job inadequately under the press of numbers. Here too, the curriculum committee can help the dean, by weighing the impact of enrollment on other parts of the curriculum and by helping faculty, students, and even parents to see the problem in terms of the college as a whole, not the fortunes of a single unit. A department should not be encouraged to grow at the expense of the total offerings of the college and its intellectual coherence; that coherence is the responsibility of the curriculum committee.

Revising the Curriculum

We come now to the single most contentious issue in the college: revising the formal requirements for students to graduate. A common dictum is "deans may come and deans may go, but the faculty are a permanent reality." To this we add: "Faculty may stay for decades, but that only makes it harder to revise the academic reality they brought with them."

Why revise the curriculum? The answer, simply put, is because no department, no college, lives in a perfect world. Every department manages its major and other offerings not only based on the essential features that any major in the discipline must have but also based on the size and specialties of the faculty, over the long term as well as in a given year. Faculty turnover, changes in the discipline, and the addition of new courses and emphases gradually alter the shape of the department's offerings, yet the requirements for the major may not change for a decade or more. In addition to the major and the graduate program, the department also offers courses for general consumption, whether for GER or simply for the curious. These have a lower priority and are probably the first to suffer neglect or compromise under pressure.

Meanwhile, because this issue plays out slightly differently in each department, the college gradually finds itself with a curriculum that has fragmented into incoherence, particularly with regard to general education requirements. Indeed, the reasoning behind those requirements probably also needs reconsideration as the larger academic picture evolves. Periodic rethinking of the whole curriculum is absolutely essential to the health of the college, but it cannot be completed—in fact, it probably will not even start—without the dean's active encouragement and participation.

How often must a college undergo this painful process? Painful it most assuredly is, calling for the departments as units and the faculty as individuals to assess what they do well or not so well, what they can contribute, how important that contribution is (or seems) to the college as a whole, what enrollments or activities they are willing to concede to others, and in general to face not just their place in their discipline but their place in the college's mission. As with program reviews, the goal is not to identify winners and losers, though that is precisely how the results will strike most participants. If there is a process in place for ongoing review by a curriculum committee as we already suggested, distortions will not have a chance to grow severe, and the remedies will be commensurately easier. But even, or especially, with frequent fine-tuning of individual units, the common responsibility of the college, the GER, will be somewhat out of alignment in five years, limping seriously in eight, and decrepit after fifteen.

Odd as it may sound, revising the curriculum should not be a task that is simply assigned to the curriculum committee. That body already has a sizable role to play in the management of the programs and in offering advice to the dean. Besides, the systematic reconsideration of the college's curriculum as a whole is a major event; it will get more attention and greater participation if it is entrusted to a special committee. Some members should be elected by the faculty, others appointed by the dean after consultation with the executive committee, and there should be representation from the curriculum committee. Student participation in the discussions is also very important, although in the end, usually only faculty have a vote.

The charge to the committee must be a public document, widely discussed before the committee begins its work. If there is any impression, however erroneous, of secret agendas or special deals, the process is doomed. Likewise, the faculty should receive frequent progress reports. These need not be detailed or have any suggestion of finality, but they should keep the college community informed of the sorts of issues the committee is addressing, the principles on which it is proceeding, and what help it needs from colleagues and students.

If there is no time frame or deadline for resolving disputes, the process will be endless. It is not unlike the most fractious peace negotiations: unless all parties are convinced that there is nothing left to gain by further debate and delay, the debate and delay will continue. The dean should address this issue before the process starts, and have agreement on when the committee will file its report (not more than a year from the time they start work, although some task forces have taken up to five years!) and when the faculty should complete its debate and action on the report. After all, if the process starts after five years, and takes another five, the curriculum will be ten years old before people agree on how to begin modifying it—and modification will also take time. Without a firm hand in the dean's office, curricular reform can be a black hole of parochial dithering and acrimony.

Deans of smaller colleges may be responsible for general education requirements, a somewhat different task from deans of colleges in larger institutions. In particular, deans of liberal arts colleges may wish to develop or revise core curricula as a means to interest prospective students and parents who are looking for the "something special" offered by the institution. Another motive might be to link the newer technical programs to the original liberal arts focus of the institution. A good way for the dean to begin this type of undertaking is to form a broadly based, but reasonably sized, committee, as described earlier, work with them to develop a set of goals for the general education, and then provide descriptions of the programs offered at several comparable and well-respected institutions. If possible, a grant or gift to fund at least one aspect of the project should be secured and announced—such as faculty time, a pilot program, or instructional technology. This will help the dean with the essential task of generating faculty support for curricular change.

One last but important thought: the wise dean offers clarity about what resources are available for curricular revisions and assurances that those resources will be forthcoming once a plan is ready. Otherwise, neither the committee nor the general faculty can be confident in proposing changes, and departments will be very reluctant to put anything on the table that they might have to fund by cannibalizing present operations. Probably a good bit of the changes *will* come out of current practice, but clarity and commitment from the dean make it far easier to reach closure on this most difficult of faculty interactions. Revisions in general education normally do require new resources. Better to accept this inevitability and plan for it, if change is really necessary.

Suggestions for Further Reading

Astin, Alexander W. *What Matters in College: Four Critical Years Revisited.* San Francisco: Jossey-Bass, 1993.

Katz, Richard N., & Associates. *Dancing with the Devil: Information Technology and the New Competition in Higher Education.* San Francisco: Jossey-Bass, 1999.

Lunde, Joyce Povlacs. *Reshaping Curricula: Revitalization Programs at Three Land Grant Universities.* Bolton, Mass.: Anker, 1995.

Oblinger, Diana G., and Richard N. Katz (eds.). *Renewing Administration: Preparing Colleges and Universities for the 21st Century.* Bolton, Mass.: Anker, 1999.

Rudolph, Frederick. *The American College and University: A History.* New York: Knopf, 1962.

Rudolph, Frederick. *Curriculum: A History of the American Undergraduate Course of Study Since 1636.* San Francisco: Jossey-Bass, 1977.

CHAPTER ELEVEN

WORKING WITH STUDENTS

As academics we all know that students are our main reason for being in the profession, but in the flurry of budgetary and other resource concerns, tenure and promotion reviews, capital campaigns, and the many other tasks that occupy time and attention, a dean especially needs to remember the students. Most deans teach at least occasionally and stay connected through that experience. Others form student advisory groups to stay abreast of their concerns. Many colleges have an assistant or associate dean with specific responsibility for student academic affairs—a fine idea as long as the dean stays informed, and doing so should be a delightful part of the job.

Even on small campuses, many student issues fall to a separate dean of students who oversees extracurricular programming, housing, support services such as career counseling or placement, nonacademic disciplinary cases, and the like. Academic deans coordinate with these offices in areas involving joint programming, such as student-run radio and television stations, and work with certain student problems that, for example, require special academic arrangements.

Yet academic deans have their own set of student matters to address. This chapter will consider four important topics: the college dean's responsibilities to students, important student-related functions of the college, the kinds of student problems a dean should be prepared for, and what students can teach the dean. Involvement in the welfare of students differs enormously by the type and size of the college; our aim is to cover the basics that apply most broadly. We assume that discipline-specific issues will be addressed in other, more specialized, sources.

The Dean's Responsibility to Students

The dean's responsibility to students lies in four primary areas: curriculum, advising, quality of teaching, and technology.

Curriculum

The most succinct description of a dean's responsibilities to students is to offer them a good education—sound in the fundamentals, up to date, and tailored to their needs and goals. The heart of that enterprise is the curriculum, which we have taken up in more detail in the previous chapter. For our present purposes we may note that the curriculum is the meeting point between faculty and student effort in the one purpose that has brought both groups to campus. As steward of the college's mission, the dean needs to ensure that the academic programs designed and approved by the faculty are accessible to the students and provided in the most effective and responsible way possible. This includes issues from the quality of course content to the adequacy of teaching.

One of the trickiest issues is availability of courses. Students need to take specified courses for specified programs. The corollary of this truism—that we must therefore offer the courses we require them to take—is less simple than it sounds. In many large public universities, students find it very difficult to graduate in four or even five years, not because they have academic problems but rather because required courses are not offered frequently enough to handle the demand from majors, much less from other interested students. A dean from the California system said she thought it was now almost arithmetically impossible to graduate in less than ten semesters in most fields at the major campuses. Surges in student enrollment have corresponded with reductions in faculty, especially regular, senior faculty who teach upper-level major courses. The result is waiting lists for required courses. In disciplines with strictly sequenced prerequisites, missing a required course early in the sequence delays everything else. Although the problem may seem to be one of resources—it is cheaper to hire part-time or non-tenure-track instructors, but they do not do as much of the specialized work—for the students it is a form of academic deprivation. Students end up taking only a partial schedule, take far longer to graduate, and are on campus less each term, eroding both academic and social engagement in the life of the campus.

After the dean has worked with department chairs to deploy as much instructional power as the budget will permit, the next remedy may be to limit the number of majors in the program. Although this is not an attractive alternative, it is better than allowing students to pay tuition while being prohibited from making normal progress toward the degree.

Another remedy is to forge cross-registration agreements, or even formal consortia, with neighboring colleges. This may increase the range of courses that are formally available to students without increasing the size of your own faculty. Of course, if the exchange is lively, there will be more students from the other campuses, and those surges may not come where room exists to accommodate them. Conversely, it takes a lot of time and energy to travel to another campus two or three times a week to take a course, and a student's overall performance may suffer from the effort.

Advising

No matter how much thought and effort goes into the curriculum, however, no array of courses and programs helps the student without good advising. Students who have committed to a major and enjoy an active relationship with an adviser benefit in many ways from the relationship, the most obvious being better planning and course selection. Equally valuable, students who get good advising are much less likely to drop out when they run into problems.

The dean's role is to be an advocate for faculty advising, to encourage it, require it, recognize it, and reward it. Many colleges from all categories—large and small, private and public—have central advising offices for students who have not declared a major or need help in resolving special problems. Those who staff these centers, whether professional advisers or faculty members, can offer training and support to faculty in the departments. Without such an office, the issue of identifying advisers, training them, and keeping them up to date becomes more problematic. Each department should have a formal system for advising students. It need not be elaborate, especially in smaller departments with relatively few majors, but all who offer advising must be well-informed and available when needed. The DEO should be responsible for assessing the quality of advising in the department. The dean meanwhile can ask for documentation of advising in faculty evaluation reports, and even offer recognitions such as an annual college award for excellence in advising comparable to awards for teaching and scholarship.

Quality of Teaching

Students not only think it reasonable to be able to take the necessary courses but also have an equally strong conviction that the teaching in those courses should be good! We have already discussed teaching evaluation (Chapter Nine) as a component of faculty development. The dean's advocacy is equally important vis-à-vis students. Most faculty like to teach, and many are remarkable at it, but those with less commitment but just as much tenure can go along without suffering permanent damage. Students who endure indifferent or incompetent teaching may never get through college—and that is a high price for them to pay for other people's inadequacies on the job!

Ironically, everyone is on the same page but no one believes it. The students certainly want good teaching but are certain that most faculty are too busy to care about it; faculty agree it is necessary and for the most part work very hard at delivering high-quality instruction. Deans know how important teaching is from every angle, from intellectual responsibility to student satisfaction to faculty success to legislative and alumni support. But we have all seen faculty members roll their eyes when the dean starts pontificating on the importance of teaching—not because they think it is a trivial topic but because they believe the dean's commitment is purely rhetorical. If the college requires thorough evidence of quality, and acts on it, word will spread quickly through both student and faculty ranks that the standards are serious. For example, when students are asked to evaluate their course regularly, they get the message that the college cares about the quality of instruction. Similarly, when these evaluations and perhaps peer reviews are included in the faculty members' annual evaluation, they are likely to be concerned about the outcomes.

Of course, faculty are not the only people who teach students. At research universities with large graduate programs, a *very* significant fraction of all student credit hours comes from teaching assistants. In foreign language and mathematics, where TAs teach most or all of the basic courses for distributional requirements (such as the first two semesters of Spanish, or freshman calculus), TAs may account for teaching 65 percent of all enrollments. If a department is to take its teaching responsibilities seriously, these novice teachers must receive adequate training, ongoing supervision—and due recognition for some of the best teaching on the campus! If there are teaching awards for faculty on a campus (and there should be), there surely ought to be at least as many for graduate teaching assistants, who face more students with less protection than any faculty member. Finally, strong teachers bring almost as much distinction to a college as its leading researchers; when alumni contribute their opinions about the people who contributed to the success they now enjoy, it is not hard to guess which faculty the alumni remember.

Technology

We have already mentioned the resource issue in Chapter Eight, but should touch on instructional technology again from the perspective of the dean's responsibility to students. This is not a simple issue. Although a university or college assesses its facilities against its competitors, students assess them against the world in which they will be pursuing a career: in such a calculus, the college rarely comes off well. A college video facility will not have the level of equipment found in a network studio; so also with the graphic arts program and many others. For hands-on work with the latest technology, then, students will do better to find an internship in the commercial world. Accordingly, the dean must work with the department chair to define the level of technology appropriate to the educational goals of the program and then find the resources to attain that level. If the institution is located in a populous area, there are surely businesses ready to donate used equipment for the tax write-off, especially if it will be used to train their future employees. Here, professions of poverty are not only true but profitable. At the other end of the spectrum is the notion that technology capable of providing simulated experiments thus eliminates the need for hands-on labs. Simulations are indisputably wonderful tools with astonishing sophistication, but virtual dazzle cannot fully substitute for real work with microscopes and specimens.

One rule of thumb in setting priorities is to consider where the technology will help the greatest number of students; another is what level of competency is necessary for study in a given field. In some cases a consolidated facility can serve, for example, all the social sciences. In others, the presence of instructional technology may have depended on the entrepreneurial skills of the DEO, resulting in a less than rational distribution of these resources in the college. The dean's job is to evaluate and take control of the situation for the benefit of the students.

The Dean's Office and Students

Students come into contact with the dean's office at several key moments.

Recruitment

Most academic deans are responsible for recruiting new students, or at least for defining the target and standard of attracting the best students possible. For this, the dean needs to be knowledgeable about college programs, including admission requirements, majors and minors, special opportunities, and so on. It helps to be familiar with what is sent to prospective students. A new dean can ask colleagues about typical questions from prospective students and parents. If possible, the dean may take the campus tour offered to visitors. In smaller or more specialized colleges, the dean may also interview candidates for admission.

Because recruitment is a two-way process, the dean might examine recruitment materials critically and observe the performance of those who are interacting with candidates, whether admissions counselors, assistant and associate deans, or faculty members. Sometimes discussion veers too far into requirements and regulations, neglecting the aspects of the college that would be most attractive to applicants. Current students are peerless assessors of the effectiveness of recruitment activities; in fact, they can be the best recruiters of all.

Diversity

Deans generally look to enhance the diversity of their student bodies. In fact, part of a good education regardless of special field is learning to value people from ethnic, racial, economic, national, and regional backgrounds different from one's own. The dean should examine the profile of students, faculty, and staff and ask what differences would enhance diversity. As to students, the dean can communicate these thoughts to the campus admissions office, but there is work as well to do within the college. Word of mouth is enormously important in recruitment, so the dean can begin by assessing the experiences of students from diverse backgrounds during their years on campus. This can be done best through personal interaction—bringing together small groups of students or conducting exit interviews with graduating seniors. Because all parts of the community are linked, quite possibly the most important step is further diversifying faculty and staff (see Chapter Five).

Students and parents from minority backgrounds are rightly concerned about support systems to help with academic and social adjustment. If the college lacks adequate programs in this area, it falls to the dean to find a way to develop them. An important example is the National Science Foundation, which funds programs to enhance the education of disadvantaged students wishing to pursue careers in science and mathematics. Partners in business, industry, and state government are often willing to assist students in business, engineering, and teacher education. These funded programs normally include support groups, counselors, tutors, and social activities. Alumni from minority backgrounds can also provide advice and perhaps help in recruiting, and they may give support by returning to campus to talk with current students. In the end, listening is perhaps the most powerful action a dean can take, closely followed by a public commitment to enhance the diversity of the college in specific ways.

Remedial Facilities

Students at many institutions need support services to provide help with specific course problems and in some cases more broadly to catch up from weak preparation in high school. Because these needs often involve basic skills, arts and sciences colleges in particular underwrite assistance centers for the most common subjects: writing, mathematics, and foreign languages. Deans in other colleges are concerned about these services because their students need them as well. A new dean should visit these operations to develop a sense of their work and the kind of students they serve, and also consult with selected department chairs, faculty members, and students to determine their effectiveness. At times a new need may surface, such as a means to help students at all levels with statistical analysis. In short, the dean's responsibility is to ensure that appropriate academic support services are available to students, no matter where those services are housed in the institution.

Recognition of Student Achievement

Some colleges hold convocations in the fall to welcome new students to campus. These are festive occasions with faculty, dean, and president in academic regalia—new students are always impressed by their first sight of academic processions, however much they profess to downplay it! The dean presides and uses the occasion to begin a meaningful college presence in the students' world.

At the other end of the year there are the festivities of commencement, with many specialized activities swirling around the main ceremony: the academic honors ceremony for those who have distinguished themselves, honor society luncheons, parent receptions, fraternity and sorority gatherings. In many larger universities, the main stage commencement is so vast and impersonal that the colleges hold their own separate events in addition to the central official bestowing of degrees. The dean presides and makes remarks to wrap up the years of association with this graduating class. The program may also include recognition of distinguished alumni and valedictory speeches by outstanding students. The most powerful part of these "regional" events is that every graduate marches across the stage before classmates and parents, and receives his or her diploma personally from the dean. After a central ceremony in which hundreds or thousands of students rise together and are granted degrees en masse, this moment of personal recognition and photo op for proud parents is what they recall most vividly of their graduation. If time is a factor, it is better to scale back the speeches than skimp on the student parade!

A college honors ceremony for student leaders in various activities can be among the highlights of the year, recognizing both the students who have completed their work and those who succeed them on the newspaper, the student council, or other areas. The dean's presence and congratulations mean a lot to the students, and even more to parents.

Some deans seek donors to make special awards at these events—for example, to the most promising prelaw student entering the senior year—but recognitions need not be monetary. The most prestigious, Phi Beta Kappa, is purely honor and distinction. With a blend of dignity and relaxed humor, these occasions create an intimate atmosphere that parents and students alike appreciate. Faculty members are often reluctant participants in ceremonial occasions, especially if there is more than one event crammed into the weekend, but DEOs should serve as a press gang to secure the necessary troops (the honor can be passed around from year to year), and the troops often end up enjoying the celebration with students and parents.

Student Problems

The most challenging, but perhaps most compelling, part of the dean's interactions with students lies in problem solving. Five particular areas require our attention: academic appeals, requests for exceptions, and related matters; academic dishonesty; disabilities; free speech issues; and sexual harassment.

First, a general observation. When a student comes to the dean's office with a problem, he or she should find a welcoming atmosphere, even if the concern turns out to be one that the dean does not handle personally. It is actually better to have a staff member, preferably an associate dean, who handles academic problems and student concerns because experience and consistency are so vital to a fair hearing. In a college of any size the cumulative bulk of student academic problems can easily overwhelm the dean's already-busy calendar.

Academic Appeals

By the time an appeal of a grade or even dismissal from a program reaches the dean's office, the student has presumably tried without success in several lower venues, and so the case probably is not clearly in the student's favor. Yet an appeal merits full review, if for no other reason than to satisfy the student that the case has received thorough consideration. There are other good reasons, too, such as the possibility that the student has been treated unfairly along the way, the victim of negligence or worse from a faculty or staff member. For example, a faculty member who uses faulty evaluation procedures has quite probably given an inexact assessment of the student's performance, but the general problem of method can make specific charges of bias difficult to prove. In a more flagrant instance, a dean discovered that graduate students were being dismissed from an M.F.A. program solely on a vote of the faculty, which was taken without regard to grades, a violation of graduate school policy. Such problems as these may never surface without student appeals.

Every year, graduation time brings on a deluge of requests for exemptions from requirements or special substitutions for them. These requests can be very emotional, obviously, especially if a student with a problem has told his or her parents that all is well. It is easier to decide when there are circumstances beyond the student's control, but each case deserves review and action. Learning how students went astray can highlight problems in advising, irregular course offerings, or even the structure of degree programs (allowing students to progress, for example, without the prerequisite courses and then holding them accountable at the end).

Perhaps the most painful cases are those students who never were admitted to a major or program but managed to take and pass all of the courses required for the degree, or those who accumulated more than enough passing hours for graduation by taking the prerequisites for admission to several programs but never settled into a major and completed all requirements. This is at heart an advising problem, because the student should have had a faculty or college office adviser up to the point of picking a major, and then a departmental adviser after that. Still, it happens—especially in large colleges or even large departments—that students drift away from any supervision of their progress until it is too late. Perhaps what was needed was a more individualized program of study, not conforming to any one major but still academically responsible. Some colleges permit such individualized majors, approved by a faculty committee and the dean's office. But the student may simply be an academic castaway, whose dilemma points up the need to look for ways to tighten the registration and advising process.

At the risk of seeming cynical, deans and faculty learn quickly that a startling number of students give falsely optimistic accounts of academic problems to their parents. Thus deans are often confronted over the telephone, in person, or in writing by angry parents who know only what their children have told them. They have known their child all of his or her life, and are dead certain that this could not be that child's doing. Stupidity or malice on the part of the college are the only possible explanation for an issue that comes to light a week before graduation. No matter how personal the attacks, the dean must stay calm and pledge to look into the facts of the situation. She must be sure to get a waiver of confidentiality from the student before sharing the facts or even the outcome with the parents, and then report back as quickly as possible.

Sometimes this takes several iterations, and even then the parents remain dissatisfied. They would like to substitute their judgment for the decisions of those who run the program and in this highly emotional context they are likely to believe that whatever requirements are at issue are unreasonable. If after reviewing the matter, and bringing all of the parties together, the dean concludes that the student has been treated appropriately, it is important to sustain the academic requirements of the faculty. Of course, if the president becomes involved, the situation may be taken from the dean's hands, but it is always the dean's duty to defend appropriate faculty judgments.

Academic Dishonesty

The problem is not always one of omission, or one of accident. One of the most distressing activities on campus in which the dean's office gets involved is the pursuit and punishment of student academic dishonesty. Allegations of academic dishonesty often require several levels of review, possibly including the college. Virtually all institutions have disciplinary procedures that must be followed scrupulously; no worse academic fate can befall a student—not even flunking— than being found guilty of cheating or other academic misdemeanors, which can lead to expulsion.

At a minimum, the dean's role is to remind faculty of means to reduce cheating and of proper procedures should they encounter it. Especially by communicating through department chairs, the dean should ensure that faculty members are supported when they make charges and know that the institution will follow through with an investigation. In this area and a related one—students' violating academic policies and procedures—the dean must see that students are treated consistently and fairly, and that the intervention of parents, coaches, or even a trustee does not contaminate the process and excuse a violation. Having an experienced person on the staff keep tabs each semester on these types of cases, and brief the dean regularly, is one way to stay alert to potential problems and trends.

Disabilities and Illness

Because of a number of factors, including the Americans with Disabilities Act, an expanding range of diagnosable disorders, and an increasing willingness to acknowledge medical problems in this area, a rising number of students arrive with identifiable emotional or physical problems that affect their academic performance. They share a perception that faculty members are slow to accept these as a reason for special treatment. Fortunately, tests that diagnose learning disabilities are widespread now and have gradually formed an objective basis for establishing a student's right under law to accommodation. Faculty can and should be encouraged to accept the results. Most colleges now have a regular channel through which students can report a learning disability, consisting of a diagnosis from a physician and a statement of the kind of accommodation required (the exact form the accommodation takes will vary depending on the nature of the course), with the opportunity for further information from a professional if the faculty member needs it.

Some students arrive with emotional disorders, are on medication, and may need to be hospitalized during the term. Others require accommodation for a variety of physical disabilities. In addition to the obvious ones, students are prone to chronic fatigue syndrome, mononucleosis, Lyme disease, and other debilitating ailments. They are not necessarily being irresponsible when they say they lack the energy to complete their assignment or even contact the professor. The dean's role is to advocate for affected students and insist that they be treated with sensitivity and respect. Faculty members should be familiar with the services offered to students so that they can refer them to appropriate offices for help. Not all are medical. The female student who tells her teacher that she is being stalked by a former boyfriend and needs a safe place to live, for instance, likewise needs a proper referral. If the faculty member is unsure about a student's needs in a certain situation, he or she should know of an office to contact for advice. The more active and vocal the dean—in newsletters, through department chairs, in talks to faculty groups—the better equipped everyone will be to assist students with these types of problems.

Free Speech

Rare is the college on which issues of free speech never arise; some colleges face the issue regularly. Students in a variety of disciplines or organizations want to invite controversial speakers to campus, the school newspaper espouses an offensive viewpoint or crusades for a cause that creates widespread distress, a student art exhibition contains work that the artist intends to cause offense and is by most standards obscene. The trustees complain to the president, who contacts the dean. How do experienced deans handle these situations? First, it helps to have a sense of humor. Second, though it will do little good, those who are offended should be reminded that students have been doing these things from the beginning of time, and unless the activity in question infringes on the legal rights of others, the crisis of the moment will pass. Third and surely most important, punitive action violates freedom of expression, which is a constitutional right, and incidentally, what colleges are in business to foster. Last but not least, punitive action almost invariably makes the situation far worse. The offensive material gets more attention than its creators had hoped for and others, seeing the splash, join in. The best course for the dean caught at the microphone is to aver that the piece of work in question is not to her or his taste, but defend the right of the students to express themselves. The faculty members closest to these situations are usually concerned and quite experienced at handling them, but they know the limits of their ability to control students without creating larger problems. The dean should consult with them for relevant information, then stoutly defend freedom of expression.

This is not to say that students cannot learn from mistakes in this area. Many a student newspaper has been chagrined to learn that advertising has been accepted from a source whose ideas are hateful; many a paper has foolishly run a column by a sophomore who thinks it is clever to deride the disabled. In these kinds of situations, however, the most effective chastisement comes from fellow students who are offended and say so. Naturally, the dean should come out emphatically against hate messages of any sort in the college.

The Problem of Sexual Harassment

As we mentioned in earlier chapters, and will discuss more fully in Chapter Twelve, deans today need to be alert to the legal implications of their actions. Students have sued over such matters as poor advising, disciplinary penalties, and dismissal. These suits may involve the college, but more often they are aimed at the department or institution. But the student legal issue of greatest concern to academic deans seems to be sexual harassment, most often between instructors and students (which for the sake of simplicity is the assumption in this discussion). Most institutions provide information and seminars to the teaching staff on this issue, and it is probably treated in the faculty and student handbooks. In any case, we underscore the importance of working with the university counsel to understand the legal parameters of this most explosive issue. Our advice must necessarily yield to the local policies governing a particular institution—all the more reason to consult the university counsel.

Along with the authoritative voice of the university counsel, the dean's voice, presence, and commitment are important in addressing the problem, for example with special workshops for department chairs, communications to faculty and staff, and resources for advisers. The message is simple enough: sexual harassment will not be tolerated and will be investigated thoroughly and dealt with promptly (at many institutions it is grounds for dismissal).

Sad to say, there will still be enough complaints to occupy a distasteful chunk of the dean's time. Therefore the dean must become thoroughly familiar with the campus procedure for handling reports of sexual harassment. Information will come in a variety of ways. If department chairs are aware of such situations, they should inform the dean immediately, but the stories may also come to faculty advisers, the office of women's affairs, the dean of students, or possibly the academic dean's office directly. Because sexual harassment is a legal matter, it cannot be handled under the table. Upon learning of a problem, the dean has as a first duty to contact the institutional officer appointed to deal with these cases. This person will determine the best way to proceed while keeping the chief academic officer and the faculty union, if there is one, informed.

If there is a campus office specifically responsible for investigating sexual misconduct, the matter will be handled there with the dean available as needed. If not, much of the investigation and negotiation may fall to the dean. There are several principles to keep in mind. First, the offended party should put charges in writing, and must be assured of protection against any retaliation. Second, on submission of a complaint, the dean and department chair should meet with the student to ask questions and develop as full a picture as possible of the situation while taking careful notes. Many students wish to have a friend or parent with them at such meetings, and this should be allowed. At no time should the student feel that he or she is under the gun for making a complaint; instead, the object is to obtain sufficient information to determine whether sexual harassment (as defined by the law) seems to have occurred.

Once the dean has the student's version of events, the faculty member in question needs to come for a discussion. There are differences of opinion as to how much the accused person should be told about the subject of the meeting. It seems only fair to give notice of the matter, but doing so invites complications that may make it harder to get at the truth. A good rule of thumb is not to discuss even the nature of the agenda in a phone call, but simply to ask the person to come in on an urgent matter. If it becomes necessary to state the general topic (for instance, a student has filed a sexual harassment complaint against you, and the first step in these cases is to inform you of the charges for a response), provide no further details. Reassure the person that he or she will have adequate time to consider the complaint in detail after the initial meeting but that it is imperative to begin the discussion in person. Institutional procedures about bringing others to such meetings vary. Sometimes legal counsel is allowed, sometimes a faculty colleague of the person's choosing, sometimes a member of the faculty union. Normally a copy of the charges is given to the faculty member at this time, and he or she is asked to respond to them by a reasonable deadline.

Inevitably there will be significant disparities between the student's account and the faculty member's, leaving a need for additional evidence but also an extraordinarily delicate need for discretion. For example, if the student sought help from someone immediately after the incident, this is often taken as an indication that something upsetting did occur. The dean may want to see records of any other complaints that have been made against the faculty member or by the student against another person. Perhaps colleagues in the department have noticed unusual behavior by the faculty member or the student, and such information can help round out the picture, but every step of this path runs the risk of overstepping the faculty member's rights—or the student's. It is very important to check with legal counsel about which lines of inquiry are sanctioned and which are improper.

During this process the dean is drawn into a role of counselor to the student and parents, trying to keep things calm, and yet the charges have not been substantiated, and the faculty member may well be entirely innocent of the allegations. The dean needs to maintain as much distance as possible from accepting either version until the competent authority has reached its conclusions.

Among the most uncomfortable scenarios is the faculty member who acknowledges the events but does not understand the gravity of the situation. "If I had pursued her, and she objected, I would obviously have stopped, but she initiated it all." He may not accept the fact that pursuit by the student is no excuse for compromising behavior. And one of the most common responses is that the faculty member did not realize that he or she was making the student uncomfortable. Then, of course, there are the cases when both parties admit that they had a relationship that went sour, with differing accounts of how, why, and what then ensued.

In the end, if the allegations are sustained, the dean needs to answer these questions: What kind of harm has been done to the student? For example, has he or she been too uncomfortable to attend class or suffered other academic effects? Then, given the particulars of the harm, what is the appropriate remedy for the student? Perhaps to be put in another class, assigned to another adviser, or given an opportunity for late withdrawal? Finally, has the faculty member's behavior been deliberate, as in pursuing an inappropriate relationship, or has it been thoughtless, perhaps a misguided attempt to help a seemingly troubled student? Just as the remedy should fit the damage, so the punishment should fit the offense.

In many cases, however, it is easier to address the student's situation than the faculty member's. Many institutions reserve dismissal for the most egregious behavior, such as having an affair with a student under one's supervision, or in another power relationship, or repeated proven offenses. In these cases the faculty member may be encouraged to resign rather than undergo a formal hearing through the faculty judicial process.

For less serious offenses, such as bestowing social invitations, gifts, or other types of unwanted attention on a student, faculty members may be put on leave, paid or unpaid, and allowed to return only after completing a counseling program. Those who receive the lighter punishment, however, should be given notice in writing that another such complaint could lead to dismissal, and a copy of that letter should be kept sealed in the personnel file. This is very important because, as experienced deans know, harassers frequently are in denial about their behavior, and they may not *recall* having been warned. Full documentation of the event obviously should be kept, preferably in the dean's files and in those of the chief campus personnel officer.

Now for a very difficult follow-up question: How much information about an employee's history of sexual harassment can or should be shared with potential employers? There are issues of liability if a former employee commits the same type of offense at a new location and referees from the previous institution said nothing, even though the referees were aware of the problem. However, if cases are settled by the person's resignation, with no official determination of guilt, the dean's responsibility is clouded. Some legal opinion holds that whereas one cannot commit these matters to written statements, one can invite telephone calls for follow-up. During such calls, it is appropriate to indicate the general nature of the issue if the caller has gathered some details, and the dean can confirm or deny them without divulging additional information. The line between professional responsibility and protection of privacy is vague in these matters, so ultimately the dean uses judgment based on a sense of the seriousness of the situation and whether the offender seems to have learned from the mistake.

There are times when faculty colleagues will rush to the defense of someone who has been accused of sexual harassment, wanting to dismiss the behavior as trivial or protest that the punishment was unfair. These things can also reach the student newspaper. Deans should never discuss personnel matters, and that is the end of it. The dean can offer the supporters a hearing, but not a response. Without making the statement a comment on the present case, the dean's position is simply that no sexual harassment is tolerated in the college, period.

Learning from Students

In the schematic world of faculty and students, faculty are assumed to be the teachers and students the learners. In reality, both groups know well that this is not merely an oversimplification but is actually false. In the classroom and the lab, faculty continue to learn their subject anew through students' eyes and perceptions. Any faculty member who does not learn something in every course from students is not paying attention to the course!

Likewise, away from the classroom students can teach a dean much. They move through many of the same activities and contexts as faculty—classes, library, labs, advising, exams—but they see each from a different angle. Student course evaluations, for example, are notorious for their quirkiness, largely because the multiple choice questions on the evaluation sheet preclude more thoughtful comment. If, in contrast, a graduating senior is asked to talk with someone in general terms about the quality of teaching she has had, her reflections are often insightful, fair, and useful, not centered on how Professor So-and-So did in

Accounting 101, but on the strengths and weaknesses of teaching as this college practices its craft. Taken collectively, even a dozen conversations each year amount to a fascinating course for the dean on the current state of teaching. Certainly one can say the same about advising.

Less obvious is the importance of student observations on course development. Asking students to critique course or program design, said one insecure teacher, is like asking customers to vote on the ingredients in the entrees at a five-star restaurant. But, one might reply, if the ingredients are second-rate, the customers will vote with their feet anyway and you will never know what the problem was. In most colleges students sit (with or without vote) on standing committees such as curriculum, and their contributions there serve the place well. Individual faculty from individual departments see the overall academic program from a single location on the disciplinary map, whereas students must experience it as a whole. They know problems and possibilities that may escape faculty and deans alike.

One important way to profit from students' wisdom is to provide them with leadership opportunities, such as service on college committees and advisory councils. In many colleges there is a tradition of such opportunities, but students' participation often flags if they perceive their efforts gain neither attention nor regard, and their organizations likewise begin to atrophy. The dean can help to revitalize the situation by talking to student leaders and other groups to uncover the problems and determine a way forward. Students love to grapple with the urgent topics of the moment, and are also thinking ahead to careers. If the dean taps into these interests by asking the college council to survey students about their views on advising and to present their findings—and does something with those findings—participation may flourish again.

In short, the dean can learn much from students about their life in the college. They are usually ready to share their opinions and experiences if asked. They help us keep perspective on our daily round of duties, and even tickle our funny bones now and then. Many students today are juggling far more in their lives—jobs, parenthood, responsibility for parents and siblings—than we ever had to do when we were students. The wise dean appreciates their efforts and makes sure they are treated with the respect they deserve.

Suggestions for Further Reading

Astin, Alexander W. *What Matters in College: Four Critical Years Revisited.* San Francisco: Jossey-Bass, 1993.

Dziech, Billie Wright, and Michael W. Hawkins. *Sexual Harassment in Higher Education: Reflections and New Perspectives.* New York: Garland, 1998.

Higgerson, Mary Lou, and Susan S. Rehwaldt. *Complexities of Higher Education Administration: Case Studies and Issues.* Bolton, Mass.: Anker, 1993.

Kaplan, Matthew (ed.). *To Improve the Academy: Resources for Faculty, Instructional, and Organizational Development.* Vol. 18. Bolton, Mass.: Anker, 2000.

Kurtz, Mary Elizabeth (ed.). *Am I Liable? Faculty, Staff, and Institutional Liability in the College and University Setting.* Washington, D.C.: National Association of College and University Attorneys, 1989.

Kurtz, Mary Elizabeth (ed.)."Sexual Harassment: Suggested Policy and Procedures for Handling Complaints." *American Association of University Professors Policy Documents and Reports,* 1995.

CHAPTER TWELVE

LEGAL ISSUES AND OTHER SPECIAL CHALLENGES

Why do special sessions, workshops, and seminars on "Deans and the Law" fill to capacity no matter how many times they are offered? To those in the job, the answer is obvious, and to new deans, it quickly becomes so. Deans find themselves in potentially litigious situations almost routinely, and a certain number of lawsuits do come to pass. In this chapter we will look at how deans should prepare for this aspect of the position and handle complaints and grievances. We also look at the special challenges faced by women or members of underrepresented groups. In our view, these points all address the issue of professionalism on the job and the focus necessary to deal with some of the most trying situations.

Legal Issues

The dean's involvement in legal issues falls primarily into a few categories, including references in searches, faculty inequities, and termination.

The Dean's Responsibility

What do deans need to know about their campus legal counsel? Some institutions employ one or more attorneys to handle the bulk of their legal business, whereas others prefer to hire counsel as needed. All deans should know how these matters are handled, whom to inform of a potentially litigious situation, to what extent her or his actions are covered by institutional counsel, and when personal legal counsel is needed. Many deans purchase umbrella policies to extend their personal liability coverage beyond that offered through homeowners' policies. Doing so allows them to protect themselves where the institution may not (such coverage excludes criminal acts, however).

The dean's responsibilities regarding legal issues are crucial to the welfare of the college. Much depends on the campus situation, of course, but normally the dean has to know the essential laws affecting higher education to ensure that college policies and procedures comply with them as well as with institutional policies and procedures and to see that such procedures are carried out fully and fairly. Because many campus legal actions arise from breach of procedure, the dean should commit to memory the procedural requirements of key policies such as tenure and promotion review, grievances, sexual harassment, termination of staff and nontenured faculty, academic dishonesty, grade appeals, and so on. Normally this information is found in the faculty handbook and other compilations of institutional policies and procedures. Acting on any of these issues without a firm grasp of both the evidence and the procedures can be disastrous. Likewise, the dean must document thoroughly any involvement in such procedures, bearing in mind that anything in the files might eventually need to be defended in a courtroom. E-mail should be limited to correspondence about factual matters, and none of those private or sensitive. If fax machines are used, they should be secure in areas where only authorized employees may enter. Although it is not possible to protect oneself completely from lawsuits, with good habits the dean can prevent frivolous suits from succeeding. Acting in good faith consistently can help because it is usually not against the law to make an honest mistake.

Besides knowing important procedures inside and out, the dean also has the responsibility to know the law in certain key areas. Even those who have been department chairs will want to consult an up-to-date manual (such as Weeks, 1995) in which many of these legal matters are laid out in detail. If in doubt about any of them, the dean should seek help from the institution's counsel. The laws differ in their applicability to public and private institutions. Therefore, a dean who shifts from one type of institution to the other needs a briefing on the new legal environment.

As former faculty members, deans presumably know the basics of the Family Educational Rights and Privacy Act (known otherwise as the Buckley Amendment) but still may not be sure how this affects the college office. Whereas faculty advisers and certain members of the college staff are authorized to consult student academic records, this is only for specific purposes such as advising. Furthermore, because state laws also apply to the release of student transcripts, a dean who has changed locations should check those as well. Unfortunately, the dean cannot assume that college faculty and staff are abiding by these laws consistently, so that occasional checks and reminders, for example about posting grades only by numbers randomly assigned to students, can ward off potential problems.

Indeed, the larger role for the dean in legal issues is simply reminding colleagues of their relevance. For example, the dean's office is the first level of review for requests to search and interview for positions. These should be checked, among other things, for conformity to the campus affirmative action guidelines, and returned to the department chair when they do not. The dean does no one a favor by agreeing that such guidelines are too stringent or that the effort to locate a qualified minority candidate for a position is doomed to fail. Such procedures not only are mandated by law but also work to the benefit of the college, whether or not a search committee can appreciate that fact.

References in Searches

For senior appointments, one normally requests permission to make calls, but both callers and referees are understandably cautious about what can be said. All questions and answers must relate to job performance (Black and Gilson, 1988). Although one cannot directly ask whether the candidate has a reputation for shady or offensive behavior or worse, one can ask whether the referee would hire the candidate for a similar position and for the reasoning behind the answer. Moreover, the question of what it is proper to ask a candidate (and what *not* to ask) requires periodic review and updating. Both the department chairs and dean's staff need to work on this. To illustrate the sensitivity of the subject, one faculty candidate complained to the dean that, in asking what kind of housing he might be seeking, the department chair was trying to discover his sexual orientation! In short, questions aimed at personal information irrelevant to the job are forbidden. However, there are numerous questions that could be taken personally even if they are not so intended. To regulations and common sense, add an extra dose of caution.

Faculty Inequities

Deans also have the obligation to keep an eye on comparative salaries in each department and thereby to ensure that inequities are addressed if they appear. This requires reviewing salaries by rank, years of service, and gender before the budget is finalized each year. If the dean inherits an egregious case of salary inequity it make take more than one year to resolve the problem fully, but a good faith effort should be made and a plan to complete the process adopted at once. Individual appraisals should also be checked for bias. Some chairs, for example, assign a lower merit increase when a faculty member will be receiving a promotion increment. This is simply not fair as it effectively nullifies the promotion bonus.

We have already described the college's responsibility in promotion and tenure (see pages 163–166 in Chapter Nine): namely, to ensure that faculty members have benefited from appropriate and timely review according to procedures and that each department's process is in accord with institutional policy. This is not easy to do. Some department chairs, either out of laziness or to avoid a potentially contentious situation, report that the appropriate reviews have taken place when they have not. More than one dean has learned too late to ask for copies of all such reviews for the college files. Some departments ignore their own procedures when the candidate is someone they want, or do not want, to promote despite the evidence.

Likewise, departments have been known to plead ignorance of institutional procedures in their handling of tenure and promotion when they do not agree with the steps required. One departmental faculty committee and chair had *never* provided candidates with copies of their letters as the institutional procedure required. The violation probably would have gone undetected but for a rejected candidate who had made an oddly inadequate response to those letters on appeal. It turned out that he had never seen them. The department defended its actions on the grounds of past practice, which of course included willfully ignoring institutional regulations. Even an alert dean cannot catch every problem, but a good many will surface on careful scrutiny of the materials.

Termination of Employees

When a department chair wishes to terminate a staff member, he or she normally consults with the dean about the situation before taking action. This is the time to review proper termination procedures and consult with the campus personnel office. Especially with new chairs, the dean needs to stress the importance of following these steps and reporting any problems that occur along the way. Even though the department chair wishes to be rid of the person, the dean must insist that institutional policy be observed consistently—for reasons of fairness and compassion as well as legality. In any event, the dean must be careful to follow any relevant provisions of the Americans with Disabilities Act. If the issue is a substance abuse problem or mental illness, many institutions have a treatment option with the possibility of returning that must be offered prior to dismissal.

The Age Discrimination in Employment Act has also affected higher education by prohibiting a mandatory retirement age, and in many instances, placing the dean in the middle of negotiating retirement buyout packages. Last, the provisions of the various statements adopted by the American Association of University Professors on professional ethics, conflict of interest, academic freedom and artistic expression, sexual harassment, and procedural standards in faculty dismissal hearings require the dean's attention. Most faculty members have only a vague knowledge of these guidelines until problems occur. Assuming they are accepted on a given campus, the dean can encourage discussion and understanding of AAUP principles through dissemination to ward off trouble.

Grievances

Deans need both analytic and diplomatic skills to succeed as chief mediators, and teaching assignments are among the most likely sources of grievances that find their way to the dean's office.

Dean as Mediator

As the leader of the college, the dean plays the role of chief mediator, like it or not. In most instances the central administration expects the dean to resolve personnel problems. The most useful asset in this role is a clear process for handling complaints and grievances. Every institution should have such a process, but in our experience the procedures vary greatly. The route of appeal up the supervisory food chain may be detailed, but procedures for a fair hearing are less so. Obviously the college process must conform to the institution's provisions. Because the dean is often the first stop in an appeal, however, it pays to have a consistent way of handling disputes, especially when the institutional process is vague. Such matters as the maintenance of careful records, how the case is to be presented (in writing, orally, or both, and in what order), who is to come for a hearing, and whether informal resolution should be sought first all figure in the process.

If the dean has no professional experience with conflict resolution, he or she may find helpful the training sessions that are offered by higher education associations and legal organizations. A sense of fairness and empathy, however, can go a long way. The dean asks, "How would I feel if this had happened to me?" or "Was a personnel policy violated when a staff member was told that his appearance was unprofessional and he would be put on probation if he did not change?" We all know that such cases are usually not one-sided, so the dean's role is to try to understand what happened and to find a mutually satisfactory solution. It is probably more effective to propose a compromise separately to the conflicting parties, work out an agreement, and then bring them together to finalize the details. In disputes between a faculty member and department chair, which are the most common conflicts to reach the dean's office, sometimes the agreement goes so far as to move a faculty member to another department until a change occurs in the chair position. Shifting personnel, especially faculty, is a drastic way to solve a problem, but often by the time the dispute reaches the dean's office the relationship has deteriorated to the point that this is the only feasible action.

Teaching Assignments

Another common source of grievances is teaching assignments. These can arise for several reasons and take an amazing variety of forms. Generally speaking, faculty are quite accommodating about their teaching assignment, as long as they receive reasonable consideration for preferences. However, some faculty have very strong views on such specific issues as what time of day they should teach or in which classroom; others either insist on giving a favorite course (a graduate seminar on current research, an old chestnut that requires little time for preparation or updating, a course with the ideal size enrollment) or stoutly resist teaching courses that they regard as outside their special field or beneath their dignity. If the DEO does not give satisfaction, the problem boils over to the college office, where the term "academic freedom" almost inevitably comes up. By this time, no amount of explanation can convince the aggrieved faculty member that academic freedom is not about schedules or enrollments, or even about one's place in the departmental rotation. The dean should be extremely wary about leaping into these intradepartmental grievances, and to the extent possible back the DEO in managing the teaching program of the department.

A more subtle variation on the problem occurs when individuals try to make academic policy on their own by in effect creating a program in which they are the sole faculty member—making themselves indispensable for a set of personally designed courses and unavailable for other, less appealing assignments. The department as a whole, with the support of the college, must keep appropriate control over program development and avoid any such privateering. At bottom, the faculty must meet the requirements of the department rather than the other way around. One compromise solution is for the dean to support the provision of a special topics course, which allows the rogue faculty member to teach pet subjects on a controlled basis, while explicitly reaffirming the DEO's authority over all teaching assignments.

Sexual Harassment

We have saved sexual harassment cases for last because they embody aspects both of the law and conflict resolution. Some institutions have one person at the campus level assigned to deal with all sexual harassment cases, and fortunate is the dean who enjoys that arrangement. Others report that although the number of cases reaching the dean's office may be few, they are dreadful to resolve, and the aftereffects may linger as long as either party stays at the institution.

Unquestionably and emphatically, sexual harassment is illegal. It can take many forms, from an offensive work environment to unwanted advances to a request for sexual favors in exchange for advancement. Much less clear is precisely whether a given moment or act constitutes illegal behavior, and equally difficult is the fact that the harasser is not always aware of how his or her actions are perceived by the other party.

It bears repeating that whenever a sexual harassment complaint reaches the dean, he or she must take action, first to investigate and then to address the situation. We have discussed situations involving students (see Chapter Eleven). But besides that kind of incident, deans most frequently encounter inappropriate relationships between two faculty members or between an employee, faculty, or staff member and an immediate supervisor.

Workplace Romances

Workplace relationships seem always to carry the potential for trouble that, if it occurs, finds its way to the dean's office. The dean cannot and should not function as moral watchdog but might be alert to certain kinds of situations that often lead to problems. When faculty colleagues from different departments develop a consensual relationship, there is no a priori cause for objection. When the individuals are peers in the same department, there is again no cause for alarm, but if one is tenured and the other not, the situation has been touched by an implicit power differential. Though sensitive, it is still workable as long as the more senior member abstains from any deliberation or decision about the partner.

The problems, however, can arise and multiply quickly should the couple break up or the junior member inherit the enemies of the tenured partner. Most incendiary is a breakup when the senior member of the couple speaks ill of the junior one, who then alleges sexual harassment. The department chair is caught in the middle and the dean has to sort out the mess. Whether or not there is any finding of harassment, resolution may involve finding a way to protect the junior faculty member, perhaps with a tenure and promotion committee that includes appropriate faculty from outside the department. Assuming the charges are sustained, the senior faculty member should be reprimanded, with a warning about the possibility of termination proceedings should the harmful behavior continue.

Power Relationships

Relationships between supervisor and employee are inherently dangerous because they always involve the power relationship of assignment, evaluation, reward, and judgment. If the personal relationship is to continue, there must be some resolution to the supervisor-employee issue. One newly appointed department chair arrived on campus only to fall in love with a new assistant professor, and wondered why the dean forced him to step down when he acknowledged the relationship. This chair thought the dean could "work something out" because, in the department he had left, the chair was married to one of the faculty members. He did not understand that it is one matter for the dean to make arrangements in advance of appointing a chair, where the relationship is known and can be accommodated, and quite another to be presented with an untenable situation that fairly flaunts the new chair's bad judgment.

Colleagues usually notice an improper relationship long before it comes to the dean's attention. They often claim that the faculty member is showing favoritism toward the employee in the relationship. Thus the dean is obligated to intervene at the first report of an emerging problem, usually by calling in both parties individually to talk about the situation. The normal remedy is to change the employee's supervisor either by reassigning the employee or by relieving the supervisor in the relationship of that responsibility.

Even when there is no personal relationship, an employee can feel harassed when a supervisor or senior colleague is persistently or excessively critical and the cause seems to be gender-related. Sadly, this is one reason chairs are often reluctant to appoint junior faculty to positions requiring any decision making affecting senior faculty. When a senior member's overbearing behavior goes too far, it may lead to a sexual harassment complaint about the hostile work environment. Sexist behavior may not equate to sexual harassment, but the dean is likely to be confronted with a number of cases that present variations on this theme. In any case, the immediate goal is to put an end to the behavior. Sometimes talking to the offender and explaining the gravity of the actions will suffice, but threats of more serious steps may be necessary. A stern letter describing the unacceptable conduct, and the consequences if it does not cease, with copies to the department chair, the victim, and the offender's personnel file is one effective remedy.

Following Through on Actions

Such a letter must not be an idle threat. The dean must be ready to follow through with real action against repeat offenders. Every report tells us that many harassers are repeaters. Whether this reflects some inner urges beyond their control or callously deliberate behavior, once the dean has evidence of a pattern of misconduct, there is little choice but to begin dismissal hearings. The university may require that counseling be offered, but if the person does not believe there has been any wrong done, the counseling will be of little help. One dean reported sitting through a painful dismissal hearing for a tenured professor who had been the object of a series of proven complaints from female students over the years, only to hear the harasser observe that "it seemed as if the students were talking about someone else." That statement said it all.

Dealing with a Hostile Climate

Deans at many institutions, even some of the most prestigious, encounter faculty who resist bringing members of the opposite sex into their ranks and create a climate that works against the success of the newcomers. Women or men can find themselves assigned menial tasks, excluded from normal professional interactions with colleagues, criticized for minor problems that would normally be overlooked, assigned punitive teaching loads or schedules, or given unreasonable service assignments. Thus burdened, these struggling faculty members find themselves held to higher standards than others and given unfair evaluations.

The dean needs to be alert to departments with a gender imbalance in the faculty, to head off problems before they become acute, by paying close attention to written evaluations and other comments from the chair, having lunch with new faculty as a general practice, and getting a sense of the kind of reception they have experienced. Often a department chair does not realize the implications—of assigning a new female assistant professor to share an office with a non-tenure-track instructor on the grounds that there is no other female assistant professor available as officemate, for example—but the dean can explain the condescending signal that such an action sends.

In contrast, if there appears to be collusion between the chair and faculty to drive out certain individuals who, in their minds, "don't fit in," the dean needs to take more drastic steps, perhaps even installing a fair-minded colleague in the department as temporary chair, or if none is available in the department, from elsewhere, until the climate can be changed. Such a shift in behavior can take years but is absolutely essential for the survival of the department as a working unit. The dean's job is to see that departments do not persist in discriminatory behavior, which can in many circumstances fit the legal definition of sexual harassment through comments made or actions taken toward individual faculty members.

Dealing with Impediments

An extremely frustrating—but far from rare—experience is to know about instances of sexual harassment where the victims refuse to press the case. This situation occurs most often between students and faculty members, and apparently more so in cases involving homosexual advances. When victims will not or cannot report their experience, deans feel as if there is a ticking time bomb in the college that they are helpless to defuse. Although at most institutions formal proceedings cannot begin without a written complaint, the dean can talk with the faculty member about the accusations and explain that further such complaints will lead to dismissal proceedings. If the faculty member actually acknowledges the relationship but insists there is nothing amiss, it is appropriate to put the warning in writing so that a formal record of notification is on file.

No less frustrating for the dean are the department chair and faculty who defend an accused colleague in the face of irrefutable evidence, trying to excuse an improper relationship as a private matter between consenting adults. Many a dean has had to pursue cases under these circumstances, with the chair characterizing the proceedings as a witch hunt and the faculty doggedly attesting to their colleague's good character. As one dean put it, the dean must stand firm on matters of sexual harassment no matter how many enemies this creates among the faculty. It is the law. That simple fact is the best defense, and putting the faculty on notice to that effect is doing them a favor even if they do not immediately recognize it as such.

The Harassed Dean

And what if the dean is the target of sexual harassment? Female deans learn early on to develop a thick skin against slights of word and deed. If they took umbrage every time a male colleague called them "honey" or they were referred to as the "lady dean," they could never get on with the job. Women have to learn to distinguish between those people who are well-meaning but ignorant of how to deal with women in a dean's role and those who are truly sexist. A supply of humorous comebacks can ease these situations and get a key point across at the same time.

The bigger challenge comes when the dean is faced with sexist attitudes from further up the hierarchy: the provost or president, or a member of their staff.

Here much depends on the seriousness of the incidents. It is a real but manageable slight when the president shakes the hand of every dean except the one woman dean; she can step forward and extend her hand or let the incident pass, whichever makes her more comfortable, without much harm either way. It is another matter when—as has been reported—the provost repeatedly criticizes her, takes note of her appearance, style of briefcase, and choice of automobile, and states his preference for wives who stay at home. What about offensive touching by the president's executive assistant? When that kind of behavior, or worse, persists, the dean needs to tell someone about it. One dean who was treated in this manner recounted each incident after it happened to an associate dean, and both kept logs recording the events. Even if the dean feels helpless to initiate any action against the superior immediately, careful records of this type will be valuable when the time is right.

How does one decide it is time to act? Basically, when justice becomes as important as keeping the job. It helps to inquire whether others have received similar treatment, because if so, the case can be advanced more easily. The dean should take the evidence to the institution's chief personnel officer or the campus official with authority for sexual harassment cases for consultation about how to proceed.

We should stress that such cases are not limited to women. A male dean who is single, for example, may find himself the object of unwanted attention. One dean's professional life was made so untenable by a vindictive female vice president with whom he refused to have a relationship that he ended up leaving the job. His complaints to the provost were not taken seriously, and he continues to feel victimized by the experience. We suspect that, generally speaking, women are more sensitized to the issue of harassment than men and therefore quicker to lodge a complaint with the appropriate office. But given the impact of a hostile work environment on deans of both genders, men would do well to follow the same formal complaint procedures as women are advised to do.

Special Challenges for Women and Minority Deans

A dean's job is never an easy one, but here we wish to address those challenges faced in particular by women and minorities, as reflected in both personal reports and current literature. First, some general points. As individuals from underrepresented groups at the decanal level, both women and minorities face special scrutiny. They are all aware of this fact, and most realize that there is little to do about it directly. Perhaps the most useful response is to turn awareness of the scrutiny into an asset. That is, because the dean fully expects to be observed with special care, he or she can confound knee-jerk critics with especially careful and impressive performance, choosing opportunities that present the dean to best advantage. The dean should also maintain a professional demeanor whether or not he or she is comfortable in a given situation and thereby claim control of the situation. Of course, all deans can use these strategies but they are a special help to women and minorities, or any people who face undeserved critics.

Another shared challenge is dealing with lack of respect, which can take a number of forms. One dean noticed that whenever she talked with parents about the problems their students were having, the parents persisted in addressing her by her first name. She decided not to make an open issue of it, because she felt that doing so would make it harder to resolve the situation quickly, but communicated through her formal and businesslike tone that she was not on a first-name basis with them.

Similarly, women and minorities often find that parents, department chairs, and others to whom they must say no, often will not accept their decisions and insist on going to the next level. A useful response to this kind of accusatory statement is to encourage them to do so, with a simple comment that the dean will notify the superior that they are coming and will brief that person on the situation before they arrive so that the meeting can be more productive. Often disgruntled parties rethink their behavior in the interval and either change their tone dramatically or decide against pursuing the issue.

Because minority and female deans more often come from disciplines outside the sciences, this feeds an assumption that they cannot understand scientific, quantitative, and technical fields. These departments are still predominantly male, and whereas they may have a strong Asian representation, they are generally not accustomed to working with African Americans or Hispanic Americans. The proper response is that no dean knows the details of every field in the college. What any dean needs, as we have noted elsewhere, is the ability to gather and analyze relevant data for decision making. If a department is as good as it claims to be, it should be able to demonstrate that objectively in terms that a dean can understand—without reference to field, or gender, or ethnicity!

The big challenge for women, however, despite real improvement and much more rhetoric to the contrary, is that they usually report to a man. Male provosts frequently avoid a close working relationship with female deans partly because they are unused to relating as mentors to professional women, and partly, it seems, because they are afraid of appearances. They avoid the kind of frank feedback and advice that they are quite comfortable giving to men because they do not know how women will react. In the words of one woman, they simply will not meet you halfway.

In making this point, we are describing a problem that women often sense but cannot specify. A useful strategy is to ask the (male) provost to tell about his experiences dealing with certain issues or making career choices. This way the dean can learn how he thinks and perhaps pick up some useful tips as well. She might also ask how her performance compares to others with similar responsibilities or even inquire about his vision of an ideal dean.

In other words, by steering away from a personal reaction to her, it is possible to elicit much of the information she needs to know. Then the lack of a mentoring relationship diminishes in importance. When the dean reports to a woman, a direct mentoring relationship may be easier to establish, if for no other reason than that communication is likely to be easier, as Deborah Tannen's research suggests (Tannen, 1991, 1994). Whether or not this works to the dean's satisfaction, there may be other women at, say, the vice presidential level, who would be willing to talk about career issues from time to time.

An African American colleague points out that intensified expectations, both positive and negative, often greet the arrival of a new dean who is a woman or a person of color. Some in the campus community will feel pride at the selection, whereas others will feel besieged and fear that the new leader will be partisan. This colleague recommends that new deans in this situation be selective in making changes and exhibit scrupulous fairness in all of their dealings with people and programs. He also suggests mastering the governance procedures and traditions of the campus and using them "to promote excellence and to accomplish new horizons of fairness" (Pitts, 1999, p. 178). Friends and enemies alike may try to persuade and manipulate the dean, so he or she should listen to constituents with a healthy skepticism. This is good advice for all deans, but for those who are presumed to arrive with an agenda, it is crucial to success. The good news is that women and minorities are discussing these matters openly and addressing them forthrightly while laying a solid foundation for the future.

By now it may seem that the dean's job consists mainly of walking unprotected through legal and behavioral minefields. Certainly that is not the case. Our purpose in this chapter has been to highlight some of the less pleasant challenges that can arise on any campus. If deans take the time to educate themselves and their colleagues about the legal issues—and particularly about the resources available to address those issues—they will be able to solve problems more quickly and more effectively, and clearly announced policies will help keep crises to a minimum. This is an ongoing process, requiring considerable expenditure of both thought and effort, but definitely worth the investment. Of all the opportunities for leadership that a deanship faces, this is among the most demanding and important.

Suggestions for Further Reading

Abadie, H. Dale. "Dismissals, Non-Renewals, Terminations." In George Allan (ed.), *Resource Handbook for Academic Deans* (pp. 113–115). Washington, D.C.: American Conference of Academic Deans, 1999.

Black, Dennis R., and Matt Gilson. *Perspectives and Principles: A College Administrator's Guide to Staying Out of Court.* Madison, Wis.: Magna, 1988.

Dziech, Billie Wright, and Michael W. Hawkins. *Sexual Harassment in Higher Education: Reflections and New Perspectives.* New York: Garland, 1998.

Eames, Patricia, and Thomas P. Hustoles (eds.). *Legal Issues in Faculty Employment.* Washington, D.C.: National Association of College and University Attorneys, 1989.

Fitzgerald, L. *Sexual Harassment in Higher Education: Concepts and Issues.* Washington, D.C.: National Education Association, 1992.

Goonen, Norma R., and Rachel S. Blechman. *Higher Education Administration: A Guide to Legal, Ethical, and Practical Issues.* Westport, Conn.: Greenwood Press, 1999.

Gordon, Michael, and Shelby Keiser. *Accommodations in Higher Education under the Americans with Disabilities Act (ADA): A No-Nonsense Guide for Clinicians, Educators, Administrators, and Lawyers.* DeWitt, N.Y.: GSI Publications, 1998.

Kaplin, William A., and Barbara A. Lee. *The Law of Higher Education: A Comprehensive Guide to Legal Implications of Administrative Decision Making* (3rd ed.). San Francisco: Jossey-Bass, 1995.

Kurtz, Mary Elizabeth (ed.). "Sexual Harassment: Suggested Policy and Procedures for Handling Complaints." *American Association of University Professors Policy Documents and Reports,* 1995.

Mantel, Linda H. "Women Who Are Deans, Deans Who Are Women." In George Allan (ed.), *Resource Handbook for Academic Deans.* Washington, D.C.: American Conference of Academic Deans, 1999.

Nelson, Cary. "Sexual Harassment." In Cary Nelson and Stephen Watt (eds.), *Academic Keywords: A Devil's Dictionary for Higher Education* (pp. 232–257). New York: Routledge, 1999.

Olivas, Michael A. *The Law and Higher Education: Cases and Materials on Colleges in Court.* Durham, N.C.: Carolina Academic Press, 1997.

Pitts, James P. "Academic Deaning Despite Difference." In George Allan (ed.), *Resource Handbook for Academic Deans.* Washington, D.C.: American Conference of Academic Deans, 1999.

Riggs, Robert O., Patricia H. Murrell, and JoAnn C. Cutting (eds.). *Sexual Harassment in Higher Education: From Conflict to Community.* Washington, D.C.: ASHE-ERIC Higher Education Report No. 2, 1993.

Rossbacher, Lisa A. "Harassment." In George Allan (ed.), *Resource Handbook for Academic Deans.* Washington, D.C.: American Conference of Academic Deans, 1999.

Tannen, Deborah. *You Just Don't Understand: Women and Men in Conversation.* New York: Ballantine, 1991.

Tannen, Deborah. *Talking from 9 to 5: How Men's and Women's Conversational Styles Affect Who Gets Heard, Who Gets Credit, and What Gets Done at Work.* New York: Morrow, 1994.

Watkins, Bari. "Affirmative Action/Equal Opportunity." In George Allan (ed.), *Resource Handbook for Academic Deans* (pp. 109–112). Washington, D.C.: American Conference of Academic Deans, 1999.

Weeks, Kent M. *Complying with Federal Law: A Reference Manual for College Decision Makers.* Nashville, Tenn.: College Legal Information, 1995.

PART FOUR

BEYOND THE COLLEGE

CHAPTER THIRTEEN

THE PROVOST

A generation ago, in most freestanding colleges, the dean was also the chief academic officer of the institution, often with the added title of academic vice president or some variant. That person reported directly to the president and between them they managed the intellectual and fiscal fortunes of the college. That remains true in many small institutions, but for universities, and even for larger independent colleges, the enterprise is far too extensive and complex to use such a minimalist administrative approach. In most cases now, the chief academic officer (CAO) is the provost or academic vice president, on whom devolves responsibility for the whole academic mission and much else (see the following section). The title varies considerably, but the most common variations are vice president (or vice chancellor) for academic affairs, or provost. For simplicity's sake we will use provost, recognizing that the three designations are not quite identical.

There is no single professional relationship more important for the success or failure of the dean's efforts than the person to whom the dean reports. This is not merely because the provost is the dean's immediate administrative superior, important as that is. The provost is the dean's boss, or perhaps landlord: the college is a living space that in the last analysis belongs to the provost, and the dean is currently responsible for its upkeep and periodic renovation. Cause too much unwelcome noise, or let the property fall into disrepair, or fall behind in the payments, and the landlord may decide not to renew the lease. In contrast, if the property gains in public appeal and measurable value, then nobody is more pleased than the person upstairs.

The dean serves at the provost's pleasure, and although either dean or provost may decide that it is time for that pleasure to end, neither party should reach such a conclusion accidentally or erroneously. The more the dean understands what the provost does, and the clearer the lines of communication between them, the better the chances for a long and productive collaboration. It sounds axiomatic, but deans are constantly lamenting, "I had no idea the provost thought *that* was what we had agreed to!" or "My provost is such a smart person, I cannot believe she does not understand how a college works anymore. After all, she used to be a dean."

That last point is crucial: most provosts are former deans. This is the good news and the bad! Because the provost has served as dean, and presumably done so successfully (otherwise why is she now a provost?), she has a good understanding of how a college works, and that will be invaluable in taking problems, ideas, solutions, and ambitions to her. No need to translate academic ideas into administrative jargon, no need to explain the faculty and departmental ethos that informs the topic of the moment. All true. It is equally true for precisely the same reasons that the provost will be absolutely sure what is best for the college in these circumstances. The advice will be cast circumspectly ("Now, this is your college and you know it far better than I do, so you will obviously want to resolve it as you see fit, but if I may just offer a suggestion. . . . "), but the more important the issue, the more likely that the provost has faced just such a challenge before and handled it adroitly. The line between the roles of supervisor, colleague, and mentor is constantly being blurred with all the subtlety and irony that is the hallmark of academic discourse. In many ways, the hardest single feature of being a dean is learning to benefit from what the provost can offer in all three roles, and to avoid losing one's autonomy in converting administrative reporting into academic apprenticeship.

The Provost's Role

Although the provost is obviously a crucial figure in the life of the academy, from the perspective of most faculty members, even many department chairs, the provost is a quasi-mythical figure in a not very interesting myth. The provost is invoked as the cause and explanation of unpopular campus policies, as the reason for a failed promotion, and for other sources of discontent. The provost is also associated in the popular imagination with the disembodied and unappealing arcana of running an academic enterprise. In short, the provost is like a dean but even more remote and terrible.

These views have in common that they are incomplete and serve primarily to impose distance between the chief academic officer of the campus and the academic community for which he or she is responsible. Even worse, remote and ill-understood figures on an ill-drawn map tend to be depicted as ogres rather than angels or magicians, much less colleagues. On the academic great chain of being, the dean is the first to have frequent contact with this person, and so on a large campus faculty can pass a satisfying career without ever meeting the provost. That is a pity, because the ambitions, standards, and problems of all the academic units on campus meet in that office. A new dean, however, may be unsure about the scope of the provost's role.

That scope is very wide. In practical terms it is often wider, or at least more complex, than the president's. Often the president is so fully engaged with external activities that interpret the institution for the wider community—such as alumni relations, fundraising, or legislative relations—that the full scope of on-campus activities falls to the provost. Even more daunting, as the second officer of the university the provost will normally stand in for the president as scheduling or emergencies may demand. The provost may also speak for the president's office on campus, setting priorities and promoting policies that reflect the president's views and consequentially which may, in fact, seem inconsistent with previous actions from the provost's office.

The provost's central responsibility is as the chief academic officer, meaning that all academic programs report to that office. So also do all academic support units, such as the library and information technology, academic computing, and the university press, but there is much more. The provost normally also has responsibility for the campus budget, policies, and decisions about resources not only for academic programs but for the entire enterprise. This is a crucial fact for the dean to bear constantly in mind; the key notion, often overlooked precisely because it is so obvious, is that the provost must see the situation of each college or school from a campus perspective. It is no dismissal of the college's concerns to weigh them beside the needs of the other colleges, the library, the deferred maintenance on labs and classrooms, the financial aid office, and the hundred other imperatives that crowd the provost's world. It is to take them as seriously as they deserve. Thus, though any dean will inevitably see his or her college's priorities as paramount, all the others reporting to the provost likewise take the same view of their provinces.

Reporting to the Provost

Although the dean is accountable to the provost for all aspects of the college's welfare, there are specific areas in which that accountability is more tightly exercised, and others where the dean enjoys relative independence—unless and until there is cause for the provost to take a closer look and a keener interest.

Areas of Relatively Close Accountability

The few areas of close scrutiny by the provost include the budget, health of academic programs, faculty development, and the dean's overall performance.

Budget. Although faculty and dean alike will promptly and sincerely insist that the most important function of either party is the responsibility for academic programs, none of the dean's obligations is observed with greater care in the eyes of the central administration than the stewardship of the budget. This does not mean that the central administration consists of philistines but that the fiscal fabric of the university is the indispensable foundation of all activities, academic or otherwise.

The dean is truly the steward of the college's resources and should feel no hesitation or resentment in accounting for them to the provost. In universities with a mature college structure, where the campus has devolved responsibility for most resources—particularly faculty lines and instructional expenses—the deans like to believe, and some act as if they do believe, that the college budget is their own turf. In their view, neither faculty on the one hand nor provost on the other should know too much about it, because their only conceivable purpose in knowing must be to make the dean carry out bad decisions or to diminish the budget and therewith the college in general. In fact, of course, it is both appropriate and essential that the dean be able to elucidate the college budget for the provost with greater clarity, and in greater detail, than for the college faculty or the budget committee. After all, the budget comes from the provost after specific and exhaustive justifications, and he or she will actually want to know what became of those brilliant ideas!

And in a large array of institutions, including both freestanding colleges and even some research universities, the purse strings are kept so tightly in the provost's office that the deans cannot hold open faculty lines or even money for instructional surges in the college. Every shift in the budget requires not only permission from the provost but the money with which to make the change. In these circumstances, the provost's office expects very close accountability of all fiscal matters because the dean is really managing a piece of the provost's budget rather than a separate college budget.

Health of Academic Programs. The academic program lies at the heart of both jobs, dean and provost, and both officers naturally focus on its welfare. Not surprisingly, many deans report that this obvious area for cooperation is the primary source of friction. For the dean, it is the most important arena for making a difference in the mission and quality of the college, and it seems like the undisputed turf of the individual school; for the provost, the academic program is the unifying fact of the campus, and the schools or colleges are dependent on each other for everything from courses (for example, statistics for psychology, business, and epidemiology) to whole programs (general education requirements). More fundamentally, programs cost money and the provost is the arbiter of resources for competing academic aspirations. The issue is all the trickier because the curriculum is the property of the faculty, and the dean is steward of their intellectual decisions as much as of the fiscal resources received from the campus.

Given these parameters, the provost expects the dean to report promptly and in detail about plans for the college's academic programs. In fact, these topics come up in every regular meeting between the two officers. The provost almost certainly has wisdom to offer from years of experience and a unique perspective as the campus CAO, whereas the dean has the perfect opportunity to lay out his or her hopes and intentions, raise questions about resources (any ambitious innovation will also take new resources), and ask the provost's help in working with other deans across the campus.

Faculty Development. As deans reflect on their accomplishments, all hope to see contributions in several fields: curricular evolution, rising quality of students, expansion of research grants, fundraising, and facilities. None of these is as satisfying or as immediate as successful faculty recruitment. Shaping the population of the faculty not only has a decisive impact on the core purposes of the academy but gathers a community that may potentially work together (or at any rate side-by-side) for thirty or forty years. What is true of the dean is commensurately more applicable to the provost, and it should come as no surprise that the key phases of faculty development—recruitment and advancement—are of keen interest to the chief academic officer of the campus. All promotions are vetted by the provost, and on virtually all campuses, candidates for tenured positions will be interviewed by the provost (in most institutions, all finalists—even for junior positions—are interviewed by the provost or an associate). Surely then, the provost must know a great deal about the faculty.

In fact, the provost has much less direct contact with the general run of faculty with some exceptions, such as members of the senate or the campus advisory committee on promotions. This means the faculty he or she knows most about are probably atypical. On the one hand, they include the provost's advisory committee, which is often made up of exceptionally strong faculty with a broad understanding of the campus, and distinguished faculty to whom the provost turns for advice. On the other hand, they include such groups as the senate, which, if anecdotal evidence from all kinds of colleges means anything, tends to attract a disproportionate number of members who have gravitated to committee work over scholarship (obviously this is not true of senate members as a category!), and faculty who are appealing failed promotions or other concerns. In the view of a surprising number of deans, the provost has an oddly skewed perception of the interests and attitudes of the faculty. This in turn means that the dean needs to be well acquainted with the faculty in all its variety and concerns and must share those details with the provost as the two of them work to advance the quality, condition, and achievements of the faculty.

The Dean's Performance. No explanation is necessary for this item being on the provost's list of things to watch closely. Everyone else from faculty to parents to staff thinks, or at any rate talks, about the dean's performance all the time, so the one person who is responsible for assessing and rewarding that performance may reasonably be expected to note and appreciate what the dean is doing. The health of the college and eventually the campus depends on it. We will talk more about the uses and risks of the evaluation process later in this chapter when we discuss performance reviews (see pp. 241–243).

Areas of Relative Independence

Then there are the tasks vital to the health of the college, and creating its distinctive personality and habits, but not normally the object of interest outside the college—except of course when they go awry and produce a crisis, or go remarkably and produce a triumph. In such circumstances the provost is stirred perforce to cope or appreciate. The clearest example is the routine administration of the college, seldom noticed even by most of the faculty. Likewise faculty governance: in some colleges, chiefly the smaller, independent entities, faculty governance is a right exercised proudly and vigorously. In larger institutions, especially, it seems, in research universities, the faculty place such citizen roles at the bottom of the list of professional priorities. In any case, the traditions of a college's self-governance are usually regarded as its own. It would be a foolhardy provost who reached uninvited to tamper with faculty governance (and there is always the chance that the astonished provost would be the only person attending the meeting!).

The dean's relations with the departments and programs of the college and their mutual relations also should not be subject to casual intrusion by any force outside the college, even the provost. But the proud or ambitious unit that believes it is misunderstood or taken for granted may take its indignation to a higher court. On one campus, a mathematics department that believed its size entitled it to greater weight in the college, despite its mediocrity and sluggishness, went to the provost and complained that the dean was undermining the department's ability to provide sufficient general education courses for the campus. The real issue was that the dean had expressed his dissatisfaction with the department's research record and said the faculty were taking refuge in GE teaching obligations as a way to avoid their duty as scholars. What came to the provost was an allegation that the dean did not care about general education or quality of teaching, and did not understand the importance of science. Would he please reach in and ameliorate the dean's treatment of the college's largest and most important department? Fortunately, the provost understood the impulses behind the complaint and said he would refer their concerns to the dean. The latter called their bluff by offering to enhance the GE teaching capacity of the department in proportion to the increase in the faculty's scholarly productivity, the funds to come from the provost only if the dean requested them. The result was some gain on all fronts: an uptick in research effort, an infusion of skilled undergraduate teachers, and a reaffirmation of the relationship between provost and dean in internal affairs.

Establishing a Relationship with the Provost

In all probability, new deans work for the provost who recruited them, and this implies a certain level of confidence at the outset. The dean must set about justifying that confidence not so much by a flurry of impressive actions as by building a trusting, cordial working relationship with the CAO. Most issues demanding action are simply the current manifestation of long-term conditions, and it is the long term that will determine the health of the college as well as the value of the dean's leadership.

Of all the advice a dean might get, the least appealing is "arrange more meetings." Yet the only way to build a sure, steady relationship with the provost, based on knowing each other's judgment and circumstances, is to meet on a regular basis. The frequency and length of the meetings will vary according to the size and complexity of the college and the number of deans reporting to the provost; in the case of large colleges such as engineering or medicine or arts and sciences, the dean might aim for an hour at least every three weeks and more frequently as either party may request. Once the pattern is established, the meetings serve many purposes: regular updates on the general situation, conversation to head off impending problems, and evolution of planning as vague notions turn into ideas, schemes, plans, and proposals over several sessions. Some provosts prefer to have at least a sketch agenda for each session; others say that unless there is a pressing issue that dominates the day's conversation, an informal flow is best. Again, if the relationship is secure and open, the tone of the interaction will vary from supervisor to mentor to colleague, which is very beneficial for the dean and useful for the provost.

A new dean tends to take into these meetings a welter of detailed information about the college, as evidence of complete readiness and unlimited energy, but unless the provost asks to be overwhelmed with detail it is better to be prepared but show restraint. The provost is unlikely to want the full panoply of numbers and names in a discussion of ideas, and of course can always request the details as they become relevant. In fact, by turning a conversation with the provost into a scrutiny of minutiae the dean is almost conceding that the matter is not under his or her management, that any action depends on getting an explanation as well as permission from the provost. There will be times when that is wise, but it should certainly not be the norm if the provost is to have confidence in the dean's independence of judgment and leadership.

Still, as the new dean gets to know the college better and becomes immersed in its needs and priorities, it is hard to put into perspective the urgency of renovating the chemistry lab, hiring faculty for the gerontology program, or funding the humanities center or the environmental law program. The dean thinks that the merits of these cases are obvious, to the department as well as the college, and surely any sensible person will support them. So how difficult can it be to persuade the provost to approve these requests? Hard on the heels of this confidence comes its opposite. Everyone knows that resources are limited, and all the other deans will be pressing their own imperative projects. The provost will probably give theirs higher priority (large colleges are sure the provost already sees them as money pits, whereas small colleges are sure there will be nothing left after their larger rivals have their way). The moral of the story is not to underestimate the place one's college holds in the provost's view of the campus. Just as it is imprudent to take a request for granted, it is both self-defeating and impolitic to assume that the provost does not understand the college's needs or holds them in low regard. Defensiveness and aggression should be kept equally at arm's length.

Every administrative presentation is part of a narrative. What narrative will this college present in laying out its circumstances and its accomplishments, resources, and intentions? This is not a matter of fabricating data or arguments; any ordering of information draws the reader into a sequenced understanding of the questions, patterning even the pages of a budget into a story. That narrative should pick up on the college's story, which is already in progress. The issues that gave shape to the dean's interviews as a candidate with the provost and other officials probably indicate their basis for understanding the college. But in this process, the newcomer must be sure to avoid comparisons or contrasts with the last dean's accomplishments, style, relations with the central administration, or choice of issues. If the new dean's eagerness for new internships with prominent local businesses is interpreted as a criticism of the previous dean's inability to build good relations with those firms, rather than as a decision about present educational opportunities, then the college's new agenda will become entangled in a comparison of personal qualities. The new dean's plans are thus doomed to be seen as either unfinished business from the past or novelty for its own sake, rather than the next chapter in the stewardship of the college. Such a distinction is particularly tricky since the campus conversation will be rife with comparisons between the old dean and the new. The dean cannot prevent this imposition of a new mythology among the faculty and staff but can make sure it does not enter into his or her own discussions with the provost.

The Importance of Communication and Candor

Once the channels of communication are established, there is an unending flow of topics to keep track of for both provost and dean. How to sort these matters out in order to handle them with the provost? One dean at a small private college observed that she tended to sort issues in her own mind as "past, present, and future," referring not to the date a project reached completion but to the time frame in which it was most important. A report on open questions from the past year, the crisis of the moment, the planning process for two years down the line— whether dealing with faculty, budgets, students, or facilities, the temporal focus held together topics that emerged from the college in the same context. This, she reported, made it far easier to get the provost to see the larger picture through the eyes of the college rather than the lens of the campus.

In addition to organization, repetition and candor are indispensable features of the dialogue. The provost has many scattered concerns, and mentioning a subject only once—even in an elegant and detailed memo—rarely suffices. Unless the topic is an emergency, it will wait in the queue for the provost's attention, probably farmed out to an assistant for a preliminary look. At the next meeting the provost will have a hazy recollection of hearing about the topic but feel caught off-guard if pressed for details or a decision. This does not mean the provost does not care or is inattentive. On the contrary, repeating an inquiry without any sign of impatience or alarm is probably just what the provost is hoping for.

As for candor, the provost does not need to hear an issue laid out in deferential tones, with key but awkward features omitted because of misplaced delicacy. Any chair who has heard half a story from a faculty member and later felt deluded into the wrong answer can recognize the problem. The only feature of reporting more important than repeating it until it has been understood is to state it candidly from the beginning. The provost appreciates the time candor saves, and it is a reaffirmation of mutual trust. In any case, academics are accustomed to vigorous, even bruising debate, and tend to value bluntness as a form of collegiality. Provosts have not forgotten how faculty talk, and they have built their own habits of discourse from that experience. But oddly enough, deans are sometimes nervous about being really candid with the provost, lest they seem too casual and forward—or maybe not sufficiently corporate in demeanor. Not least, the dean may hope for candor in return and that will make life easier for all concerned!

In person or in writing? The protocol is changing rapidly now that e-mail is such a basic tool and combines the speed of direct speech with the permanence of written documents. Obviously, significant documents such as annual plans and reports, personnel recommendations, and the like will always be presented in hard copy, but virtually all routine communication now goes via e-mail. Is a message an ephemeral contact like a phone call or a durable record like a letter? Does the provost think of e-mail as a variant on the phone or the mail service? The dean's views on this are less important than the provost's, so it is a good idea to find out at the outset. A good rule is that if there is likely to be any reason to refer back to a communication, e-mail creates a record for clarity, protection, and ease of reference—and also saves time at the next meeting. A concomitant effect on both deans and provosts, however, is that they are getting far harder to see in person just because business can be done more efficiently and quickly through an exchange of messages. As a result, faculty complaints about inaccessible deans are on the rise, whereas deans lament that they are actually *more* accessible because faculty do not have to wait for a convenient time to meet—the e-mail system is open twenty-four hours a day!

Even with the best of intentions on every side, communications with the provost can break down, sometimes with alarming effects. It hardly matters whether the provost has explained his or her wishes poorly or the dean misheard, or the reverse. A dean who is suddenly the object of a provost's displeasure quickly learns the full meaning of the phrase "serves at the pleasure of the provost." The dean can do no more than clarify, without rancor or defensiveness, the facts of the situation. Posturing and threats to resign are the worst possible tactic (next to overtly accusing the provost of bad faith). If the relationship between dean and provost is solid, the storm will pass and there may even be some further gain in mutual regard. If not, then the dean's days in office are numbered and won't be extended by either truculence or subservience. If, in the worst case, the dean finds that the provost is not trustworthy or honorable, then the breakdown of interaction may turn out to be the ideal opportunity for the dean to depart with integrity intact and the full support of the faculty.

Performance Reviews

Everyone acknowledges the value of performance review, although almost everyone believes this is another case where it is better to give than to receive. Yet there is no substitute for clear, substantive comments from those to whom you report, reflecting on how you have done your work, both in general terms and with reference to particular expectations or ambitions.

Regular and Accurate Evaluation

If performance reviews occur at a regular time each year, they become part of the rhythm of the year and detached from any particular crisis, achievement, or problem. Because the year is otherwise filled with irregularly spaced surprises, an oasis of planned reflection has several beneficial effects.

First, the review allows the provost to acknowledge the dean's role in what has gone well. This is not the same as expecting flattering praise for everything that has not gone amiss. Much of the year's activities consist simply of meeting one's established responsibilities, and the provost has every right to expect a record of solid, timely performance of those duties. Nonetheless, because the ideal of these achievements is precisely that they be accomplished without flourish, they tend to pass unremarked, and although it would be absurd to look for constant comment on routine matters, everyone appreciates some explicit acknowledgment of a job well done, even when it is a well-established and familiar job. This may seem an obvious point, but it is astonishing how many deans report that they get no comment from their provost except when things go awry.

Even the more impressive achievements of a year may draw no reaction. The solicitation of a major gift, for instance, is a gradual process. Until the gift is confirmed, it is a work in progress and hardly a matter for premature congratulations. A personnel problem—perhaps a difficult promotion case, a delicate early retirement arrangement, or a staff grievance—can feel like an administrative root canal until it is finally closed. In the meanwhile, appreciation for what has not yet worked out is rare, and the flow of formal reports likewise offers no appropriate channel for recognition of what has gone into the establishment of a program, the hard-won approval of a plan, or the securing of a gift.

Conversely, a substantive annual review allows the provost to raise concerns about any specific action, not as a cry of alarm in the heat or aftermath of a crisis, or as a confrontation over the solution to an active issue, but rather in the context of the dean's overall performance. In this way the provost can address smaller, individual concerns before they begin to pile up and seem part of a cluster or even a pattern of troubling decisions, a source of serious worry or disenchantment, and eventually grounds for changing deans.

Understanding the Annual Review

At the same time, it is important to understand the limitations of an annual review. Although the dean serves at the pleasure of the provost and the president, appointment is normally for a specified term, most commonly five years culminating in an overall review of that period. But each individual year brings successes and frustrations, and the agendas of all concerned will surely be different in the first year when a newly appointed dean is making initial assessments of the college and in the fifth year when he or she will be expected to have made important progress on well-developed plans. An annual review focuses on the record over the past twelve months, even though both parties will inevitably fold that period of months into an evolving assessment of the total record.

Precisely because academic administration is such an odd blend of the routine and the startling, it is hard to tell what longer-term significance an annual review has. There is a temptation to assign a very positive review in a given year more value than it has in the long run. A good rule of thumb is to be far more skeptical about an unqualified encomium (if it ever happens!) than about a stern critique. The praise may be genuine and deserved, yet very local in its significance. It may not reflect the provost's overall assessment, and to read it as the new baseline will only make the next, more severe critique feel cruel and unfair.

Conversely, a review with strong critical elements can feel like the prelude to removal. Again, it is better to probe the issues to see how fully or fairly the criticisms are counterbalanced in the provost's mind by recognition of achievements or at the least by any explanatory factors. If the issue is specific—for example, a program initiative that has foundered or a proposal that draws sharp comment—then the review can turn to ways to make more satisfactory progress in that area, without either dean or provost seeing the one issue as emblematic of overall performance.

Written Evaluation and Follow-Up

All the reasons that make regular performance evaluation important also make it imperative to get a written version of the final assessment. The provost and the dean will remember the conversation differently no matter how clear and intense it was at the time. Assuming the review identified specific concerns, or produced commitments in either direction to correct problems, those agreements are a part of the college's prospects as well as a record of the dean's evaluation. If for any reason the dean does not continue in office until the commitments are carried through to completion, both offices need to have an unambiguous record of what was agreed to. Conversely, if the evaluation is strong, the dean will not only want, but is entitled, to have the provost's approbation set down as a formal comment on the year's progress, and all the more so after a full-dress fifth-year review that serves to justify renewal or nonrenewal.

Yet it is a distressing fact that most annual reviews lead to nothing more than a formulaic letter of thanks (used for all deans who will continue in office) and next year's salary figure. Indeed, even the periodic full review is sometimes a secret affair, with no appointed faculty committee and no specific comments to the dean at the end. Being a dean is not a permanent condition and can end in various ways (see further in Chapter Sixteen), from resumption of full-time faculty status to another deanship, a provostship, or retirement. If the only written evaluation from the provost made available to the dean is a letter that ends the appointment, it is likely to be a puzzle as well as a disappointment—to the dean and probably to the faculty. None of this is necessarily the result of malice, but may simply arise, especially in private institutions, from old habits of discretion and informal management styles. Accordingly, the dean should explicitly ask the provost for written annual comment both on the current year's performance and with reference to issues raised in earlier reviews.

In return, the provost has every right to expect action from the dean on the concerns that surfaced in the review process. They are now on record, and the provost's letter ought to have laid out his or her expectations and a timetable for making progress in meeting them. Both parties can then continue the candid and productive interaction that is the sine qua non of a dean's relationship with the chief academic officer.

Suggestions for Further Reading

Birnbaum, Robert. *How Academic Leadership Works.* San Francisco: Jossey-Bass, 1992.
Bowen, William G., and Harold T. Shapiro (eds.). *Universities and Their Leadership.* Princeton, N.J.: Princeton University Press, 1998.

Hoekema, David. "Evaluating Deans." In George Allan (ed.), *Resource Handbook for Academic Deans* (pp. 25–30). Washington, D.C.: American Conference of Academic Deans, 1999.

Keeton, Morris. *Shared Authority on Campus.* Washington, D.C.: American Association for Higher Education, 1971.

Martin, James, James E. Samels, and Associates. *First Among Equals: The Role of the Chief Academic Officer.* Baltimore: Johns Hopkins University Press, 1997.

Readings, Bill. *The University in Ruins.* Cambridge, Mass.: Harvard University Press, 1996.

CHAPTER FOURTEEN

OTHER DEANS AND DIRECTORS

All deans are faculty members, and glad of it. Most faculty members are not deans, and even more glad of that. Thus, even though deans and faculty are not different life forms, there is an undeniable, sometimes uncomfortable gap between them.

For the faculty at large, this gap simply reflects puzzlement that the dean has taken on an alien role, as a full-time administrator, doing things that most others do not want to do, and because of the strangeness of those functions, do not value terribly highly. The common reaction (*sometimes* mercifully unspoken) is: "I suppose we need to have a dean, but I am sure glad I do not have to do it. What would make a successful academic, a good faculty member, go off and do something like that? Must be the money, or maybe he is just burned out academically."

If the dean comes from the outside, he or she has no history with the faculty as a colleague, and is known only as the hired administrator. Over time, that sense of academic strangeness diminishes but never goes away entirely as long as the dean is in office. Being in charge (how wonderfully ironic that sounds to a dean's ear!) of the college is always a faintly adversarial relationship that no amount of teaching, scholarship, bonhomie, or familiarity overcomes.

All the more so in the dean's own department. Here is the focal point of any faculty member's institutional identity, with college membership usually a distant second. Thus the dean is technically a member of a department, and perhaps a highly valued scholar-teacher, but insofar as one is dean, one is of reduced value to one's own disciplinary colleagues, the very ones who know how much better it would be to have the prodigal child home working in their own fields. The feeling of deprivation (or neglect) shrinks when deans teach in their home departments on a regular basis, even one course a year, or at least participate in seminars and other incidental activities. Most departments, too, take a secret pride that the academic leader of the college is from their own tribe. If a dean stays in the college after stepping down, the department, welcoming and accommodating, is often a wonderful home in which to resume normal faculty life.

That pride of connection, however, is frequently tested as the dean tries very hard to be objective, without favoritism toward the home department. A common lament in the department runs along these lines: "She is a very fair person, and I know she is trying to be balanced, but she bends over backwards and we end up with less than we would get from a dean in any other department!" Meanwhile, there are faculty in other units who say: "She sure is taking good care of her own department. How come they got to hire again this year?" Maybe if both reactions are present but rare, things are going pretty well. Certainly, the dean needs to keep some distance from any single department, particularly his or her own, while working to sustain a solid relationship with every unit based on trust, knowledge, and proven support.

Deans as a Natural Cohort

The isolation of being a dean weighs all the more heavily if one is the only dean, as in a freestanding liberal arts college. Above is the president and perhaps the provost, and out there are the faculty. But to whom does the dean talk about being a dean? Associate and assistant deans are invaluable colleagues. There are very few topics one would not try out on the decanal staff. But the deanship is different from any one of the associate or assistant positions. What if only another dean will do? One answer is to talk with deans elsewhere. We will return later in this chapter to a discussion of regional and national organizations of deans, groups that provide benefits for administrative colleagues across the country.

In universities with multiple schools and colleges, the answer is easier. All the academic deans on campus form a natural cohort of shared interest and—in theory at least—mutual support. The number of deans, not counting associates and assistants, on a Big Ten or Pac Ten flagship campus for instance may run to twenty or more. That is a considerable population, as many colleagues as in a fairly large department, but there are important differences between colleagues in a department and decanal colleagues.

First, though all are deans, they direct very diverse operations, from a compact college of nursing with twenty-five faculty to the sprawling arts and sciences with six hundred or the medical behemoth with well over a thousand. Some have departments, others are unitary. The budget of the largest will be perhaps a hundred times greater than the smallest. These factors make for far greater divergence in function than among colleagues in a department, and deans are commensurately less confident that understanding what the next one does may actually be helpful to them.

Second, the disciplines are as different as the size of the colleges. In a department, whereas one colleague's specialty differs from the next, they are all chemical engineers or economists or microbiologists. Deans as a group are more like an institute in which everyone comes from a different department.

Third, departmental colleagues, being in reasonable proximity, have frequent casual contact in the hallway or lounge as well as planned meetings. Deans are scattered each in his or her own bailiwick, and although phone and e-mail are at their fingertips, their cluttered schedules can turn what should be a quick comment or question into an exercise in frustration.

Despite these differences, deans do share at least three characteristics that do not depend on the size or field of their individual colleges.

First, although each deanship has its unique features, other deans are still the only people on campus who hold the same title and have the same basic job description. They are the only source of wisdom on deaning from experience (except perhaps for the provost). They all report to the same person, in many places playing a common role as the provost's advisory cabinet on academic affairs. Taken together, the deans have the responsibility to students and faculty for the administration of academic programs across campus.

Second, because all deans come out of either a different role or another institution (those who move from a previous deanship), everyone is learning on the job. Obviously, faculty learn on the job too, but that is a deepening and expanding of professional training that was a prerequisite for being hired. How many deans have credentials in higher education administration when they are selected and take up their new responsibilities? (However, see the following section on seminars for new deans offered by national organizations.) This amateur status of deans binds them together, often into a circle of amicable and supportive colleagues. Inevitably, that amity fades from time to time under pressure of competitive effort; deans are no more universally likable than any other group, and some search committees simply make mistakes. But on the whole deans feel free to ask each other for advice or assistance. We quickly recognize the local curmudgeon (or *grand seigneur*); learning to work around the problem colleague helps bring the rest together effectively!

There is a third aspect to deanship that unites them: relative brevity of tenure. The half-life of a dean is actually less than four years with important exceptions such as agriculture and medicine, where the average tenure is considerably longer. This awareness of being temporary occupants of the office, so great a change from the endless security of faculty tenure, may raise the specter of Dr. Johnson: "When a man knows he is to be hanged in a fortnight, it concentrates his mind wonderfully." Some days, that dictum does not seem very humorous. One dean at a large university recalled a meeting of the deans and directors with the provost, during which the latter said: "Look to your right and your left. As they used to say in less happy circumstances like the Black Death, one of the three of you will not be here this time next year." The dean added wryly, "As so often, the provost underestimated the problem."

Without any assurance that one's appointment will run longer than the initial term, there is a great urgency to identify priorities, develop plans, and achieve results—rather like returning to the exhilarating panic of a probationary faculty member. Again and again, deans who do not find favor with the provost are told that it was because they were too slow in getting things done, even if all accomplishments to date were done well and carefully and following an approved plan. It is extremely important that a dean's watch tick at the same rate as the upper administration's. The deans collectively, by comparing notes and working together on projects that meet in the provost's office, can often recognize if there is a problem in this regard, when an individual dean might not.

There is one other bond worth mentioning: the deanship is the last rung on the academic administrative ladder from which any significant number of people return to active, productive faculty status. Certainly a few provosts—or even presidents at smaller colleges where the whole community is still closely knit—have made that return, but after a sufficient number of years of detachment from real faculty activities, the reversal is hard and the results can be discouraging if not embarrassing. Deans know that their career path may still move in any direction, and keep their options open accordingly (see further on this topic in Chapter Sixteen).

Directors

First cousin to the dean is the director. Indeed, the two are often spoken of together. The modern university is replete with directors, as the number of specialized units for teaching, research, and academic support has shot up. Broadly speaking, degree-granting units are headed by deans, other units by directors. Most of those are centers or institutes housed in a college or school, particularly research centers in medical schools and institutes for specialized fields (such as

African studies). Here, we are interested in units that appear at the same level on the campus administrative chart as the colleges and have directors.

The largest and most prominent unit on campus with a director is the library, whose chief is analogous to a dean. Library staff indeed often have tenure or its functional equivalent, and senior staff have a long tradition of both teaching and published scholarship—not only in the specific professional field of library and information science but in the traditional disciplines. The intimate connection between the quality of the library and the quality of academic programs makes the director of libraries an indispensable party to any conversation about program growth anywhere on campus. More recently, the other crucial unit for academic support is information technology, which holds the key to successful pursuit and use of knowledge far beyond the collections of the library.

In addition to these units, whose contribution to the academic strength of the campus is obvious, there may be other campus-level operations reporting to the provost, such as museums or the university press. Many campuses have distinctive units at the campus level. For example, Emory's roster includes the Carter Presidential Center and the Yerkes Primate Research Center. The list may also include specialized laboratories. In some cases the executive officers may hold the title vice provost or its equivalent, but they still sit with the deans in the provost's cabinet.

All these entities are part of the intellectual and educational mission of the campus directly under the CAO, and in that context their heads work alongside the deans. Where this arrangement applies (not all provosts work jointly with deans and campus-level directors), perhaps the most important shared activity is contributing to campus-level planning for both program development and resource allocation. A museum has clear relevance to the academic programs of the colleges, both teaching and research. This fact in turn has implications for collections, staffing, college-related educational programs, outreach to the community—not to mention facilities and maintenance. As with the library, the nexus with faculty and student needs is very close.

Of course, the parallel of dean and director is only partial. Units such as museums and academic computing do not have their own degree programs or responsibility for faculty and students. They can, however, lend crucial support to all of these, from staff who teach specialty courses to collaborative planning with the deans for new premises or special equipment.

Working with Other Deans

A discussion of working with any group or individual seems to start with the formulaic utterance: plan to meet regularly. In the case of the deans, this is often easier said than done. A monthly meeting under the gavel of the provost serves the formal purposes we just mentioned, but once a month is not very frequent contact for the cohort of deans whose responsibilities are so intertwined. Moreover, even assuming the provost invites the deans to suggest agenda items, they are attending the provost's meeting, not shaping their own discussions.

The deans also need to meet at their own call, on their own turf, and with their own agenda. Not all discussions of plans, exchanges of ideas, or offers of collaboration need to take up the provost's time—and it is only sensible to try out ideas without rehearsing them for the provost until they have gained shape and support. Once these meetings are established, the deans should invite the provost to join them sometimes. This is not a matter of secret plotting or backroom muttering, and the invitation reinforces the fact that the deans are working for the provost and want to discuss their ideas with him or her.

Every now and then, however, comes a provost who feels uncomfortable (insecure?) about any rogue gathering of deans. One dean, with a mixture of frustration and amusement, recalled mentioning in passing to his provost that the deans were planning to get together once a month for breakfast, just to keep up with each other. The provost immediately said, "That is a fine idea. I'll have my assistant contact all of you about agenda items. Now, next week is no good because I will be out of town. . . . " That was that for deans meeting apart from the provost.

The monthly breakfast is still a good idea, whether the provost is anxious about it or not. It is helpful to make it casual—no set agenda, so business can come up as it may. Sometimes it will be just personal chat and building of relationships. That will pay dividends when there are more problematic conversations to get through.

Cooperating on the Academic Agenda

One immediate benefit of discussion among the deans is learning more about areas of natural overlap in function. What courses or programs are the product of collaborative effort by faculty in two schools? Some are obvious enough, such as the general education responsibility of arts and sciences on behalf of the entire campus. Or perhaps economics is housed in the business school, meaning that an arts and sciences student majoring in economics takes ten or twelve courses outside his or her own college.

A large number of students pursue a double major (music and chemistry, history and French). If the campus has a unified arts and sciences college, these will all be inside the same college, but if, as often happens, there are separate colleges of humanities, social sciences, and natural sciences, then it takes coordination to maintain and improve program requirements, availability of faculty, and other considerations that cross college lines. Further, a few hardy souls each year actually take a double degree, earning one baccalaureate from engineering and another from arts and sciences, or one from agriculture and another in business. These are almost invariably individual efforts rather than established combinations. But what opportunities do the deans and their respective faculties have to encourage, enhance, improve—or for that matter, discourage—particular combinations?

Closely akin to shared programs are shared faculty appointments across college lines. It is not hard to think of attractive linkages between almost any pair of colleges. Putting the pieces together is harder, however. For example, imagine an appointment between psychology and public health. Psychology assumes the entire salary is hardwired; the only question is how much each college covers. But public health assumes that each faculty member will generate 50 percent of annual salary from grants and contracts, and because psychology is covering 50 percent, that is the limit of the institution's salary commitment; the person will need to generate the entire public health half of the salary each year. Teaching loads create similar puzzles. Psychology faculty teach four courses per year, public health faculty teach two courses. Thus psychology assigns one course a term, and is amazed when the faculty member says, "That is a full year's load for public health. I should only do one for you and one for them." Or, "If I teach two for psychology, that is my full load, and I do not owe public health any teaching. Besides, they do not even put up any salary for their half!" Add to this puzzle the matter of where tenure and salary decisions reside, who provides office and lab space, and it becomes clear why cross-college appointments are not common!

In addition to students and faculty, colleges also share facilities, equipment, and specialized libraries, and the staff to run them. Overarching all these collaborations is the issue of equitable cost sharing.

Among the benefits of cooperation between deans is the opportunity to learn in greater detail about how other parts of the campus work. Faculty know colleagues from all over campus, perhaps even collaborating on teaching or research, and hear anecdotes about life in the other schools, but that information is inevitably filtered and fragmentary. Few faculty have any reason to learn of the administrative system or plans or talent in other schools. In that sense at least, a dean selected from within has no real advantage over the dean brought in from the outside. And the very fact that the deans want to learn more about one another's schools means they will run into undeveloped areas for collaboration, as well as notice useful administrative practices they can apply back home.

In view of all these intersecting interests, each dean should keep in close touch with the others as academic plans develop. Before we create the design for the new environmental studies program—in fact, before we get too involved in the planning process—where else are there faculty who may be helpful? Are there students in other colleges who may need this course in law and public choice? Will outside interest create enrollment pressures? While respecting the boundaries of other schools and colleges, deans should look diligently for ways to contribute at the campus level and not just in the college, even with programs that may seem germane only to a single school. Discovering that a program is interesting to other deans and other colleges may open up prospects for sharing resources and bring the new program on-line sooner, perhaps in a better form than was originally imagined.

Finally, so much of what we do affects students that we should always ask what intentional or unintentional effects any decision will have. We get good at answering that question in our own schools, but the ripple effect of one college's actions out to other colleges is harder to predict. Consultation among the deans prevents accidental damage, such as dropping a course whose principal clientele lies outside the college or one that will be crucial to a program another college is planning but has not announced yet.

Even beyond this mechanical level, if the workings of a college are something of a mystery to the average faculty member, we must realize how much more peculiar they seem to the average student. When there is collaboration in describing programs, spelling out requirements and opportunities, and advising, students can be saved from falling into needless difficulties. Such efforts help students see where colleges overlap or intersect, how they are different or divergent. Eventually, as the students have reliable comparative information about academic expectations, career options, and so on, they can reach the best possible decision about what and where they really want to study.

The Wider Community of Deans

Finally we come to wider linkages of deans that bring support, advice, and practical help through at least three kinds of affinities.

The Multicampus System

For deans in a university with more than one campus, the academic administrators at the other campuses form a natural community that oddly enough may do little to work together or even share information except at the most rudimentary level. The campuses may be quite different in mission, size, and scope, as with the University of Wisconsin with its flagship campus in Madison, a major urban presence in Milwaukee, and an array of smaller sites around the state. The individual components may be virtually separate universities, as in the State University of New York with sixty-four institutions of every size and description, or the University of California or Texas. These conglomerate university systems are an amazing resource for any dean belonging to them both for the number of colleagues in equivalent fields (chiefly but by no means only arts and sciences) and for the diversity of situations the deans collectively handle.

Regional Clusters

These may arise from any of several causes, and take varied form. One model is the consortium built around a metropolitan area or some other natural regional boundary. The Atlanta Regional Consortium for Higher Education, for example, includes twenty institutions including the University of Georgia, Georgia Tech, Spelman College, the Institute of Paper Science and Technology, the Atlanta College of Art, and the Columbia Theological Seminary. Most consortia are more homogeneous in type or size of member institutions, but some are even more wide-ranging, including both schools and colleges (such as New England Association of Schools and Colleges). These clusters not only allow mutual assistance with courses, cross-registration, and shared program development but offer a perfect chance for comparable deans to work together.

Another form of affiliation is the competitive conference, such as Big Twelve, SEC, or Big Ten (the latter was originally and remains in its constitution primarily an educational affiliation, not originating in athletic competition). The great advantage of this grouping is that the universities or colleges in a given conference share many features of mission, size, and quality, making exchanges of both information and students relatively easier to arrange.

National Organizations

Last, national organizations of deans in various fields provide networking opportunities, annual meetings, publications, and seminars on pertinent topics. Among these are the Association to Advance Collegiate Schools of Business (AACSB International), the Engineering Deans Institute of the American Society for Engineering Education (ASEE), the Council of Colleges of Arts and Sciences (CCAS), the American Conference of Academic Deans (ACAD), and the Council of Graduate Schools (CGS).

Here are a few illustrations of the opportunities these organizations offer. CCAS, in addition to its annual meeting, has seminars for sitting deans during the year, as well as sessions on working with the media, seminars for chairs, and seminars for new deans each summer. Deans who have become involved in their respective organizations find advice, practical help with problems, and a wide array of new colleagues in their adopted careers. For the dean at a freestanding college in particular, this kind of connection puts an isolating situation into a supportive, educational context.

Suggestions for Further Reading

Austin, Michael J., Frederick L. Ahearn, and Richard A. English (eds.). *The Professional School Dean: Meeting the Leadership Challenges.* New Directions for Higher Education, no. 98. San Francisco: Jossey-Bass, 1997.

Bowen, William G., and Harold T. Shapiro (eds.). *Universities and Their Leadership.* Princeton, N.J.: Princeton University Press, 1998.

Facione, Peter. "Fundraising and Entrepreneurship." In George Allan (ed.), *Resource Handbook for Academic Deans* (pp. 152–156). Washington, D.C.: American Conference of Academic Deans, 1999.

Keeton, Morris. *Shared Authority on Campus.* Washington, D.C.: American Association for Higher Education, 1971.

Readings, Bill. *The University in Ruins.* Cambridge, Mass.: Harvard University Press, 1996.

CHAPTER FIFTEEN

EXTERNAL RELATIONS

The fastest-growing demand on most deans' time is in the realm of external relations. This is not simply because with every graduating class there are more people who have a connection to the college, although that is certainly true. The scope of a dean's activities off campus, the variety of persons and groups with whom the dean deals, and the time each requires, have all increased dramatically in the past decade. Now a dean's calendar sometimes looks rather like a president's in terms of off-campus appointments. As we mentioned earlier, the dean quickly builds a network of contacts in the community both by conscious effort and by accepting invitations from various organizations (see Chapter Four). These range from onetime speaking engagements or short-term consultations to long-term memberships in civic or cultural bodies. They are a valuable source of information for the dean as well as a way to lend visibility to the college itself.

In a sense, all these connections, every effort of outreach, have the same purpose: to explain to people who have an interest in the college, but limited or outdated knowledge about its components, what it is doing, and what it hopes to be with further support. The nature of that support varies from disseminating informed stories to contributing large sums of money. Many individuals at different times occupy several places along that continuum. Whereas even a decade ago much of the fundraising effort in most colleges still fell to the president, and direct contact with the media was rare for a dean, both are now standard fare in good times and bad.

Alumni

By far the largest population connected to any but the newest of colleges is its alumni. In a huge enterprise such as a Big Ten arts and sciences college, where the current student population may run to fifteen thousand (on a campus of forty thousand or more), the alumni number well over one hundred thousand, and for the campus as a whole the number over time rises above the half-million mark. That number swells at more than a simple arithmetical pace, for two reasons.

First, as access to higher education has broadened, the flow of students into college has expanded. Even relatively small places find themselves twice the size they were twenty years ago. For example, 70 percent of all Emory graduates have passed through the campus since 1980! This means that if a college's methods and channels for staying in touch with alumni have not been completely overhauled in the past decade, they are obsolete.

Second, the very definition of alumnus has changed. Once upon a time, an alumnus was someone who graduated from the college. But as the number of students who started college ballooned, so did the number who did not finish. Of course, even if the graduation rate remained constant, this would be true, but the dropout rate has also risen for various reasons, many economic or family-related and quite unconnected with academic failure. Now the term *alumnus* refers to someone who has *attended* a college, with no necessary implication of a degree.

The reason for this is, in part, a simple egalitarian impulse: the central distinction between completing a program or not completing it is reflected in the granting of degrees. Does the university or college also want to maintain invidious distinctions between the graduate and the former student for the rest of their lives? But in large measure, to admit the obvious, the more inclusive approach grew from the hope of garnering contributions from the largest possible circle of donors. Every college and university is in a capital campaign, or will be soon, and the circle of those who may remember a place fondly is not limited to the degree lists. Unquestionably, big-time athletics have driven campus after campus to include everyone who can afford a parking spot near the stadium and wants to wear varsity colors. From their ranks come some of a college's most ardent and generous supporters, giving to academics as well as athletics. No wonder that colleges are eager to think inclusively and use the term alumnus in less narrow ways, and no wonder that an increasing share of the dean's attention goes to alumni!

The primary relationship with alumni is as the extended family of the college. Alums carry the memory of a distinctive, formative phase in their lives, encountered only on the college campus, and it is especially vivid—whether pleasant or not—for students who came directly from high school. The connection wanes in most cases, but frequently revives in later years. Time after time older alumni, out of college for forty years or more, speak of a resurgence of memories, and of interest, in their alma mater. Class reunions are a deeply emotional activity, closely akin to family reunions. Deans often have a role at these events, highlighting new developments and reconnecting alumni to the college they knew.

By dint of sheer numbers, whether they are well- or ill-disposed to their alma mater, alumni are a potent force in the ongoing fortunes of the college. They may send their own children to the campus, and recruit others as well. Many are willing to speak eloquently on behalf of the college to garner support or contributions, and are themselves a continuing source of contributions. They can influence legislators and touch public opinion. They can be called on to participate in forums, advise search committees, and help assess the reputation of the college.

Finally, a college should see its alumni as still linked to its central purpose: the development of the life of the mind. A well-designed program of seminars and short courses for alumni, on and off campus, draws alums who appreciate being regarded as educated minds, not just pocketbooks.

The dean, then, needs to build and maintain personal contact with the alumni. This involves a good deal of travel, cocktail parties, and cookouts, hosting events at the homecoming weekend, and other forms of conviviality. When traveling on business, the dean should make a point of either hosting an occasional gathering of alumni or looking up some of them for a brief personal visit, which may be purely social and informative, not necessarily turned toward solicitation of a gift. Meet and remember, stay in touch and appreciate: this is the mantra of the dean. As the graduates of a college prosper professionally and personally, the college grows in stature. The dean can benefit from the success, wisdom, and expertise of those graduates. We will return to this topic shortly.

Parents

Students are adults, and are so regarded by the university or college. Few undergraduates arrive at campus before they turn eighteen, and a steadily rising number at public universities, especially urban campuses, are considerably older than that. Many have already started once and broken off, and have returned in their mid- to late twenties with renewed focus and perhaps family responsibilities of their own. Others put college off until they attend to other urgent purposes, and attend for the first time at age twenty-five or older. The university or college treats students as adults in protecting their privacy as laid out by the Buckley Amendment and other legislation. In short, the college campus is deemed a gathering place for adults, not merely an extension of high school for advancing youths.

Still, legions of fresh high school graduates come to college, and standing behind them are parents, with the full measure of pride and anxiety that has always characterized parents watching their offspring leave home. Public universities run the gamut from residential to commuter, full-time and part-time, and there is a greater feeling of independence, even anonymity, among the students making their own way on a vast campus. Here we are concerned only with parents of undergraduates, for all practical purposes the parents of students in the traditional age cohort (eighteen to twenty-two). In private colleges especially, where the freshman class is still virtually all age eighteen or nineteen and just out of high school, and all living away from home, the interaction between college and parents is more active and more critical.

One extremely important link in a private school is financial. The parents are probably paying for most or even all of their offspring's educational costs, which at a private college will total well over $125,000, even assuming a student graduates promptly in four years. Parents have every confidence that their son or daughter is able to do well, and they want to be sure that the college is doing its part with good teaching and advising, modern facilities, and sensible career counseling—in short, that they are getting their money's worth. With each year of attending a first-tier private school costing about the same as a new luxury automobile, that concern is easy to understand.

There are four main occasions when the dean is likely to have direct contact with parents. Each contributes to a productive relationship that can carry through the student's years on campus and even sometimes far beyond.

The Shopping Phase

As students and their parents weigh options for a college, a sizable number take a tour to visit their top preferences, especially if there are several within reasonable driving distance of one another. This adds a great deal to the free but less informative virtual tours that so many colleges offer on their Web sites. During the visiting and application season, many a campus hold all-day events aimed at answering questions and making both parents and prospective students aware of their special attractions. Among all the faculty, student leaders, and campus administrators who put their best collective foot forward is the dean, who often speaks briefly to the assembled visitors (numbering hundreds each time) and then mingles over cookies and punch to greet and charm.

Nobody would expect the dean to recall names or faces from this activity, particularly because these visitors may not yet have even applied, much less been accepted. But the dean's personal appearance and remarks have a powerful effect on parents who are quietly wondering whether there is any person who can provide assurance and authority once their son or daughter leaves home. We all know that universities and colleges no longer stand *in loco parentis* for their students, but tell that to a parent whose seventeen-year-old is looking to leave the nest!

Parents of New Students

Before the new class of students arrives, more and more private schools hold some kind of social event in cities where there is a concentration of new and returning students. This is an excellent opportunity to create various kinds of contact. Parents of first-year students can meet others whose sons and daughters are going to the same school and start to build a community of local interest. New students can meet some of those who will be their classmates and have a familiar face to look for when they arrive. They can also meet advanced students who can answer their questions and take some of the strangeness out of the place. The dean, again, is a pivotal figure in this event, now welcoming the students as members of the college community and meeting parents who have a definite relationship to the college. This is the time to learn some names and hear some concerns, and to assure parents that the dean's office—no, the dean—will be there to help. Parents, no less than their sons or daughters, want to know personally someone they can call if necessary. Relatively few parents will avail themselves of this offer, but the assurance is invaluable. The relationship is personalized in these events to link parent and dean.

Parents' Weekend

During the fall, the campus probably has a parents' weekend. Usually, this is the chance for parents to see the campus for themselves (if they did not visit in the selection phase) and more specifically see how the student is "really" doing. Now the connection to the campus has moved beyond the hypothetical or anticipated to the actual. A chat over punch and cookies with the dean this time is a visit with an acquaintance; it is not the moment to take up specific problems, but it can offer a chance to express concern and invite further discussion later.

No doubt this all sounds highly improbable: just think how many students there are! What does the dean know about any of them, and how many parents can he or she pretend to remember from a sweltering reception in Houston last August? In fact, the number of parents who pursue any such conversation is small, and the parents are always the first to reintroduce themselves, without expecting the dean to have total recall. The rest simply appreciate the continued appearance of a familiar stranger who cares enough to come out and welcome them.

Good Times and Bad

Except in fairly small colleges, the main interaction deans have with students comes at the two opposite extremes: when they distinguish themselves by winning awards or earning other special notice, and when there are problems serious enough to work their way up to the dean. In the first and happier of these situations, it is a pleasure for the dean to meet with the outstanding student, tell him or her the good news, and learn more about one of the top achievers in the college. With undergraduates, the dean ought to drop a note to the parents, including them in the round of congratulations.

In the other scenario, it is not appropriate for the dean to contact the parents unless the situation is life-threatening or legally demands it. But in the case of undergraduates at least, we have already mentioned how student problems may be creatively reported home (see Chapter Eleven), resulting in heated confrontations with distraught parents who become ardent critics of the college when their child's standing is threatened, especially when conduct or academic honesty is involved. In such situations, when the dean has to wait out the storm of accusation and disbelief before beginning to work through the problem, it is a huge advantage for both parties if the parents have met the dean or at least heard him or her speak and there is some framework for mutual recognition and trust. Previous acquaintance will not make an honor code violation go away, but it engages both sides as allies to help the student-child rather than feud over authority and credibility.

Parents also exert a powerful force in the wider community, whether voting as citizens of the state on issues that affect education or as individual ambassadors of the institution to their neighbors and friends. Like alumni, parents will spread their views of the university by word of mouth, and their own testimony can help to influence other families as they make their college decision.

The commitment of parents to a college or campus is sometimes almost startling in its intensity. Even if they have never attended the university, they can be as attached to it as alumni. Perhaps this is not so surprising: they have quite possibly put as much money into the place as an alumnus. Moreover, as college becomes accessible to more people, every year brings to campus more students who are the first in their family to go to college. Conversely, this means that there are more and more parents who did not themselves attend college. For these parents, the campus becomes a sort of proxy alma mater in which they take vicarious pride.

The dean, then, has a large group of committed people with whom he or she shares an interest in the progress of the students. Without ever stepping in to curtail the student's independence or presume on the temporary bond that this produces, the dean can gain much from working with parents. Not the least is the generosity of time and money that comes from grateful parents. The opportunity for building a connection to parents lasts only as long as the student is on campus, but the carryover can last for many years.

College Publications and Publicity

All colleges and universities advertise their programs and other assets, both to attract the best possible students and to provide information for other browsers. In addition to the traditional printed catalogue and view books, nearly all colleges have Web sites that offer a swifter, more detailed, and more sophisticated gateway to the campus. Because these publications serve as an official statement of the college's programs, they need to be current, complete, and accurate as well as attractive and convenient.

The dean should be sure that all public descriptions of the college's activities are appropriate and accurate, and be involved in any changes in the college's self-presentation to the outside world. Prospective students, or applicants for faculty and staff positions, use these resources when deciding whether to apply for admission or whether to seek a position in the college. On-line resources in particular can make or break a college's outreach by the quality of information and presentation. Both catalogue and Web site should include greetings or other comments from the dean, who embodies the college for the casual visitor.

Less universal than the catalogue or Web site, but still very common, is the college newsletter, produced anywhere from once a year to monthly and sent mainly to alumni and donors. It provides an excellent opportunity for the college to focus attention on recent accomplishments, current plans, student honors, remarkable faculty work—whatever is noteworthy in the life of the college. The newsletter is probably the main source of information on the college for the majority of alumni, who are scattered across the country and rarely visit the campus and after a few years have no ongoing contact with faculty or staff.

Given the importance of the newsletter for reaching alumni and donors, and its potential for building support for the college, no issue should go out without a message from the dean, pointing out matters that the dean wants readers to be aware of. The newsletter should describe new initiatives for the college, report on accomplishments, and feature successful alumni. The immediate goal may be to boast or to beg, or anything in between, but the long-range goal is always to keep alumni and donors interested in participating in the life of the college.

Some colleges use the general mailing of the newsletter to showcase individual departments by including a copy of one departmental letter or brochure each time. In this way, the departments' special voices can be heard, and over time the readers will come to know all parts of the enterprise.

Alumni remember the campus from the student perspective, and they are always most interested in what students are like now. They recall faculty also from the student perspective, and are eager to be impressed by what today's faculty are doing. Accordingly, when the dean meets with alumni or writes to them, the best strategy is to put interesting faculty and remarkable students front and center. Alums generally do not remember the dean, and almost certainly not the current one.

An important caution: graduates who return to campus constantly comment on how much has changed since their day. This reflects a blend of fact and nostalgic bad memory, but the comments highlight the importance that former students attach to the college as they remember it. In talking with alumni, and in the mailings that go out from the college office, the dean can both acknowledge the value of those memories and showcase how the college has built on that past: to show what has changed and to underscore what has persisted over the years. When parading the quality of current students and faculty, and basking in the glow of constant improvement, however, it is important not to present this as a change from the low standards of the past when these alumni were students. Many a dean has fallen into a self-congratulatory routine, only to find that the alumni are not impressed but offended. Better to take an approach that does not rely on contrasts with the past. How is the college competing for current applicants? Being equipped with modern advantages for competing in a modern world is no reason for slighting the talent, the loyalty, or the success of older graduates. It is a mistake that costs both friends and funds.

Instead, along with a healthy pride in its current achievements, the college should celebrate prominently the success of its alumni with special recognitions at homecoming and other alumni-oriented events. This not only pays tribute to their accomplishments but also reminds all the alumni that the college still knows they are out there doing good things and wants to keep in touch.

Finally, the dean should point to the growing academic diversity that keeps the college in the forefront of its peer institutions, as well as the demographic and economic diversity that has put a degree from this college within reach of so many talented students. This is quite possibly the real story of change from a generation ago, and it will be the basis for an institution's competitive success in the next generation. Texts, pictures, and general information figures should highlight success in achieving diversity matching the changing national scene.

Advisory Councils

Advisory councils are a very important source of information and support for deans in all kinds of colleges, and even for individual departments. They engage the varied strengths of a select group of people with the wider community. Some members arc donors with an interest in the college but no special expertise who can heighten community awareness of projects on campus and thus bring friends as well as dollars. Others have expertise (business executives, scientists, professional artists) to contribute to discussions about programs, and probably also have contacts with prospective donors. Usually, these councils meet two or three times a year for a day or so to discuss the college's activities and plans, meet with faculty and students, and revitalize their commitment to the college. In some cases, membership on a dean's council has proved to be a stepping-stone to a seat on the board of trustees.

Depending on the nature of the college and what the dean wants to gain from the council, the membership may vary considerably. The two most common types draw on alumni and business leaders in the community; a few graduate schools have councils made up of current faculty from the school and graduates of the doctoral programs who are now teaching elsewhere (a very few even invite graduate deans from other schools). The focus of this kind of council is on scholarly issues, the training of scholars and teachers, and the refinement of graduate programs.

The rules to remember are simple: have a stated mission for the council, pick members cautiously, treat them well, take their advice seriously, and rotate them off to make room for more. Giving the college exposure to an expanding circle of informed friends is more important than seeking the advice of any one individual through this channel. Once the dean has established a personal relationship with a councillor, that advice will always be available whether or not the person continues to sit on the council. With these admonitions in mind, council meetings can be among the most enjoyable activities of the year for the dean—and one of the most profitable in every sense.

Media Relations

Any college that is doing its job right will have newsworthy events that attract the media. Good, clear exposure in the media is a great help in getting the college's story out to the wider community. The campus should be glad of a strong working relationship with the press, giving information and explaining it readily for the community at large.

But likewise, any college that does not do its job right will have the media on its doorstep, and almost every institution falls into this unhappy situation from time to time. Fortunately, most campuses have an office to deal with public relations, including the media. That office can usually provide appropriate information and fend off further questions when discretion is necessary—personnel issues, for example. But if the story is at all interesting, and particularly if it is tantalizing (the rumor of a scandal) or distressing (a bad accident or a death), the reporters come to any office that might have a story to tell. That includes the dean's office. But most deans, despite being comfortable in front of a microphone, lack experience or training with the media and make the crucial, if typical, academic's mistake of talking too much. The results in the hands of the media can be disastrous. One of the most dangerous outlets is the campus student newspaper, which combines an understandable zeal for chasing down a good story on campus with a lack of finesse and experience. Stories in campus papers are notoriously shaky in their accuracy, especially in understanding the way the campus administration actually works. They are also very frequently the first ones to put out a story, which can set the tone for subsequent inquiry from others.

The basic principle in such situations is far harder than it sounds: the dean needs to decide on the message he or she wants to convey to the media before meeting any reporters and stick to that message without prevarication or elaboration. Because the press will be contacting several people, it is also important to coordinate with the campus administration so that the institution provides a consistent perspective. This is not at all to suggest that anyone should distort the truth but simply that the campus should know what has happened, and however discreet or full an account it decides is appropriate at the present stage of events, that account should not be cluttered with internal inconsistencies or premature assessments of cause, responsibility, or solutions.

Once a story hits the front page or the evening news, or worse, the national media, festooned with contradictory remarks or images of visibly rattled administrators, it almost does not matter whether the story is true or is subsequently amended or even disproved. The damage is done. Worst of all perhaps is the story that gets turned loose, unverified and uncontrollable, on the Internet or via an e-mail campaign.

In short, the media can greatly enhance the good rapport a college has with external constituencies or greatly magnify its woes. The dean absolutely must be able to function smoothly and professionally in this context. One cardinal rule is not to use the press as a means of conducting on-campus business—debating issues on which the campus is divided or trying to force someone's hand by a pre-emptive announcement of a decision. Some campuses are afflicted with senior administrators, even presidents, who use the media as a weapon on campus instead of a resource to communicate off campus. The wise dean will take the high road and shun this form of institutional "culture."

Dealing with the media is tricky enough, and important enough, that some institutions provide training sessions for its officers. So do some professional organizations. The Council of Colleges of Arts and Sciences, for example, runs an annual seminar on deans and the media. Whatever form it takes, any type of training will help.

Development

In an odd but widely accepted euphemism, *development* has come to mean the pursuit of financial support from friends and agencies, as if other activities that build relationships and make friends and find other forms of support were not equally valid development of the institution's condition.

In fact, anyone involved in development knows that questions of financial support cannot be addressed in isolation, and gifts rarely come with no context or contact. The cultivation of gifts requires tireless preparation and endless attention. The matter can be put even more succinctly: fundraising is one aspect of a sustained relationship built over time. If that relationship is sound and grows from contacts for other reasons, material gifts are a natural, almost inevitable result, if the resources are there to allow for fiscal generosity. The real resource under development is the human capital of alumni, friends, and interested parties who want a connection to the enterprise.

Development is not a crude, abrupt method of preying on the rich or the unsuspecting to separate them from their savings. It is an investment of time and attention, care and regard, with the prospect of a substantial return of interest. The difference between cultivation and eventual solicitation, rather than simply tracking down and asking for a gift, is roughly the same as the difference between a banker and a bank robber, in both tone and technique.

As recently as 1989, the only discussion of a dean's role in development was as a sidekick to the president, and that mainly in private schools (Tucker and Bryan, 1999). Now deans of every stripe are engaged in development, as leading figures, and for as much time as they are willing to commit. Of all the activities a dean takes on, this may be among the least familiar, and for many it is the least comfortable. Many deans acknowledge that they are frankly uneasy asking individuals to contribute substantial amounts from their personal resources to the college. Without developing a real relationship first, it seems so crass, and yet once a personal relationship has been built it seems like a betrayal of trust suddenly to ask for money. "I cannot ask him, I hardly know him" becomes "I cannot ask him, he is my friend." Both feelings are understandable to those who have never been involved in fundraising; it can feel like turning into a highwayman or con artist. The first concern is very appropriate. Asking people for large gifts before getting to know them, learning about them, and understanding their interests as well as their capacity for giving, is not only indelicate but unproductive. Anyone who has been harassed at the dinner hour by telemarketers understands this point. The second concern arises in part from a natural (even commendable) squeamishness that, candidly put, diminishes with success. As the dean becomes better acquainted with the prospective donor, and talks more specifically about the college and its purposes, there should be a real kindling of interest, even of desire, to participate in those purposes. By the time the dean presents a proposal for a donation, the donor (in textbook conditions) is eager to be a part of the action and genuinely grateful for the opportunity to give. Many a dean has attended a groundbreaking ceremony at which the donor who has committed millions of dollars to the college says "thank you" even more often and more fervently than the president or the dean.

In addition to the comfort level that comes with experience, there are also opportunities for training, such as the seminars for deans given by the Council for the Advancement and Support of Education (CASE). Various deans' organizations also offer fundraising sessions at their regular meetings. And many campuses, large and small, give training and workshops for those who will be engaging in development.

Collaboration

Support from the campus is vital, because development is very much a team effort, from the board of trustees through the president's office to other senior officers. Coordination of all aspects is absolutely essential. The dean needs to work closely with both the president and the vice president for institutional advancement (the title varies greatly, but this is the senior officer in charge of external relations, from alumni to the press to donations).

The college must have its own plan, closely related to its strategic plan that has already been approved as a blueprint for the coming years. Ongoing consultation with the department chairs always generates many useful ideas, far more than any development plan can hope to achieve. The dean also needs to learn about previous development efforts: What projects were pursued, and to what effect? Who has already been asked and either agreed or declined? Have the priorities of the college changed in the past five years, or more importantly, would they change if major support were available for particular dreams?

Any plan the college formulates must fit into the campus plan and gain approval from the campus as conforming to institutional goals, priorities, policies, and practices. How will each part of the proposed plan be carried out? In particular, which office will be responsible for each facet of the campaign? If several offices, even several deans, are interested in talking with a donor and each pursues a different project without prior agreement on who should proceed, the result can be disastrous. The donor could be approached by three people, all professing to represent the university and each asking for something different. Predictably, the donor will shrink from all requests and wonder why the university cannot speak with a single voice. The president then has the unenviable task of overcoming the mix-up. No dean wants to be a participant in any such scenario—especially the follow-up by the president.

In contrast, the president can be the problem rather than the solution. Many a dean reports frustration with a president who virtually kidnapped the dean's best prospects and sequestered them for campus priorities, so that any major prospect automatically became a presidential prospect and the dean was left to find another lead, only to have that one similarly swept up into the institutional stratosphere. There is little the dean can do in the face of such exercise of presidential power, except to maneuver the college's priorities in such a way that they emerge as the president's own ambitions. The senior campus development officer can be of some help in mediating these rifts, but they can be disheartening and eventually even defeat the dean's attempts at college development. Consider the following scenario. A dean has formed a good relationship with a potential donor, who is an alumnus of the college and has shown interest in the plan for a new anthropological museum. The dean wants to proceed to the next phase of the process by working up a proposal and setting it before her, but the president decides that the campus will ask her for the naming gift for the new alumni center. The dean can argue the college's case—and surely will—but may very well see the only known prospect for the museum gift vanish without ever being able to give the donor the choice. The process of allocating major prospects is political, intense, and always frustrating to someone. In this example, if the donor agrees to the gift, the dean feels all the more keenly that this could have been the solution for the museum; if the request fails, the dean is sure that it would have worked if only they had asked for the museum.

Staff

From the broad sweep of annual fund campaigns seeking $50 or $100 contributions, through small and medium individual donations, to the grand naming gift for a new building, every level of development takes time, which means staff. Ideally, there should be staff dedicated to each of these levels, working directly with the college as well as with the campus development office. More likely, outside of the large universities, the college has one full-time development professional for major gifts and relies on personnel in the central development office for other functions. In smaller colleges, the development staff will coordinate with the dean but probably report directly to the president. However the staff is deployed, their two primary tasks are to locate and learn about prospective donors, and to manage the effort so as to make the most of whatever time the dean can commit to fundraising.

The level of giving determines the kind of work needed. For an annual fund the dean should set the tone, write the letter, explain the goals, and provide encouragement to the volunteers and staff, but it will hardly be feasible to be involved in the mechanics at this level. Whether the college is large or small, independent or part of a university, there will be a wide range of potential gifts and prospects being cultivated. The dean needs to focus on working at the upper end of that range. These are the gifts that require the greatest preparation by both staff and dean and will only succeed with personal handling by the college leader.

In order to do their job, the development staff must be fully briefed on the college's plans and priorities. The senior development officer should meet frequently with the dean and be a full participant in college decanal staff meetings. By the same token, the development officer must be well informed of campus activity so as to advise the dean on options, timing, and strategies.

The Dean's Role

Clearly the dean's role spans the entire development effort, from setting priorities and planning to directing and working with others, cultivating friends, and finally asking for gifts in person. Much of the work overlaps with the ongoing alumni contacts: travel around the country, meetings with groups large and small as well as with individuals to report on the college's activities, days when all three meals are business meetings with individuals or corporate representatives, presentation after presentation of "The Plan," and finally offering the right person the opportunity to make a mark on the college's history with a gift for something they are genuinely eager to support. At smaller colleges, deans not only put together the requisite wish list but may also write preliminary case statements. These are all components of development.

But nothing in this list is more important than being meticulously informed. This means knowing the campus's plans and priorities in order to contribute strongly to the overall institutional effort. It means having frequent, detailed reports about the progress of the college effort, being ready to step into any situation without hesitation about either the project or the donor. It means knowing the staff's strengths and limitations in order to direct the staff skillfully and make sure that everyone knows what needs to be done. And it means having detailed familiarity with each and every proposal.

In addition to the professional development staff, the dean has a powerful resource in the faculty, who are among the chief beneficiaries of donors' generosity. Indeed, most of the splendid proposals that donors see originate in the imagination of the faculty. Their zeal for the project is probably greater than anyone else's because they know far better than others what it will take to achieve their goals, and how valuable that achievement will be. Often a faculty member is the strongest possible advocate for a proposal, and the dean should be ready and eager to take advantage of that enthusiasm by inviting that faculty member to explain the proposal in person. A personal presentation by the expert scholar makes a powerful impact on a donor.

If the engine of development is preparation and knowledge, its fuel is enthusiasm and confidence. One problem side effect of "we can do this" or even "we must do this" is the assumption that "this" will surely happen. The result is a challenge in managing expectations at every level. The dean must not expect too great a display of miracles from the development staff—and vice versa. The campus understands the problem but has put the full weight of its ambitions behind a dazzling proposal and has only limited tolerance when no major gift emerges. Faculty and staff and students hear so much about the college's commitment to the wonderful arts center or research building that they cannot imagine not having it. But major campaigns for such buildings take years to complete, and every year seems to increase concern, and eventually cynicism, that nothing will come of all the talk after all. Part of development is underscoring what a valuable purpose the college is working toward, but at the same time it helps if people remember that precisely because the new building or scholarship program or endowed chair is so important and costly, it depends on extraordinary generosity, and that does not simply appear when summoned like a trained pet.

How much of a dean's time should go to development? The answer obviously will vary from one place to the next, and even from one season to the next. If the dean is a skilled campaigner, the development office will want as much of his or her time as it can possibly get: during a capital campaign, not less than 25 percent and during critical phases involving frequent trips, as much as 40 percent in the short run. Although such a schedule may well be necessary to secure the gifts in prospect, it is a tremendous drain on both the time and the energy the dean has to devote to the internal leadership of the college. It essentially reproduces the external orientation of the president, without cutting out any of the internal responsibilities of the dean.

But even though every dean sometimes feels painfully pressed by the demands of development, it is an enjoyable aspect of the position because it puts the dean in touch with many interesting people who have the success of the college at heart and it involves many enjoyable activities. Moreover, securing a major gift brings a very special satisfaction of putting into place a significant piece of the college's future.

Thus although the heart of the dean's job is to be chief academic officer of the college, the responsibilities range far more widely than the confines of the college, and far more widely than academics. For all the talk of ivory towers and the "real world outside," the institution is very much a part of the wider community. That relationship requires deft handling and constant creative attention to family, friend, and stranger alike.

Suggestions for Further Reading

Axtell, James. *The Pleasures of Academe.* Lincoln: University of Nebraska Press, 1998.

Bérubé, Michael, and Cary Nelson (eds.). *Higher Education under Fire: Politics, Economics, and the Crisis of the Humanities.* New York: Routledge, 1995.

Graham, Hugh Davis, and Nancy Diamond. *The Rise of American Research Universities: Elites and Challengers in the Postwar Era.* Baltimore: Johns Hopkins University Press, 1997.

Hall, Margaret Rooney. *The Dean's Role in Fund Raising.* Baltimore: Johns Hopkins University Press, 1993.

Rodgers, James Ellison, and William C. Adams. *Media Guide for Academics.* Los Angeles: Foundation for American Communications, 1994.

Tucker, Allan, and Robert Bryan. *The Academic Dean: Dove, Dragon, and Diplomat* (2nd ed.). Phoenix: American Council on Education/Oryx Press, 1999.

CHAPTER SIXTEEN

BEYOND DEANING:
BUILDING A BALANCED CAREER

Because the average length of a deanship is less than four years, this discussion of the aftermath could be the longest in the book. Of course, many deans serve longer, and in more than one post, and often late in their careers. Nonetheless, just as a considerable stretch of academic career comes before a deanship, so another important segment often comes after. This chapter addresses some questions about maintaining an active academic identity while in the dean's office, planning ahead for the next professional step, disengaging from the role of dean, and stepping into a satisfying subsequent role that may make use of the experience gained.

Maintaining an Academic Identity

Among the most important decisions deans make for themselves involve which teaching, scholarly, creative, and professional commitments to maintain. Oddly enough, the decisions come more often by default than by choice. The new dean is swamped with new activities and knows that familiar academic functions are bound to fade into the background for a while. Gradually it becomes apparent that this most familiar role has faded further and further away. If nothing is done, a once-flourishing academic career sinks beneath the surface.

Academic staleness may come from assuming too soon that the deanship is a stepping-stone to a provostship or a presidency, leading to needless neglect of all but administrative activities and goals. Most often, however, the challenge consists in trying to excel at the new role, and simply having no time for academic pursuits.

The converse is equally risky: blithely assuming that somehow there will still be enough time for a full, vigorous research program and thus committing to projects and deadlines that are unrealistic. When these commitments are not met, and other people are adversely affected, word quickly spreads that this dean is no longer reliable as a working scholar. Connections, invitations, and opportunities are no longer there, leaving even less chance for the dean to engage in the life of his or her scholarly community and inflicting permanent damage on a hard-earned scholarly career.

Discussions with other deans about juggling the academic and the administrative may only bring greater discouragement about staying alive in one's field. Worst of all, there may be pressure from above to minimize time spent on academics in order to devote full energy to the dean's duties (cynics would say to reduce the dean's options for changing his or her mind). Yet despite all the difficulties involved, academic administrators need to stay in touch with their disciplines through all of the traditional activities, including teaching, to the fullest extent possible. Obviously no dean can keep up the same level of involvement as a faculty member, but participation in the academic life of the institution is also a form of leadership. The college should be made aware of what the dean is doing and why it is important. In this way the dean serves as an example to department chairs, who may be having problems balancing the various demands on their time, and to faculty members considering administrative assignments, who wonder whether doing so may doom their academic careers. In short, deans can and should define academic work as part of the job.

Teaching

Some institutions encourage or expect deans to teach; others see it as optional or even odd. Many deans find it hard to sustain a regular course meeting several times a week, term after term. The calendar is too unforgiving, and the dean either must miss classes or show up not fully prepared. Still, given the variety of forms that instruction takes in a college, deans can be usefully involved even if their schedule precludes a traditional course. Among the options are team teaching, directing independent studies, conducting laboratory research with students, reading or supervising undergraduate and graduate theses, giving guest lectures, and leading seminars.

It is important to keep a hand in teaching, and not only for altruistic or scholarly reasons. It is a good way to stay in touch with students and to learn what their experience is like in the college, and it reminds the dean of the challenges that teaching faculty face every week. Equally important, teaching regularly in some capacity will greatly ease the transition back to regular faculty life, if that is what lies ahead. Some deans report that they keep up to date in their disciplines through teaching regularly and incorporating new materials into their courses. Finally, teaching is a good way for deans from another institution to get to know their new colleagues and develop a positive relationship with the home department.

Research and Creative Activity

The most horrifying words a dean can say are "I used to be a biologist, musician, chemical . . . engineer. . . . " These words signal a resignation from the academic community and surrender to a closed world of professional administration. Giving up a scholarly career is grossly inappropriate for a dean. There is no faster way to lose the respect of faculty colleagues, on whom the dean must form some academic judgment almost every day.

Depending on the field and the kind of research or creative activity that is appropriate to it, a number of strategies for staying active have been recommended by current and former deans. They all urge maintaining subscriptions to the best journals in the field. To stay up to date, deans can also take an assignment to write a review essay of recent scholarship or to contribute a book review. They can collaborate with another author or a group on a project. Some deans produce edited books or revised editions of textbooks. Scientists are often able to maintain a laboratory with the help of a strong research staff. Active scholars may find it necessary to narrow their focus in order to stay current and have significant results, but some progress is better than none.

As mentioned in Chapter Two, it is important to consider the options before embarking on a deanship, both to be sure that this is a step one can live with and to make the necessary preparations, such as start-up funds and laboratory space, not to mention arranging a workable schedule. Some deans resolutely set aside a half-day twice a week and even more time (perhaps exchanged with an associate dean) during the summer. Others find that hours blocked out during the workday inevitably get filled by the crisis of the moment. In practice, many deans therefore use evenings and weekends to read, write, perform, sit at the computer, and otherwise sustain their own work. One dean, a confessed "morning person," writes between 4:00 and 7:00 each morning.

No matter the schedule, the key to maintaining progress is to do some form of scholarly or creative work regularly, and under no circumstances wait passively until blocks of time appear on the calendar. One successful scholar-dean advises making contact, even if only physical contact, with one's work every day. That may sound silly, but thanks to continued contact with the work even when it is not possible to make progress on it, returning to it in the end feels more like a home-coming than a crash landing.

Deans who have changed locations usually find challenges in pursuing their academic specialties. One had to move his research away from limnology and lake management when he moved to the Atlantic Coast, although he did find plenty of water on which to base new projects. Those whose scholarship depends heavily on the availability of a research library or a specific set of archives may also need to make special arrangements for periodic access to those resources or else be forced to change the focus of their work.

In addition, as a colleague noted, the new challenges of academic adminis-tration can provide research opportunities for a dean who is interested in the workings of higher education, whether from the perspective of educational man-agement, pedagogical issues, academic programs, or any of the other topics dis-cussed in this book. There are numerous opportunities for grants at the college level designed to improve curricula, enhance instructional technology, and train faculty members in techniques such as problem-based learning.

A number of deans have written books and articles on their experiences, and they have done survey research on a range of topics from teaching loads in vari-ous fields to start-up costs for new faculty members. This kind of work may be published by academic publishers, including those specializing in higher educa-tion, in educational and interdisciplinary journals, and in newsletters published by deans' organizations. A sample of potential outlets appears in the Bibliogra-phy, which draws heavily on the work of our colleagues.

Consulting

Some deans come from fields such as engineering, business, or law, where con-sulting is part of the professional life. They continue to block out time for these assignments in order to stay active in the field and maintain their contacts and visibility. As long as the consulting work is done with the provost's blessing and falls under institutional guidelines on conflict of interest and time limits for exter-nal consulting, this can be a rewarding way to keep a hand in the discipline.

Deans from many backgrounds are sought as consultants for the administra-tive acumen they have in addition to their disciplinary wisdom—serving on grants panels because they have demonstrated the ability to make hard decisions, for example. Deans also often receive invitations for accreditation work and cam-pus visits, whether focused on a single unit, as when deans from engineering and from arts and sciences advise on the best arrangements for a computer science department, or on broader topics, such as assisting a college struggling with a long-range plan. Of course, one can only devote a certain amount of time to such activities, but when they offer the opportunity to gain a new perspective on one's own college, they are worth considering.

Scholarly Organizations and Conferences

Active scholar-deans recommend at a minimum attending the best professional conference in one's field each year, and more if there is time. One dean tries to obtain copies of conference papers, especially those that review the literature on a particular problem, because of the effort they save in staying current with the latest thinking. Presenting research papers is a somewhat harder habit to sustain, and as one dean noted, the benefit of not doing so is that without the stress of performing one can concentrate more on the other presentations.

Another alternative is to remain active in professional societies and organizations, from regional to international. A dean may be in a better position than a faculty member to serve as a leader in one of these groups because of the office support provided by the college. Whether the contribution is relatively mechanical, such as maintaining membership rosters or collecting dues, or more ambitious, like editing a newsletter, planning a conference, or holding office, the activity gives the dean some visibility in the discipline and a way to keep in touch with the organization. Deans also tend to have thicker skins than some faculty colleagues, which is always helpful in work of this kind.

In the end, preserving a functioning academic identity is at the heart of the dean's mission. It allows the vigorous pleasures of the mind that made an academic career appealing in the first place, it demonstrates by example the necessity of ongoing intellectual creativity, and it builds a bridge to the resumption of full-time faculty activity. The very skills of organizing and prioritizing that make for an effective dean also allow that dean to continue as an active scholar when he or she selects projects and opportunities that are the most feasible and will yield the best results.

Endgame

In the end, two important questions are when to leave and how to leave.

When to Leave

Through the 1960s, a person who was appointed dean might expect to keep the job until retirement. Academic administrators in general stayed in their positions for lengthy periods and it took an extraordinary circumstance, such as the student protests of the late 1960s, to motivate a great deal of turnover. There have always been institutions that appointed a new dean from the faculty every five years or so, but even that process preserved a kind of stability. The situation has changed partly because of the new demands placed on higher education administrators, and partly because of today's common expectation that the deanship is a stepping-stone to another administrative position.

As student numbers, faculty salaries, support and equipment costs, and capital construction needs have continued to grow, major income streams including endowments and government funding have not kept pace. At the same time, demands for accountability have grown and required much greater attention than ever before. As a result, many academic administrators today find themselves in high-pressure situations with inadequate resources to solve problems and move ahead. Deans are dealing with issues as varied as fundraising and program elimination, for which they are not well prepared and which may hold little intrinsic interest for them. In this book we have tried to describe the dilemmas currently inherent in the dean's position, the greatest of which may be the need to mediate between concerns tangential to the academic enterprise on the one hand and the people who are directly involved in the work of teaching and learning on the other. It is no wonder, then, that deans expect their tenure to be relatively brief, ended often by a move to another administrative position or a return to the faculty. How and when does that moment arrive?

Being fired, of course, settles the matter decisively and swiftly. Otherwise, a dean may come to the decision to leave very gradually, prompted by two kinds of considerations. Some deans sense that they have accomplished those goals that were achievable in their current place and conclude they should capitalize on that success now to advance to a higher position. Others feel insufficiently challenged, or perhaps dissatisfied working for the institutional leadership, so that they are unenthusiastic about attempting to formulate dazzling visions for the coming years. They take to chatting with former deans who have recently changed positions, and the position listings in the *Chronicle of Higher Education* become priority reading each week. These clear signs of loss of energy and optimism in the role probably signify a need to move on. Perhaps the most useful point to bear in mind is that because a deanship nowadays is seldom a long-term appointment, the question of subsequent career possibilities should not steal up like a thief in the night but be a part of prudent personal planning all along. What then are the main factors that prompt a decision to leave?

Vision Achieved. Having developed a vision for the college and worked toward those goals for some years, the dean may feel that the college has advanced to the next stage and is ready for a new vision under fresh leadership. This does not mean that everything the college dreamed of has come to pass but rather that it has achieved those goals that could be achieved in a realistic amount of time. At the end of each year, reflecting on the provost's annual performance evaluation, the dean should personally review his or her progress and hopes, and consider what challenges still lie ahead in this position. If after about three years the record of accomplishments is reasonably gratifying, with the balance either in sight or out of the question, it may be time to consider moving to the next phase of one's career.

Time for a Change. Normally the early years of a deanship are the most exhilarating, filled with the pleasure of a new role and new relationships with colleagues. The college is full of potential that can be realized by working together, and both faculty and administration are disposed to try to do that in good faith. After a few years, however, each side begins to see the other's limitations. Gradually the balance shifts from joy in things done to frustration at things left undone, together with the humdrum of routine business. Progress in some areas is counterbalanced by a feeling of regression elsewhere. This may simply be another sign of the situation mentioned earlier: the dean has achieved all that can be reasonably expected in the present environment. Merely presiding over operations carries little appeal. When this prospect opens before a sitting dean, it is time to declare victory and pass the job to someone else. Both dean and college will benefit.

Change of President or Provost. New presidents and provosts often decide to form their own administrative teams, and no dean's position is secure in these times. In some places, all deans are expected to submit pro forma resignations, which the provost generally declines to act on (but the dean should be ready to face the new reality just in case!). More often, no such plan is announced. Nevertheless, deans should be alert for major changes whenever a new institutional officer appears.

Changes under these conditions are not necessarily personal. The president has a fresh mandate from the trustees, and perhaps a very different operating style from the incumbent, and will clear away administrators who do not fit his or her way of doing business. If in the first eighteen months of a new president or provost several deans and directors resign, and the new chief executive shows a lack of interest or confidence in the college agenda, it is time to update one's résumé and begin actively looking around. Discussion about optimal administrative structuring (translation: reorganizing the colleges) is another not-so-subtle invitation for the deans to leave. The risk to a dean increases if the new person has served previously as dean of a similar college; only someone personally selected by the provost has a strong chance of meeting with approval.

The discontent may not originate upstairs. Sometimes after observing the new administrator in action, the dean concludes that the disparity in their visions or management styles is too large to tolerate and too entrenched to remove. When there is such a mismatch, there can be little doubt about which officer will move and which will remain. For whatever reason, when the dean concludes that he or she cannot work productively with the president or provost, departure is the right course of action for the good of the college.

Budget Problems. "Budgets" and "problems" seem like a matched set, so that deans develop a high tolerance for unpleasant surprises in this area, but some problems are so serious that they undermine the desire to continue as dean. The most obvious is repeated budget reductions, even if the causes are clear enough (for instance, a bad state budget, a disastrous downturn in the endowment, and so forth). Consecutive small increases or even an occasional flat budget, although difficult, are tolerable for a while, but a series of cuts that require dismantling programs and reassigning faculty on short notice is debilitating.

So, after making all the creative changes imaginable and eliminating all but the most essential programs in the college, here come further reductions. Bad as the numbers themselves may be, the department chairs and faculty begin to question the dean's effectiveness as a leader for not averting the cuts. Many a dean has faced this scenario, and with no relief in sight, decided to leave the job.

Even worse, if possible, is the imposition of a budget structure that requires formal approval from the campus for virtually all expenditures. When the funds are held in the provost's office, the dean becomes little more than a well-paid beggar. In this circumstance, it is hard to stay enthusiastic even about concrete accomplishments, much less hope to achieve further goals for the college.

Finally, colleges are occasionally saddled with an institutional problem not of their making, such as a deficit in the athletic program. These are usually a surprise because they have not arisen from the activities of the college, and there is nothing laid aside to pay for them—except the contingency funds for college projects. If the clouds over the budgetary situation look so gloomy all the way to the horizon that they block out all progress on college priorities, there is little to do but avoid the storm.

Lack of Support. To achieve a measure of success, the dean needs the support of the president, provost, department chairs, and faculty members. We have discussed (Chapter Thirteen) the importance of a strong, trusting, and constructive relationship with the provost or president to whom the dean reports, as well as substantial agreement on college goals. If there are problems in these areas, it becomes very hard to accomplish anything of lasting significance. Deans report having experienced intolerable treatment—being ridiculed, cursed at, falsely accused of unprofessional behavior, and the like. When relationships are degraded by such professional maltreatment, the dean must decide where to draw the line for the good of all concerned.

The problems may arise at any level. Deans who direct too much of their attention externally may find that colleagues perceive the lack of internal attention as a sign of disinterest in the college, and not surprisingly this returns as lack of interest in the dean's priorities. Other signs include reluctance among faculty to serve on the dean's committees or to be considered for positions in the dean's office. Whether or not the dean has had a direct role in the problem, low morale makes it very difficult to move the college ahead. If the dean cannot count on the support of chairs and faculty members, it is time to leave.

Ill Health. If a dean develops a chronic or debilitating illness that will indefinitely impair his or her ability to perform the job, this may be a reason for stepping down (obviously we are not referring to disabilities that do not interfere with decanal duties). The sight of someone hanging on who clearly is not able to cope with the demands of the deanship is depressing and helps no one. Despite any rationalizations, remaining in a position where one cannot function harms the college and unfairly increases the burdens on colleagues. This is an excruciating decision to make. The dean continues to feel responsible for leading the college, but the importance of the position is too great to allow personal wishes to prevail over practicalities. More than one administrator has persevered too long in ill health and damaged what had been a productive legacy. The time to plan for contingencies of this kind is when one is healthy. Family and close colleagues can help a dean face the situation when health problems dictate against continuing.

Last, a family health crisis may prove so distracting that it undercuts work. A leave of absence, perhaps two or three months, allows time to seek a solution to the domestic problem and stability that will permit the dean to function in office. Again, if this leads to no resolution, for the sake of the college as well as family it may be best to leave the deanship.

Nonrenewal or Request for Resignation. Deans serve at the pleasure of the president or the provost and can be asked to resign at any time. If this happens, there presumably was a reason for it, and the dean probably wants to know what it was. Yet there is little to gain by pressing for details; no one is obliged to provide answers, and in any case it is unlikely that the reasons provided will tell the whole story. The best response is to negotiate departure in the most favorable terms, a kind of mirror image of the hiring process, and step away with professional and personal dignity intact. Stirring resentment or protest will not help the college and certainly will not help the dean, even if a majority of one's colleagues think the negative decision was ill-founded.

Warning signs that were missed or ignored may be discovered on reflection. However, frustrating as it is to acknowledge, the decision may have had little to do with the dean's actual work or merit. As in the corporate world, deans and other middle-level executives are often the scapegoats when the institutional leadership has problems. Handling this awkward and infuriating situation well can lead to good references that actually reflect the dean's achievements and enable him or her to find another administrative position. The provost will be happy to see the ill-treated dean move on and may even feel some pang of guilt about the unhappy closure.

We leave aside the other logical possibility, which is that a dean is justifiably dismissed for incompetence or worse, not because this scenario is unthinkable but simply because the advice in these pages cannot help in such situations.

Retirement. Surprising though it may seem in the face of all these perils, some deans actually reach retirement age still in office. Although advancing birthdays are easier to foresee than illness, many deans suddenly find themselves at an age when retirement makes perfect sense but act as if this year's birthday were an unexpected calamity. With no mandatory retirement age, disengaging from a demanding and rewarding career is a very personal decision. Faculty can continue their research in retirement, and teach part-time, and not feel as if they have surrendered their professional identity, but administrators often see retirement as a form of going cold turkey. Far better to plan for a specific age by which to retire, discuss it with family and close colleagues, and then stick to it. This also allows the college to plan for the transition. Deans can begin discussion of the plan with the provost at least eighteen months ahead, tell colleagues informally, and develop a schedule leading to retirement. Such planning helps avoid idle speculation or even a notion that a dean has stayed in the job too long. A full year's notice should be sufficient to permit a search for a successor, so that the college will not have to endure an interim dean, although decanal searches not infrequently run longer than one season. Knowing when and how to retire is the dean's parting gift to the college.

How to Leave

No matter the reasons for the departure, a dean should go with grace and orderliness. A dean who has been on the job for several years will have a wide variety of relationships and close ties with many individuals in the college, especially the college staff, all of which need consideration. Numerous projects inevitably remain incomplete. Which must be finished? Which must be left in good order for the next dean? And which must be kept flexible to give that successor options? These questions take on added seriousness if there is no permanent successor named when the dean steps down.

Negotiating Departure. The formal process begins with a conversation with the provost or president. In preparation, it is important to think through and succinctly lay out the reasons, thus assuring objectivity and consistency in conversations with assorted people around campus. Depending on the circumstances and their relationship, the provost may try to dissuade the dean or merely offer good wishes. If the dean has sound reasons for deciding to resign or retire, it is better to resist any temptation to reconsider. The very announcement of a decision to leave affects relationships with everybody else.

The question of reconsidering is moot, of course, when the dean has accepted another position inside or outside the institution, but there may be other transitional matters, such as moving studio or laboratory equipment to a new location, finishing up work with graduate students, and the like. These, however, should be easy to settle.

The transition is far more complex and important when the dean stays on as a faculty member in the college. As we noted in Chapter Three, the basis for these arrangements should have been established when the dean first took up appointment, but now is the time to determine the specifics. First comes salary—converting an eleven- or twelve-month appointment to nine months. Some provosts agree to using ten-elevenths as the new nine-month base; others simply remove two-elevenths. A few Grinch-like figures insist that because the dean is now no more remarkable than any other faculty member, the salary will be put at the highest figure currently being paid a colleague in comparable disciplines. This may well result in an annual loss of as much as 50 percent.

What happens to unused vacation time and sick leave? Many institutions offer former administrators a sabbatical to prepare for their new role. Is that the case here? What about office and computer setup? These may be minimal requirements for any faculty member but they should not create a hardship for the department. Before negotiating specifics, it is helpful to talk with former deans who have become faculty members in recent years to learn what to expect. However, it is equally important to have one's own needs in mind and be ready to justify them.

Giving Notice. The departure date too may be negotiated. It is best to step down within one appointment year to avoid being a lame duck longer than necessary. Those leaving for another post may have to mediate between the needs of current and new institutions. Those who are staying in the college may be asked to serve until a replacement is found. This is not a comfortable situation, but if the dean has been well treated he or she may feel compelled to do the campus this favor. In contrast, there is no reason to be offended if the provost appoints an acting dean without input from the departing dean. It allows the process—and the dean—to move on unencumbered.

Making the Announcement. Once arrangements have been concluded, the dean should speak immediately to his or her closest colleagues and then issue a formal announcement. The statement should be brief and factual, including effective date and any future plans. This will lead at once to a flurry of inquiries about the "real" reasons. Quite possibly the news media will call for comments, which should all be positive.

Saying Thank You. When a dean prepares to depart, colleagues often will want to express their thanks through receptions, gifts, and so forth. Many deans privately prefer that a scholarship fund be established and would be glad to contribute to it as a token of their own appreciation to the college. Personal mementos to staff and other close colleagues are important as a gesture of thanks for all they have done to make the job easier. Not least, the dean should get in touch with donors and other external supporters of the college to thank them for their contributions over the years. Those relationships took a lot of work to build, and often acquaintance grows into friendship.

Packing to Leave. Oddly, deciding what to take when one leaves is a serious matter. Some items are straightforward:

- Files of correspondence unrelated to dean's office business, for instance, from colleagues at other institutions
- Material related to activities in professional societies
- Speeches and articles
- Copies of reports the office has prepared, along with institutional policy documents that may be helpful in the future

More problematic are issues that may follow the dean out the door and could end up in court. Personnel matters such as grievances, sexual harassment cases, or faculty terminations for cause can persist or resurface long after the dean leaves the institution, and they may require testimony. It is safest to keep one's own records of sensitive cases and make copies of official correspondence pertaining to them. This allows ongoing access to any necessary materials and avoids the risk of having them discarded or misplaced by office staff. The university counsel can give written advice on what legal protection will be provided if any of the pending cases goes to trial.

Following Up. A dean's involvement in the college's affairs does not necessarily end when he or she vacates the position. Whether near or far, the dean's office and other campus officials will need to contact the former dean for the full background or special knowledge of particular events. Further, colleagues from this former life will continue to seek recommendations and even career counseling. One touching carryover is that various people all over campus will continue to use the term "dean" in addressing former occupants of the office, a pleasant reminder of the association.

Where to Go

Because most deans understand that their jobs are temporary they spend time thinking about next steps. The choices they make depend on a number of factors, including their ties to teaching and scholarship, the attractiveness of another administrative position, their wish to change institutions, their value in the marketplace. Options they may consider include becoming provost or president, taking another deanship, and rejoining the faculty.

Lurking in the minds of a great many deans, and no small number of colleagues, is the notion that the deanship will lead to a provost's position and then on to a presidency in higher education—and indeed it does in a good number of cases. Arithmetic is against this as a general plan, however, because there are far more deanships than provostships, and the competition is correspondingly daunting. Those who are determined to pursue a higher post must be willing to persevere over several years, and perhaps, take the step up in rank at a lesser institution.

Deans who become provosts report that their main job is to do the bidding of the president (see Chapter Thirteen on the role of the provost). For this reason, some argue that the only reason to take a provost's position is the desire to become a president. To a dean who is accustomed to working closely with faculty members and students, the provost's job can seem too distant from teaching and learning. A provost can also be made miserable by a demanding president who takes credit for everything positive and blames the provost for any problems that arise. In contrast, if a provost enjoys a symbiotic relationship with the president, or is left to shape the campus according to her or his best judgment, then the job can be exhilarating and make a qualitative impact on the institution. Being a provost also provides a close-up view of the presidency. Those deans who ultimately became presidents report enjoying the top position much better than that of provost. The challenge of working with trustees never ends for the president, but the role does provide a great opportunity for leadership in higher education.

The most attractive deanships often go to candidates who have already earned their stripes at another institution. Sometimes a dean of a smaller college will move to a larger position, or to a more prestigious institution. Deans who enjoy working with faculty members and students may find this kind of move the best way to reenergize themselves while still doing what they like. The main challenge is whether one can find the necessary level of enthusiasm to face problems already familiar and tiresome. A jaded attitude will be fatal at a new position, no matter how much experience comes with it. Almost as dangerous is the temptation to re-create previous goals—especially successful ones—without sufficient regard to the local differences. In short, moving to another deanship can be like starting over again as a college dean. If this is not discouraging, a new deanship can be very rewarding and invigorating.

In most cases, deanships come with a tenured faculty appointment; but the specifics of that position may not be fully defined until one is actually ready to assume it. Usually a former dean joins the faculty of her or his academic department and assumes the usual responsibilities of teaching, scholarship, and service. At times, however, deans prefer to negotiate a joint appointment that allows them to use their decanal experience and teach courses in higher education policy. In fact, freedom from the dean's duties can offer the opportunity to reflect on and write about issues that occupied them on the job. The main concern in choosing this as an ongoing arrangement is whether one's interest in higher education issues will remain strong. It could be wiser to leave the arrangements subject to renegotiation after a specified period of time.

Whether or not the transition is ushered in with a sabbatical leave, the new role will surely be liberating. Being able to set one's own schedule, read books, work long hours in a laboratory or studio, and think about something besides other people's problems, must have a salutary effect on anyone's enthusiasm for teaching and scholarship. In addition, former deans find themselves called on as consultants for a variety of purposes. Their academic expertise will be of value, but their administrative experience can add a dimension to their qualifications as a grant panelist, accreditation reviewer, advisory board member, and the like. The most frequently asked question: How do you like teaching again? There is something peculiar in academic culture that views teaching as a semipunishment and yet expects an enthusiastic response to the question. Genuine pleasure at getting back to full-time teaching is actually another way to combat this odd notion.

Finally, deans in professional disciplines such as law may well choose to leave higher education altogether for opportunities that draw on the administrative experience. And for veterans of all stripes, academic search firms are an interesting possibility (see Chapter Three). These firms need professionals who can match candidates with positions and size up the suitability of the pairing. Accreditation agencies, both regional and discipline-related, recruit former academic administrators as staff. The same is true of the numerous higher education organizations and professional societies operating at the national level. Agencies of the federal government, among other opportunities in Washington, have included former deans on their staffs. Others join foundations or granting agencies that look for decisive individuals who know how to seek and evaluate proposals.

The Decanal Afterlife

Former deans retain a great deal of influence. They also carry a number of positive memories and possibly some regrets or even grudges. If they move to a higher position on the same campus, some may be concerned about their favoring the former college, much as faculty have anxieties about deans and their home departments.

Dean's Office

It is important to maintain cordial relations with former staff in the dean's office even after leaving the campus. Contacts with them may be limited, but they will be interested in hearing what is happening to the former dean and they may be able to offer help from time to time. Former deans who remain in the college can keep even closer relationships with some of their best friends among the staff. One odd but attested difficulty occasionally arises: a new dean who is insecure—or even simply unpleasant—may view the lingering predecessor as a faculty spy and a threat. To help forestall this reaction, the outgoing dean must be absolutely sure not to discuss the new dean with the office staff and to maintain a friendly demeanor toward him or her. Conversations with staff members are not a means to elicit information about the office, nor to provide opinions even if asked. This may seem self-evident, but it is easier said than done!

These same admonitions apply with at least equal force when moving to a higher position on campus. In that case, the former dean, now the provost, may actually select and supervise his or her own successor. The temptation to avoid is to expect the new dean to do the job exactly the same way as the old one.

Faculty Colleagues

For those who stay on campus and become full-time faculty members, colleagues inevitably begin speculating about the dean's motives for decisions or the "true story" behind a public announcement. However tempting it may be to respond to such speculation, doing so has many more drawbacks than benefits. The politic thing is to remain positive or silent about administrative policies and personnel. Advice to the department chair should only be given if asked for.

A long hiatus in teaching may well have affected the range of courses one is ready, interested, or able to take on. Rather than trying to regain the full teaching range of preadministrative years, the new colleague on the block should sit down with the chair and talk about what role he or she might best play. One successful strategy is to concentrate on a relatively small array of courses, mainly at the undergraduate level at first, particularly if the new colleague brings a specialty not otherwise represented in the department. This way, teaching is a pleasure and a benefit to the department, not a drag on its effectiveness or a source of irritation or even embarrassment to the returning teacher.

There will be other productive activities as well. The veteran dean knows the college's committees and projects and can contribute powerfully by volunteering to serve where needed. This reengagement in the full range of faculty life brings a most gratifying awareness of an ability to contribute to the welfare of the institution in a new role.

Personal Matters

Leaving the deanship is no less difficult than entering it, especially if the individual remains on the campus. Colleagues pay the compliment of assuming the new member has valuable expertise and opinions, and others assume that the veteran is still available as an advocate for the college.

One adjustment that catches many veterans by surprise is learning to live without staff assistance, at least at the level that supports the dean. This means finally learning about all the forms to be completed for professional travel, course requests, textbook orders, library reserve, and so forth. The tasks go far beyond the rote, including learning how a temperamental copying machine works, preparing syllabi, setting up a network among one's students, and handling one's own correspondence again.

Unless the former dean was a remarkable negotiator, the change in salary will be felt by the family. If the change is going to be very great, there may be other opportunities such as summer teaching or more consulting to close part of the gap. Sometimes spouses have difficulty dealing with the loss of status that accompanies the dean's position, but the benefits in flexibility of schedule and reduced pressure are likely to balance the score. It is important to convey to one's spouse or partner, at least, that this is a positive professional change, and to work to minimize any adverse impact on the family.

In fact, once the transition is completed, life after being dean is among the most pleasant in the entire academy—friends across campus, a return to activities that were the basis of a happy career for many years, perhaps greater flexibility in choosing teaching assignments and research projects. Former deans hear countless spontaneous remarks on how much happier they seem since "returning to work."

External Constituents

Finally, deans join a number of organizations for the sake of the college, and these may or may not continue to claim their time or interest. It is important to review all such memberships and resign graciously where need be, first completing any existing obligations, because in the eyes of the external community the actions of a former dean continue to reflect on the college. If one stays at the institution, there will be continuing contacts with college supporters, some of whom are now personal friends.

In the end, being dean is a wonderful adventure, giving a deeper understanding of the workings of the academy and a deeper appreciation of how remarkable a place the academy really is. The privilege of leading a college requires us to find and use talents we never suspected we had, and we can use them for whatever lies ahead. Our work in office can be as important as any contribution of our individual scholarship, because it helps hundreds of colleagues make their contributions as teachers and scholars, and improves the college years, as education and as personal experience, for countless students. That is truly a satisfying way to occupy a vital portion of a career!

Suggestions for Further Reading

Allan, George. "Helping Your Successor." In George Allan (ed.), *Resource Handbook for Academic Deans* (pp. 186–189). Washington, D.C.: American Conference of Academic Deans,

Harris, Evan. *The Quit.* New York: Simon & Schuster/Fireside, 1996.

Tucker, Allan, and Robert Bryan. *The Academic Dean: Dove, Dragon, and Diplomat* (2nd ed.). Phoenix: American Council on Education/Oryx Press, 1999.

REFERENCES

Abadie, H. Dale. "Dismissals, Non-Renewals, Terminations." In Allan, George (ed.), *Resource Handbook for Academic Deans* (pp. 113–115). Washington, D.C.: American Conference of Academic Deans, 1999.

Allan, George. "Helping Your Successor." In George Allan (ed.), *Resource Handbook for Academic Deans* (pp. 186–189). Washington, D.C.: American Conference of Academic Deans, 1999.

Allan, George (ed.). *Resource Handbook for Academic Deans.* Washington, D.C.: American Conference of Academic Deans, 1999.

Anderson, Richard E., and Joel W. Meyerson (eds.). *Financial Planning under Economic Uncertainty.* New Directions for Higher Education, no. 69. San Francisco: Jossey-Bass, 1990.

Arreola, Raoul A. *Developing a Comprehensive Faculty Evaluation System* (2nd ed.). Bolton, Mass.: Anker, 2000.

Astin, Alexander W. *What Matters in College: Four Critical Years Revisited.* San Francisco: Jossey-Bass, 1993.

Austin, Michael J., Frederick L. Ahearn, and Richard A. English (eds.). *The Professional School Dean: Meeting the Leadership Challenges.* New Directions for Higher Education, no. 98. San Francisco: Jossey-Bass, 1997.

Axtell, James. *The Pleasures of Academe.* Lincoln: University of Nebraska Press, 1998.

Bennett, John B., and David J. Figuli (eds.). *Enhancing Departmental Leadership: The Roles of the Chairperson.* New York: American Council on Education, 1990.

Bérubé, Michael, and Cary Nelson (eds.). *Higher Education under Fire: Politics, Economics, and the Crisis of the Humanities.* New York: Routledge, 1995.

Birnbaum, Robert. *How Colleges Work: The Cybernetics of Academic Organization and Leadership.* San Francisco: Jossey-Bass, 1988.

Birnbaum, Robert. *How Academic Leadership Works.* San Francisco: Jossey-Bass, 1992.

Black, Dennis R., and Matt Gilson. *Perspectives and Principles: A College Administrator's Guide to Staying Out of Court.* Madison, Wis.: Magna, 1988.

Boice, Robert. *The New Faculty Member: Supporting and Fostering Faculty Development.* San Francisco: Jossey-Bass, 1992.

Bowen, William G., and Harold T. Shapiro (eds.). *Universities and Their Leadership.* Princeton, N.J.: Princeton University Press, 1998.

Boyer, Ernest. *Scholarship Reconsidered: Priorities of the Professoriate.* Princeton, N.J.: Carnegie Foundation for the Advancement of Teaching, 1990.

Cason, Roger L. "Bird's Eye View: Typical Strategic Plan." Paper presented to the board of the Delaware Chamber Music Festival, Wilmington, Mar. 2000.

Chafee, Ellen Earle, and William G. Tierney. *Collegiate Culture and Leadership Strategies.* New York: ACE/Macmillan, 1988.

Diamond, Robert M., and Bronwyn E. Adam (eds.). *Recognizing Faculty Work: Reward Systems for the Year 2000.* New Directions for Higher Education, no. 81. San Francisco: Jossey Bass, 1993.

Dziech, Billie Wright, and Michael W. Hawkins. *Sexual Harassment in Higher Education: Reflections and New Perspectives.* New York: Garland, 1998.

Eames, Patricia, and Thomas P. Hustoles (eds.). *Legal Issues in Faculty Employment.* Washington, D.C.: National Association of College and University Attorneys, 1989.

Eble, Kenneth E. *The Art of Administration.* San Francisco: Jossey-Bass, 1978.

Facione, Peter. "Fundraising and Entrepreneurship." In George Allan (ed.), *Resource Handbook for Academic Deans* (pp. 152–156). Washington, D.C.: American Conference of Academic Deans, 1999.

Feiss, P. Geoffrey. "Working with a Strategic Plan." Paper presented to the Council of Colleges of Arts and Sciences' Deans Seminars, Spring 2000. Charleston, S.C. and Albuquerque, N.M.

Fitzgerald, L. *Sexual Harassment in Higher Education: Concepts and Issues.* Washington, D.C.: National Education Association, 1992.

Gmelch, Walter H. "When a Chair Becomes a Dean: The Rite of Passage." *Department Chair,* 2000, *11* (2), 1–3.

Goonen, Norma R., and Rachel S. Blechman. *Higher Education Administration: A Guide to Legal, Ethical, and Practical Issues.* Westport, Conn.: Greenwood Press, 1999.

Gordon, Michael, and Shelby Keiser. *Accommodations in Higher Education under the Americans with Disabilities Act (ADA): A No-Nonsense Guide for Clinicians, Educators, Administrators, and Lawyers.* DeWitt, N.Y.: GSI Publications, 1998.

Graham, Hugh Davis, and Nancy Diamond. *The Rise of American Research Universities: Elites and Challengers in the Postwar Era.* Baltimore: Johns Hopkins University Press, 1997.

Graubard, Stephen R., ed. *The American Research University.* Proceedings of the American Academy of Arts and Sciences, Vol. 122, No. 4.

Hahs, Sharon. "Setting Goals and Achieving Them: The Art of Planning." Paper presented to the Council of Colleges of Arts and Sciences Seminar for New Deans, Williamsburg, Va., June 1997.

Hall, Margaret Rooney. *The Dean's Role in Fund Raising.* Baltimore: Johns Hopkins University Press, 1993.

Harris, Evan. *The Quit.* New York: Simon & Schuster/Fireside, 1996.

Heifetz, Ronald A. *Leadership Without Easy Answers.* Cambridge, Mass.: Harvard University Press, 1994.

Higgerson, Mary Lou, and Susan S. Rehwaldt. *Complexities of Higher Education Administration: Case Studies and Issues.* Bolton: Anker, 1993.

Hines, Samuel M., Jr. "What to Read." In George Allan (ed.), *Resource Handbook for Academic Deans* (pp. 36–40). Washington, D.C.: American Conference of Academic Deans, 1999.

Hoekema, David. "Evaluating Deans." In George Allan (ed.), *Resource Handbook for Academic Deans* (pp. 25–30). Washington, D.C.: American Conference of Academic Deans, 1999.

"Ideas for Planning a Department Chairs Retreat." [http://www.calpress.com/Retreat/].

Kaplan, Matthew (ed.). *To Improve the Academy: Resources for Faculty, Instructional, and Organizational Development.* Vol. 18. Bolton: Anker, 2000.

Kaplin, William A., and Barbara A. Lee. *The Law of Higher Education: A Comprehensive Guide to Legal Implications of Administrative Decision Making* (3rd ed.). San Francisco: Jossey-Bass, 1995.

Katz, Richard N., & Associates. *Dancing with the Devil: Information Technology and the New Competition in Higher Education.* San Francisco: Jossey-Bass, 1999.

Keeton, Morris. *Shared Authority on Campus.* Washington, D.C.: American Association for Higher Education, 1971.

Keller, George. *Academic Strategy: The Management Revolution in Higher Education.* Baltimore: Johns Hopkins University Press, 1983.

Keller, George. "Examining What Works in Strategic Planning." In Marvin W. Peterson, David D. Dill, Lisa A. Mets, and Associates (eds.), *Planning and Management for a Changing Environment: A Handbook on Redesigning Post-Secondary Institutions.* San Francisco: Jossey-Bass, 1997.

Kolodny, Annette. *Failing the Future: A Dean Looks at Higher Education in the Twenty-First Century.* Durham, N.C.: Duke University Press, 1998.

Krahenbuhl, Gary S., and Patrick M. McConeghy. "The Integration of Faculty Responsibilities and Institutional Needs." Paper presented to the annual meeting of the Council of Colleges of Arts and Sciences, Seattle, Nov. 1999.

Kurtz, Mary Elizabeth (ed.). *Am I Liable? Faculty, Staff, and Institutional Liability in the College and University Setting.* Washington, D.C.: National Association of College and University Attorneys, 1989.

Kurtz, Mary Elizabeth (ed.). "Sexual Harassment: Suggested Policy and Procedures for Handling Complaints." *American Association of University Professors Policy Documents and Reports,* 1995.

Lankford, John. "Are You Ready to Move Up in Administration? Some Decision-Making Guidelines for Academic Chairpersons." *Department Chair,* 2000, *11* (2), 3–6.

Leaming, Deryl R. *Academic Leadership: A Practical Guide to Chairing the Department.* Bolton, Mass.: Anker, 1998.

Leary, David E. "Strategic Planning." In George Allan (ed.), *Resource Handbook for Academic Deans* (pp. 125–131). Washington, D.C.: American Conference of Academic Deans, 1999.

Lucas, Ann F. *Strengthening Departmental Leadership: A Team-Building Guide for Chairs in Colleges and Universities.* San Francisco: Jossey-Bass, 1994.

Lucas, Ann F., and Associates. *Leading Academic Change: Essential Roles for Department Chairs.* San Francisco: Jossey-Bass, 2000.

Lunde, Joyce Povlacs. *Reshaping Curricula: Revitalization Programs at Three Land Grant Universities.* Bolton, Mass.: Anker, 1995.

Mantel, Linda H. "Women Who Are Deans, Deans Who Are Women." In George Allan (ed.), *Resource Handbook for Academic Deans*. Washington, D.C.: American Conference of Academic Deans, 1999.

Martin, James, James E. Samels, and Associates. *First Among Equals: The Role of the Chief Academic Officer*. Baltimore: Johns Hopkins University Press, 1997.

Massy, William F., Andrea K. Wilger, and Carol Colbeck. "Overcoming 'Hollowed' Collegiality." *Change*, 1994, *26* (4), 11–20.

Nelson, Cary. "Sexual Harassment." In Cary Nelson and Stephen Watt (eds.), *Academic Keywords: A Devil's Dictionary for Higher Education* (pp. 232–257). New York: Routledge, 1999.

Nelson, Cary, and Stephen Watt (eds.). *Academic Keywords: A Devil's Dictionary for Higher Education*. New York: Routledge, 1999.

Oblinger, Diana G., and Richard N. Katz (eds.). *Renewing Administration. Preparing Colleges and Universities for the 21st Century*. Bolton, Mass.: Anker, 1999.

Olivas, Michael A. *The Law and Higher Education: Cases and Materials on Colleges in Court*. Durham, N.C.: Carolina Academic Press, 1997.

Peterson, Marvin W. "Using Contextual Planning to Transform Institutions." In Marvin W. Peterson, David D. Dill, Lisa A. Mets, and Associates (eds.), *Planning and Management for a Changing Environment: A Handbook on Redesigning Post Secondary Institutions*. San Francisco: Jossey-Bass, 1997.

Peterson, Marvin W., David D. Dill, Lisa A. Mets, and Associates. *Planning and Management for a Changing Environment: A Handbook on Redesigning Post Secondary Institutions*. San Francisco: Jossey-Bass, 1997.

Pitts, James P. "Academic Deaning Despite Difference." In George Allan (ed.), *Resource Handbook for Academic Deans*. Washington, D.C.: American Conference of Academic Deans, 1999.

Plante, Patricia, and Robert L. Caret. *Myths and Realities of Academic Administration*. New York: ACE/Macmillan, 1990.

Project on Faculty Appointments, Harvard Graduate School of Education. *Faculty Appointment Policy Archive* (CD). Bolton, Mass.: Anker, 1999.

Readings, Bill. *The University in Ruins*. Cambridge, Mass.: Harvard University Press, 1996.

Riggs, Robert O., Patricia H. Murrell, and JoAnn C. Cutting (eds.). *Sexual Harassment in Higher Education: From Conflict to Community*. ASHE-ERIC Higher Education Report No. 2. Washington, D.C.: George Washington University, School of Education and Human Development, 1993.

Rodgers, James Ellison, and William C. Adams. *Media Guide for Academics*. Los Angeles: Foundation for American Communications, 1994.

Rosovsky, Henry. *The University: An Owner's Manual*. New York: Norton, 1990.

Rosovsky, Henry, and Inge-Lise Ameer. "A Neglected Topic: Professional Conduct of College and University Teachers" (pp. 119–156). In William G. Bowen and Harold T. Shapiro (eds.), *Universities and Their Leadership*. Princeton, N.J.: Princeton University Press, 1998.

Rossbacher, Lisa A. "Harassment." In George Allan (ed.), *Resource Handbook for Academic Deans*. Washington, D.C.: American Conference of Academic Deans, 1999.

Rowley, Daniel James, Herman D. Lujan, and Michael G. Dolence. *Strategic Change in Colleges and Universities: Planning to Survive and Prosper*. San Francisco: Jossey Bass, 1997.

Rowley, Daniel James, Herman D. Lujan, and Michael G. Dolence. *Strategic Choices for the Academy: How Demand for Lifelong Learning Will Re-Create Higher Education*. San Francisco: Jossey-Bass, 1998.

Rudolph, Frederick. *The American College and University: A History.* New York: Knopf, 1962.

Rudolph, Frederick. *Curriculum: A History of the American Undergraduate Course of Study Since 1636.* San Francisco: Jossey-Bass, 1977.

Scarborough, Elizabeth. "Retirement Arrangements for Faculty." In George Allan (ed.), *Resource Handbook for Academic Deans* (pp. 125–131). Washington, D.C.: American Conference of Academic Deans, 1999.

Schuster, Jack H., Daryl G. Smith, Kathleen A. Corak, and Myrtle M. Yamada. *Strategic Governance: How to Make Big Decisions Better.* Phoenix: American Council on Education/Oryx Press, 1994.

"Sexual Harassment: Suggested Policy and Procedures for Handling Complaints." *Policy Documents and Reports.* Washington, D.C.: American Association of University Professors, 1991.

Smith, Holly M. "Getting and Keeping Good Department Chairs." Paper presented at the annual meeting of the Council of Colleges of Arts and Sciences, Seattle, Nov. 1999.

Steeples, Douglas. "So Now You Are a Dean: The First 100 Days." In George Allan (ed.), *Resource Handbook for Academic Deans* (pp. 89–91). Washington, D.C.: American Conference of Academic Deans, 1999.

Tannen, Deborah. *You Just Don't Understand: Women and Men in Conversation.* New York: Ballantine, 1991.

Tannen, Deborah. *Talking from 9 to 5: How Men's and Women's Conversational Styles Affect Who Gets Heard, Who Gets Credit, and What Gets Done at Work.* New York: Morrow, 1994.

Trower, Cathy A. (ed.). *Policies on Faculty Appointment. Standard Practices and Unusual Arrangements.* Bolton, Mass.: Anker, 2000.

Tucker, Allan. *Chairing the Academic Department: Leadership Among Peers* (3rd ed.). New York: American Council on Education, 1992.

Tucker, Allan, and Robert Bryan. *The Academic Dean: Dove, Dragon, and Diplomat* (2nd ed.). Phoenix: American Council on Education/Oryx Press, 1999.

Warren, Charles O. "Chairperson and Dean: The Essential Partnership." In John B. Bennett and David J. Figuli (eds.), *Enhancing Departmental Leadership: The Roles of the Chairperson.* New York: American Council on Education, 1990.

Watkins, Bari. "Affirmative Action/Equal Opportunity." In George Allan (ed.), *Resource Handbook for Academic Deans* (pp. 109–112). Washington, D.C.: American Conference of Academic Deans, 1999.

Watt, Stephen. "Faculty." In Cary Nelson and Stephen Watt (eds.), *Academic Keywords: A Devil's Dictionary for Higher Education* (pp. 132–152). New York: Routledge, 1999.

Weeks, Kent M. *Complying with Federal Law: A Reference Manual for College Decision Makers.* Nashville, Tenn.: College Legal Information, 1995.

Whalen, Edward L. *Responsibility Centered Budgeting.* Bloomington: Indiana University Press, 1991.

Index